Kenyatta's Country

RICHARD COX

Kenyatta's Country

FREDERICK A. PRAEGER *Publishers*
New York . Washington

BOOKS THAT MATTER

Published in the United States of America in 1966
by Frederick A. Praeger, Inc, Publishers
111 Fourth Avenue, New York 3, N.Y.

Second impression 1967

Library of Congress Catalog Card Number: 66–14714

PRINTED IN GREAT BRITAIN

FOR CAROLINE

and also in gratitude to the late

JACK BEDDINGTON

Acknowledgments

My thanks are due to the *Sunday Times*, *New York Times* and the B.B.C. for permission to use material collected on their behalf, and, above all, to my wife who typed the manuscript.

NOTE Kenya became a Republic within the Commonwealth on December 12th, 1964, the anniversary of Independence, with Jomo Kenyatta as President, and Oginga Odinga as Vice-President.

R.H.F.C.

Contents

1

Introduction— The Party Turns Out to be Over

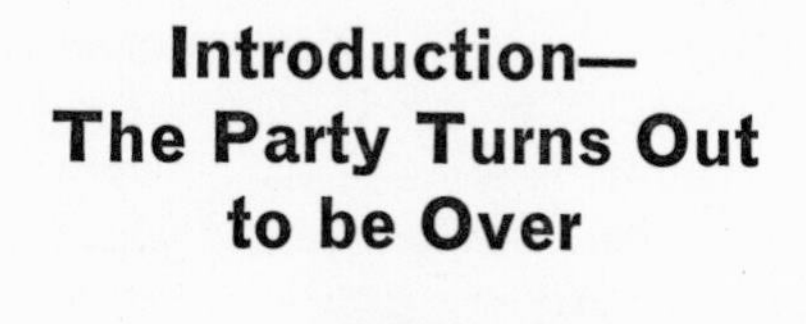

'JUNGLE JUICE MORE,' shouted the major, banging the mahogany table and looking around impatiently for a mess waiter. 'More. Jungle juice. More!' Though posted away from Kenya, and his favourite topic of the Mau Mau, he still seemed to carry a personal State of Emergency with him wherever he went, even here in the sticky, friendly heat of Lagos a few months before Nigeria's independence in 1960. At last more fruit salad was brought, lush with pawpaw and melon. Momentarily satisfied, the major returned to his theme: 'I could have shot the pair of them, both those bastard M.P.s, shot them and no questions asked. Labour Party? More like communist in my opinion. They wanted to see a Mau Mau hideout, and I was detailed to take them. "What on earth d'you bring them back *alive* for?" everyone asked me afterwards. Wish I hadn't. Told them a lot and all they did was twist it out of recognition when they got back to Westminster.' He paused to gulp down another spoonful of the Jungle Juice. 'Even so, those were great days in the Emergency. Girls all carried pearl-handled revolvers—and the way they lived it up! Old man, I can tell you they were the randiest lot of women I've seen since the war, Singapore not excluded. What a posting! Terrific parties. Adjutant rode his horse into one. Beast panicked and kicked all the furniture to pieces. A great place, Kenya.'

It was with some trepidation that I set off for this land of military legend six months later. Having made many African friends in West Africa, and even lived off dried fish and yams for a week whilst staying with the chief of a small village, I felt I would be suspect from the moment I set foot in Nairobi. Though completely English and as white as a soap advertisement, I had no doubt, after the major's exposition of Kenya life, that the settlers would sense I was tarred with the black brush the moment they saw me. At the first party I went to some unfortunate would be seized, debagged and thrown in the swimming pool by the voracious Kenya women; and it was odds on that the someone would be me. If, that is, I hadn't already been trampled into the parquet flooring by the adjutant's horse.

I need not have worried. To use a phrase which might have been coined for Kenya, 'the party was over'. At least it was almost over. The 1950's were more the British Army's party than the settlers', though at the same time the last fling of a rogue elephant tradition which the remittance men of the 1930's had created. The end of the Emergency proved to be a watershed, the moment at which the Wild West feeling was finally seen to be a dead duck, when the British tax-payers finally decided that Red Indians biting the dust were a splendid spectacle and well worth spending money to see but that settlers versus Africans fell into a different and less desirable category of saga.

When I arrived in Nairobi European lack of inhibition was giving its dying kicks and African lack of it hovering waiting in the wings. At the Equator Club a young Kenyan sang a song about *Uhuru*, the Swahili word for independence. 'No more working, no more tax, we'll sit in the sun and just relax', went one verse, and another: 'When the money's all finished and the country's on the floor, we'll get the Government Printing Press to turn us out some more'. The refrain ran: '*Uhuru*, *Uhuru*, *Uhuru* . . . *Uhuru* is good enough for me.' The African band looked pretty sick accompanying this song and it was taken off after Christmas 1960.

Three years later six young Europeans, all in their early twenties, and eight older European civil servants, celebrated the night of Kenya's independence and the end of the 'white man's burden' in the same satirical vein, at a party on Tank Hill in Kampala. They dressed up in old colonial uniforms, solar topees, fever belts and some of them in African servants' kanzus—a long white garment like a nightshirt. They sent out invitations asking friends to celebrate the ending of the 'white man's burden' and they sang songs. It was an undergraduate kind of affair, making fun of both British and Africans. But it roused the fury of Uganda's Prime Minister and the party-givers were deported. In Nairobi the *East African Standard*, long the newspaper of the settlers, the same settlers who once planted banana trees down

Delamere Avenue in order to make the Government tarmac the street, commented: 'In a new African country the official view is that the Government does not have to tolerate the presence of anybody considered undesirable.'

To my surprise and dismay this turned out to mean me. On May Day 1964 I found myself untolerated and expelled, the first journalist to fall foul of *Uhuru*, or, to be more precise, of the Minister of Information, Achieng Oneko. I was admitted to have done nothing against Kenya, it was the Tanganyikans who had disliked an article I wrote in the *Sunday Times* on the union of Tanganyika and Zanzibar. But Oneko signed the order making me a Kenyan prohibited immigrant as 'a demonstration of our commitment to the East African Common Market', which, if one pauses to think about it, is as good a piece of economic reasoning as any.

So it hadn't been the adjutant's horse that was destined to trample me into the floor, after all, just the rearing mastodon of African temperament. It is a salutary experience finding out that people you have been trying to understand see you as an arch imperialist, or what Oginga Odinga, the Minister of Home Affairs, whom Oneko was deputising for at that time, is fond of calling 'an ill-intentioned colonialist remnant'. However, as my object had been to write this book on the transition from white rule to black, much of which was already in draft, the experience was at least relevant to my theme, even if I have had to try to erase any personal bitterness from my account of what Kenya is becoming under African rule. Certainly it reminded me forcefully that the white man's party, whether private or public, good-humoured or wild, drunken or sober, was indeed finally and irrevocably over. From *Uhuru* onwards the white man was only in Kenya on sufferance, whether he was Kenya born or not, as later deportations sadly emphasised.

The whole colonial history of Kenya covered a tiny span of years, less than Kenyatta's own life. It was fitting that the first street name to be changed in Nairobi was that of Delamere Avenue, named after the pioneer settler, and that it was rechristened Kenyatta Avenue. Jomo Kenyatta saw the British in and out. He was born before the first settlement, he was among the first to object when Kenya officially became a colony in 1920, and as Prime Minister he stood in the centre of the Independence Stadium and watched the Union Jack hauled down at midnight on December 11th, 1963. In that short time a country was delimited that had no unity before, a country of great contrasts, from the white coral beaches and palms of the coast to Highland farmland like the English shires, with above that the bamboo forests and glaciers of Mt. Kenya. First the Arab slave-traders came up from the coast, penetrating the forbidding and untamed interior. The missionaries followed literally in their tracks, making the island of Zanzibar their base, just as the slavers had. Then came the Uganda railway and with it the settlers, though Delamere caught his initial view of the Highlands after taking the most unlikely route of all. He marched down from Somaliland across the unending wastes of what is now northern Kenya. Finally the reluctant administrators of the Foreign Office handed over to the professionals of the Colonial Office. It needed only the rise of African nationalism to complete the cycle. Now Kenyatta has taken on the problems of maintaining the unity the British had wrought.

This turbulent half-century of growth involved three immigrant races: Arab, Asian and European. Kenya was the first of Britain's white settled colonies to achieve African rule, a testing ground for the European's future in Africa.

Within two months the backlash of the Zanzibar Revolution made all East Africa quiver under a series of army mutinies, in which one battalion of the new Kenya Army actually turned against the Government and others were on the brink of it. But few of the European community's worst fears were in fact realised. Only a few farms were inundated with African squatters, only a few Europeans were deported, only a small proportion of politicians' speeches were violently anti-white.

It was largely due to Kenyatta that this stability was retained. The old man, the *Mzee wa nguvu*, the elder with the beard, who took the name Kenyatta to identify himself more closely with his country in the twenties, utilised its now being identified with him to balance and restrain the potent forces that threatened the new state even before it was officially born. Today the rest of the world tends to think of him when they think of Kenya, and *vice versa*, which is why I have called the book *Kenyatta's Country*, although only a small part of it is actually about him.

2
JOMO

AFTER WINSTON CHURCHILL, then British Under-Secretary of State for the Colonies, visited Kenya in 1907 he commented in a book called *My African Journey*: 'One would scarcely believe that a centre so new should be able to develop so many divergent and conflicting interests, or that a community so small should be able to give each such vigorous and even vehement expression. There are already in miniature all the elements of keen racial and political discord.'

A half-century later the man who was to inherit the problem from a succession of Colonial Governors, Jomo Kenyatta, was welcomed back from eight years of imprisonment and restriction by the women of his family dancing round the compound of his new house and chanting, in Kikuyu, 'This lovely country of ours, Kenya, has room for everybody with *Uhuru*.' Outside the fence on this cold, drizzling early morning of his release, undeterred by the police aircraft droning in circles overhead and the swarm of General Service Unit men in fatigues and red berets laconically waiting for trouble, a gathering crowd of Africans marched up and down and sang in the same primitive melody as the women: 'People were locked up while fighting for *Uhuru* but now it is inevitable. *Uhuru* is coming, Kenyatta is in the country with us, he is the leader of Africans.'

This moment at Gatundu, up on a ridge of the Kikuyu Reserve, some thirty miles from Nairobi, was incongruous, touching and unexpected. The simple emotion of the songs was evidently not the only sentiment the police had anticipated, for the security precautions had been stringent and the waiting Africans, sporting K.A.N.U.'s red, black and green forage caps and armbands, had not known whether it was that morning, or the next, or the one after, that Kenyatta was being brought down. The dozen or so Press reporters there, I among them, had been telephoned at 6 a.m., and Kenyatta told me afterwards that he himself was only warned an hour and a half before being put aboard a Police Air Wing Cessna at Maralal that the day of his return had come at last. Although the crowd grew rapidly the rioting, violence and demonstrations that the police feared never materialised. Those Kikuyu who hated Kenyatta did not raise their voices, equally there were no sudden inflammatory demands from his supporters to march on Nairobi and massacre the white men who had jailed him. As the songs indicated, it was a time of happiness at Jomo now being free to lead Kenya to independence and, however surprisingly, of racial reconciliation, prefiguring Kenyatta's statements that 'People of different races, colours and religions can walk together to build a new Kenya, a new nation.'

It was extraordinary how during Kenya's transition to independence the really significant days of African achievement, the days when the white officials conjectured aloud on the dangers of letting the lid off the boiling pot too fast and took commensurate precautions, were days that the Africans themselves on no account allowed to be marred by unpleasantness. Polling day in the 1961 Elections, when women walked miles to vote with their babies on their backs and their voting cards clutched in their hands, or sometimes in cleft sticks for safety, was one such occasion. So was the 1963 Election Day. So was the Independence Night, when a white friend of mine walking back from the stadium in the dark next to a group of Africans heard them discussing the urgent need for beating up and chasing out the Europeans of Nairobi—and yet was completely unheeded by them. Kenyatta's release was like these days, one on which the whole of Kikuyuland was set on rejoicing and nothing else.

So the women dancing in the compound, in orange and green costumes and with coils of beads bouncing in their earlobes, bobbed and jigged between policemen and journalists. Kenyatta, wearing plastic sandals emblazoned with the word '*Uhuru*', moved in and out of his new iron-roofed bungalow house, showing friends its defects compared with the one that the Government had razed to the ground during the Emergency, inspected the quantities of furniture which Asian traders in Nairobi had given him to demonstrate their loyal affection, and waved to the crowd with his flywhisk. Youth Wing marshallers obligingly kept a passage clear for the Land Rovers coming and going through the mud to the gate. The trees were thick with small boys getting a bird's-eye view of the goings-on. Achieng Oneko, tall and thin, himself released previously and now Kenyatta's private secretary, conducted groups of the family in shouting *Uhuru*, answering his cry of it in a jerky chorus. Kenyatta's grand-daughter scurried about in her blue school uniform. Inside the house, unseen, the old man's young new wife tremulously made the beds under the severe eye of his senior spouse. The same scene, with variations, was re-enacted for about a week. When I came up again four days later the area looked like the site of a fairground, maize formerly high in the shamba was now trodden flat and one could safely assume that the brewers of tea, lemonade and less identifiable drinks, whose stalls, tin basins and spirit stoves stood near the improvised car park, had found their fortunes.

When Churchill made the comments I quoted earlier, Jomo, Kenya's demon and its saviour, its Machiavelli, Gandhi and Joan of Arc rolled into one, was neither called Kenyatta nor Jomo. He was a motherless young man of about seventeen named Kamau, living on this same one of the countless steep red-earthed ridges that make up Kikuyuland, herding the cattle and tilling his stepfather's shamba. He had been given the Christian name Johnstone by Church of Scotland missionaries who helped bring him up and who saved his life when he was stricken by a serious spinal disease at the age of ten or so—he can only date his birth approximately from his own age group, having been circumcised in 1913. Despite this debt to the missionaries he later wrote of them, in his book *Facing Mount Kenya*: 'They set out to uproot the African body and soul from his old customs and beliefs and put him in a class by himself with all his tribal traditions shattered and his institutions trampled upon.' They had by then particularly offended him by their attempts in the mid-1920's to end female circumcision, a custom basic to Kikuyu traditions.

Although not of an important Kikuyu family, like the Koinanges of the Wambugus, it was as the apostle of Kikuyudom that Kenyatta became known. He identified himself with the Kikuyu mystique of the land by interpreting for Chief Kioi in a big land dispute heard at the Nairobi Supreme Court in 1920. This was the beginning of his public career. Because the Kikuyu tribal lands were more affected by European colonisation than any other tribe's, and because the

Kikuyu have a penchant for intrigue, they took the lead in Kenya politics, which were only emerging in the early 1920's. Kenyatta quickly came to the forefront of this movement, apparently seeing the force latent behind it clearly. 'Land', he wrote later, 'is the most important factor in the social, political and religious life of the tribe. . . . Communion with the ancestral spirits is perpetuated through contact with the soil in which the ancestors of the tribe lie buried.'

By 1924 the District Officer at Fort Hall had reported back to Nairobi that Kenyatta was a dangerous agitator and by 1928, when he was working for the Nairobi Council Works Department, he was General Secretary of the Kikuyu Central Association, a party which aimed to get back the 'stolen lands' from the settlers and was strongly anti-European.

The arguments about the stolen lands have been often enough rehearsed, but they still animate Kikuyu feeling today despite the massive settlement schemes devised to return European farming land to the African. The European view was that the land was empty. In 1902 the railway to Uganda had been opened, built at a cost of £5,500,000, nicknamed the 'lunatic line'. It had to have traffic and the quickest way for this to be obtained was for the British Government to encourage white settlement and development of the Highlands. The Crown Lands Ordinance, under which grants of land were made to settlers, whether freehold or leasehold, was based on native land-tenure practices and stated that land not in beneficial occupation was at the disposal of the Crown. The resultant White Highlands, so called because they were reserved for white occupation, eventually covered 10,200 of the colony's total 220,000 square miles. In 1928 the Director of Agriculture stated that 'The natives have been left in possession of the most fertile land of the colony'.

Needless to say, the Kikuyu took a very different view of it. During 1888 and 1889 a great smallpox epidemic, severe drought and a plague of locusts on top of earlier rinderpest, had combined to drive them out of the Fort Hall District and back to their homelands around Kiambu, near Nairobi. The white settlement started just after this and when the Kikuyu wanted to reoccupy the land they found it closed to them. In the words of a veteran Kikuyu politician called Harry Thuku, 'The Europeans said, "We have bought this land".'

In fact Harry Thuku was in business as a politician before

Kenyatta. He founded the Kikuyu Association and the East Africa Association and he engaged in protest not only against the 'stolen lands' but also against the system of registration, the rise of native taxes in 1920 and the forced-labour system, the essence of which was that the white farmers who needed more labour wrote to the District Commissioner asking for so many men or girls, the D.C. told the chief to send his retainers round and collect them and the tribal police finally despatched them to the farm. Since girls and men went together, this latter incidentally resulted in many illegitimate births, seduction being easier away from the authority of the village elders.

Thuku, however, was arrested and put into restriction in the Northern Frontier District at Kismayo (now in Somalia) in 1920, much as Kenyatta was to be in the 1950's, and did not return from his sojourn there and at Marsabit until 1930. Kenyatta came to prominence in the interim.

Kenyatta is in any case a more dominating type of man than Thuku. His old friend Mbui Koinange describes him as he was in the late twenties. He was a big man and he 'used to wear a large cowboy felt hat with its band decorated by beads-felt, a half sleeve khaki jacket with four pockets all with flaps. Around the waist was a huge beaded belt fastened with a large copper buckle to match, a pair of riding breeches and a pair of light brown boots.' Clad like this he roared through Nairobi's suburbs out to the African reserve after work each day on a powerful motor-cycle. Everyone in the reserve jumped out of the way when they heard him coming. It was from the beaded belt, white, red, green and black, that he took the name Kenyatta, the Kikuyu word for it, abandoning his real name.

In 1929 he went to London to promote the Kikuyu case, visited Moscow, and after a trip home returned to London in 1930 for a stay that was to last sixteen years. By this time he was engaged fully in the young Kikuyu leadership and the length of his absence seems extraordinary, although one has to remember that life for an ambitious African was extremely humiliating at the time. Most ways to real advancement were closed. When Mbui Koinange came home from an American university, the first Kenya African to get a degree, he failed to gain any acceptance in white society and the only jobs available to him were ones that no European graduate would dream of touching. Admittedly this was the period of the depression, when Europeans who are now prosperous farmers faced bankruptcy or took relatively menial jobs, like one friend of mine who was a bus-conductor in Mombasa. But there was none the less little obvious inducement for a go-ahead African who had tasted the possibilities of life in London to return to the reserves in Kenya, even though he continued to receive money from supporters in them.

These sixteen years of Kenyatta's life were varied, shot with radical politics, study, poverty, the crabbed life of cheap cafés and bed-sitting-rooms and fervent hopes of getting Kenya's problems a better hearing. In 1932 he went to Moscow again and is believed to have attended the Lenin School, at which innumerable agitators, including Mao Tse Tung, studied. He joined the British Communist Party when back in London and took a course in social anthropology at London University under Professor Malinowsky, who contributed the preface to his book *Facing Mount Kenya.* He also did numerous odd jobs, one being a small part in the film *Sanders of the River*.

Facing Mount Kenya was a sociological study of the Kikuyu, with Kenyatta's views on politics mixed in and possibly some of Professor Malinowsky's too. It puts the case against colonisation with a virulence, and choice of phraseology, which have strong undertones of Moscow indoctrination. Kenyatta may well have felt them apposite, despite his friends' assertions that he was not outwardly so very bitter at this time. 'The people', he wrote, 'were put under the ruthless domination of European imperialism through the insidious trickery of hypocritical treaties.' There was much more in the same strain, along with the details of tribal life which, when compared to the real hardships, malnutrition and disease of many African villages even now, seems somewhat over-romanticised.

The book was dedicated to 'Moigoi and Wamboi [Kikuyu clans] and all the dispossessed youth of Africa: for perpetuation of communion with ancestral spirits through the fight for African freedom and in the firm faith that the dead, the living and the unborn will unite to rebuild the destroyed shrines.' This is a conscious mysticism, one might say a mysticism cynically exploited, which is part tribalism and part modern Pan Africanism. It has the emphasis on the tribal ritual that Kenyatta said in the book he strongly believed in, expounding the idea that magic is 'one way of transmitting thoughts telepathically from one mind to another'. But it also contains the seeds of that amorphous conception the 'African Personality', with all the emotional heat the phrase conjures up today. It is Kenyatta's *Mein Kampf.*

Kenyatta appears to have been between two worlds at the time he wrote this, for all his astute use of atavistic sentiment to give force to the coming struggle for African Independence. The elders at home had begun to accuse him of losing sight of tribal tradition, so much so that when he and Koinange came to arranging for a frontispiece photograph of the author for the book they agreed that he must somehow be given an 'elderly tone'. Koinange recounts how 'Jomo wore my hyrax and blue monkey cloak. We sharpened a wooden plank for a spear.' They also invented the name Jomo. Feeling that both for this occasion and the future he needed a more traditional first name than Johnstone, 'We made a combination of vowels and consonants until we agreed on "Jomo".' The word also meant 'burning spear' and it stuck, incidentally becoming a major weapon in the armoury of those Kenya officials who were out to get Kenyatta in later years.

Meanwhile the 1939–45 war did what the Kenya Government could not do, though it wanted to: it prevented Kenyatta returning home. He spent the war in England, working as a farm labourer in Sussex some of the time, where he earned the affectionate nickname of Jumbo from the villagers and married an English wife, Edna, who remained in Britain, but who was a guest of honour at the Independence celebrations. Their son Peter has been at Cambridge, is a radical Socialist and hopes to go into Kenya politics eventually. Kenyatta also kept up with his friends in the Labour Party and with the effect the war was likely to have on Britain's Colonial Empire. Immediately afterwards, in 1946, he helped found the Pan Africanist Movement at a meeting in Manchester with Kwame Nkrumah, George Padmore and several others. Its aims, as declared, were not even full independence but were directed more against the subordinate social and economic status of Africans in their own countries. It was, however, the first freedom movement to unite the leaders from different British African colonies, the first move among them to solidarity, and Kenyatta's participation in it helped to make him something much more to his fellow Kenyan politicians than merely a Kikuyu leader. When he returned home later that year it was to join and then head a national party, or one at least less than totally Kikuyu, the Kenya African Union.

The K.A.U. had been started by Thuku in 1944, after the K.C.A. had been banned for subversive activity. In 1946 its President was James Gichuru, son of a chief who was one of the first Kikuyu to be converted to Christianity, educated at the Alliance High School and today the Minister of Finance in Kenyatta's Government. Gichuru stepped down so that Kenyatta could take the Presidency of K.A.U., which everyone pronounced 'cow', just as he was to step down from the Presidency of K.A.N.U. when Kenyatta was released from restriction in 1961.

Kenyatta had been persuaded to return home in order to lead Kenya to independence, and seems to have felt very hesitant about coming. On at least two previous occasions the money for his ticket had been sent but he had failed to arrive. Now, however, he began to achieve an enormous success, for the war years, when African volunteers had seen something of the world serving abroad in the King's African Rifles, had revived interest in politics. Soon he was addressing rallies of 30,000 or 40,000 people, the largest the colony had ever seen. Beginning with a characteristic, long-drawn-out 'Eeeee!', which drew not only attention but wild applause, he would express himself with compelling clarity: 'I want you to know the purpose of K.A.U. It is the biggest purpose the African in Kenya has and it is their mouthpiece which asks for freedom.' K.A.U.'s support, though predominantly Kikuyu, also came from other tribes, notably the Luo. Achieng Oneko, the present Minister of Information, was its General Secretary.

At the same time Koinange and Kenyatta were organising the Kikuyu Independent Schools, based on a teacher-training college which they built with voluntary labour at Githunguri in the reserve. They taught nationalism and as such were viewed as subversive by the authorities, despite the acknowledged shortage of Government-run establishments.

All this activity, both of K.A.U. and the schools, was relatively overt. But growing alongside it, organised by former members of the K.C.A., was the terrorist organisation that came to be known as Mau Mau. Kenyatta claimed then, and still does, that he doesn't even know what the words Mau Mau mean. 'What is this Mau Mau?' he used to ask in public. There are plenty of theories—that it derived from a terrorist group among Kikuyu on the Mau Summit—that it was a mouthing sound, meaning 'I will eat you up', and so on. Kikuyu loyalists tell one it started in a small way, just someone asking you to their hut for a drink and then threatening to kill you if you didn't take the oath. At all events it existed and it had two aims: to rid Kenya of the European and to put the Kikuyu in control of the country afterwards. There has been real fear among the rest of the tribes of Kikuyu domination ever since. It also put Kenyatta in jail, just as surely as the circumcision group of the forties had chosen him as its honorary leader.

The trial at Kapenguria, after a State of Emergency had been declared in October 1952, ended with Kenyatta being sentenced to seven years' imprisonment for managing the Mau Mau. It has been written about enough already. On the one hand the District Officers of that time firmly believed Kenyatta to have been the evil genius behind Mau Mau, and while admitting that the evidence was flimsy, point out that many of the witnesses the Crown wanted to call were murdered before they could testify. His friends say that while he was certainly the only African who could have stopped the spread of Mau Mau had he denounced it unequivocally, which he never did, he would equally certainly have been murdered. Many people are convinced that the trial was a travesty of justice and Mr. Dingle Foot asks why Mr. Justice Thacker was called out of retirement to preside over it. One is left with the image of Kenyatta, burly and understandably sullen, clad in his leather lumber jacket, handcuffed to a fellow prisoner and waiting to be loaded into a truck by the police. Then his life passes into a semi-oblivion, while the unquestionable bestiality of the Mau Mau, especially of African against African, follows its much headlined course until, in 1955–6 £15,000,000 of the £36,000,000 Kenya budget was being spent on prisons, police and security services.

To the enquirer interested in Kenyatta's mental make-up, and who has had only superficial conversation with the man himself about this period, some scraps of information throw sudden illumination on the lost years of 1953–61. There is a doctor, a fluent Russian speaker by chance, who was called to examine him and found that he still remembered Russian well; there are Kenyatta's own remarks about how he made a study of comparative religion, 'I have read practically all the principal religions—I read them all in prison.' There is a police officer who told me that he had been drinking himself to death in prison, never expecting release, until with remarkable self-discipline he gave up smoking and drinking and began preparing himself for his return to life. The wind of change was apparent long before Mr. Macmillan coined the phrase and, knowing that his African warders, or at least one of them, did contrive occasional communication between prisoner and the outside world, it is reasonable to suppose that the news of Ghana's independence in 1957 stirred him to take a grip on himself.

Then in 1958 Oginga Odinga, a Luo elected to the Legislative Council as the Emergency died away, raised the demand for the old man's release. Although there were some who feared his return, partly because they felt he had led the African cause to disaster in 1952, the cry compelled allegiance once it was raised. Kenyatta became the symbol of everything that the British Government was denying Kenya. At the elections of March 1961, when Africans first acquired a majority of seats in the Legislative Council, he was so much a hero among Africans that the only slogan any politician needed at the hustings was '*Uhuru na Kenyatta*'.

Indeed it was a real question whether the godlike figure he became during the last months of detention could survive the return to earth. The Governor, Sir Patrick Renison, having recently condemned him as the 'leader to darkness and death', now finding his release inescapable, ordained it in a way that could hardly have been bettered for boosting his prestige. For some eight weeks he was allowed to receive visitors, a handful at a time only, at his last place of detention, Maralal. They came in a constant stream, like mortals to the oracle, a procedure Kenyatta seems to have enjoyed, for there is undeniable vanity in his character. It immediately became clear that he was still a past master at telling people what they wanted to hear. The representatives of no less than seven religious sects came away satisfied at his future intentions and proclaiming his virtue; four major contenders for political power returned from Maralal to Nairobi and announced their unofficial appointment as his political heir; Americans found him a convincing exponent of democracy and socialists of socialism, while a representative of the white settlers thought him solicitous for their future welfare. In private conversation he certainly can be both understanding and charming.

Kenyatta's character is complex and difficult to analyse even though the reasons for his immense public appeal are clear. His very appearance is somewhat awe-inspiring. He is of only average height, but broad, and the set of his great grizzled bearded head on his shoulders bespeaks power. His voice is normally calm, deep and convincing—except when he is annoyed, and then it is harsh and tough. When talking of 'my people', as he often does, he is fatherly and benevolent.

But whether he is being devious or direct, humorous or bitter, all of which he can be within a short space, what strikes one most is the force of personality that he can project, especially through his eyes. These are very dark, pupil and iris sometimes seeming one, and yet there is an ominous pale blue green depth flickering in them. They can be dull, saying nothing; they may blink innocently from behind reading glasses, or they may be compelling, hypnotic and not a little sinister. There is nothing weary about them, despite Kenyatta being now in his mid-seventies. Indeed his intense magnetism, his development of the chanting, swaying mass meeting, and his ability to hold, almost to transfix, his listeners has often been compared to hypnosis, while the widespread reverence for him incorporates a definite element of fear.

In public he is at his best speaking extempore, being considered a magnificent orator in both Kikuyu and Swahili, though the occasions he can use Kikuyu are now few, for it is liable to arouse the antagonism of any members of other tribes who may be present. In either language he employs continual imagery and proverbs and likes to finish off with a joke and long, low chuckle—the same that in 1952 convinced police officers that when condemning terrorism he was deliberately laughing at his own words. Perhaps he was, but the practice remains characteristic of him. Indeed, Thuku told him in 1951 that he ought to go into the theatre, he made people laugh so much. Only in English does he sound uncomfortable and stilted, feeling for his words, not quite getting the pronunciation right, all of which contrasts oddly with the fluency of his writing in *Facing Mount Kenya.* On Independence Day, replying in the stadium to Prince Philip's formal transference of sovereignty, he abruptly abandoned a set speech in English and launched into a Swahili peroration, which incidentally drew tumultuous applause and finally confounded those critics who claimed he was losing his powers.

Suggestions that he was a dead letter, a spent force, began to circulate as soon as he descended from Maralal in 1961. I had a long interview with him then, in the new house at Gatundu with a policeman manning a radio out on the verandah. Whilst contemptuously rejecting ideas that he should now take six months' rest, he was very like a man finding the use of his legs again after some months in a hospital bed. 'Places like London and Manchester,' he declared, 'I know better than Nairobi now.' He occasionally contradicted himself, saying one moment of race relations, 'My philosophy is love thy neighbour as thyself', and the next, 'I have not been in touch with the public so I cannot make any comment'.

Understandably his attitudes had the underlying feel of 1952, like hesitancy to commit himself on the Mau Mau's heritor organisation, the Land Freedom Army, of which there was allegedly evidence of his having been in touch with when in restriction at Lodwar. 'I do not know what their aims or activities are, but anything that is harmful to Kenya I denounce.' He was feeling his way, shrewdly, carefully, and by the end of that first week back at Gatundu he was visibly extremely tired. The people of Kenya were demanding that the prophet should come out of eight years of solitude with all the answers to all the current political questions. At the same time he had somehow to rehabilitate himself before answering, despite not having yet recovered the insignia of his old leadership, the great gold ring for his left hand and the elephant-headed walking stick. 'My stick and my ring are locked up with the Government,' he said, and added, smiling, 'Why they locked them up too I don't know—perhaps they think they had my juju!'

Whether or not they did, he soon had them with him again and his magic began to reassert itself. For some months all he really needed to do was to put no foot wrong during his crucial re-entry to the political scene. Being a wily and extremely experienced politician, and no doubt aware of the future power his fame would give him, he accomplished this beautifully. He let others put him forward, indicating merely his willingness to serve Kenya if Kenya wanted him. For months he kept out of both political parties, K.A.N.U. and K.A.D.U., then engaged in bitter constitutional wrangling, finally accepting the Presidency of K.A.N.U. after James Gichuru stepped down for him. A Parliamentary seat was found for him through an arranged by-election, after the laws against a man with more than a two-year jail record being elected had been amended. In June 1963, after the K.A.N.U. victory in the General Election, he became Kenya's first Prime Minister, and in December 1964, its President.

Gradually, too, his flamboyance, so much a part of his character, has revived and been modified to the new situation. The lumber jacket and the sandals faded out of public life, for all that they had seemed an essential part of him since his Hyde Park Corner oratory before the war. Instead a more tailored figure now stands portly but erect before the leather benches of Kenya's National Assembly. A golden cockerel badge, symbol of K.A.N.U., sits in the lapel of his blue chalk-stripe suit. Where once there was an open-necked shirt there now hangs the red, gold, black and white striped K.A.N.U. tie. On his head, above the grey jutting beard, sits a Luo beaded hat, an honour conferred by the Luo on their leaders and in this case a visible indication that the old man is not merely a Kikuyu leader but a national one. However, the beaded belt remains, though it is hidden by his suit most of the time, and so do the stick, the ring and the heavy silver-handled flywhisk. No one, considering the overall effect, could fail to see that this is the same Kenyatta who wore a cowboy hat and riding breeches on his motor-bike, but it is a Kenyatta manicured and polished, a Kenyatta who now has a Mercedes, a Lincoln Convertible and a Rolls-Royce to choose between for his transport, a Kenyatta internationalised.

3

Harambee—
Kenyatta's Party in Power

'UHURU NA KENYATTA' was a highly successful rallying cry, the equivalent of 'King and Country'. It had, as a public-relations man would say, the right personalised appeal. In Kenyatta the Africans of Kenya began to see themselves imprisoned and, as the theme was developed, tortured, humiliated, defiled. I have seen no evidence that Kenyatta was tortured, but that is irrelevant to an emotion-raising exercise of the sort that was mounted in Kenya once Odinga had scandalised the European members of the Legislative Council by reopening the old man's case in June 1958.

The way that the campaign for his release was mounted, with the organising of 'spontaneous' public demand, should be a model for political agitators anywhere. Kenyatta was made synonymous with solidarity. The Pan African Freedom Movement of East and Central Africa honoured him as its true, if absent, leader. It rapidly became impossible for local politicians to do otherwise than base their appeals at the hustings on his release. Mboya canvassed his Nairobi constituency in the 1961 Election, aptly named the Kenyatta Election by one historian, with his supporters holding aloft a large painting of Kenyatta over the heart of which was superimposed Mboya's own face. In March of that year Mboya and Gichuru had found themselves having to answer open accusations that they did not want Kenyatta free. This was at the Cairo meeting of the All-African Peoples' Conference. Although numerous people did indeed not want him out of restriction, including the representatives of various smaller tribes, united in the Kenya African Democratic Union, that union's leader, the school-teacher Ronald Ngala, joined in demands for his release. Fears of future Kikuyu domination had to go by the board, publicly at least.

There were good reasons why this was desirable. In 1958 the rising generation of Kenyan politicians were riven by quarrelling and conflicts of tribal and personal interest. These had been accentuated by the Colonial Government's refusal to allow nation-wide political parties to function in case there was a revival of the Emergency situation. Thus an attempt made in May 1958 to register a Convention of Africans' Associations, which would have paralleled the European Convention of Associations founded by settlers back in the 1920's, failed. The obvious way to arrest the disastrous fragmentation of African opinion was to find a supra tribal figure. Kenyatta was the only possible choice, despite his identification with the Kikuyu, and a very useful one in that he was a living martyr. The pro-African politicians in Britain, Fenner Brockway, Barbara Castle, John Stonehouse and others, all knew him. He was an ideal stick with which to beat the British Government. At the same time while restricted he could meet no one, never be quoted, never make a political mistake. He was the ideal unifying factor for the Africans engaged in the Independence struggle.

There is no doubt that once he was free Kenyatta was the first to realise the dangers inherent in this, and the dying adequacy of '*Uhuru na Kenyatta*' as a national policy. Furthermore the momentum gained from his release could not last for ever. Rumours soon arose that he was a broken man, that one appearance on the American television, harassed by an inquisitorial interviewer, would destroy his international reputation. It was said, and possibly with truth, that the younger politicians could dance rings round him at the conference table. His answer, quickly coined, was a new slogan, '*Harambee*'.

'*Harambee*' means, approximately, 'let's pull together'. A purist in Swahili would insist that it ought to be spelt '*Halambee*', but since it is now enshrined on the Kenyan coat of arms as the national motto, the purist would be unlikely to prevail. He would indeed have had to run for shelter from the thunderstorm of '*Harambees*' that accompanied *Uhuru*. The old man himself began all his open-air speeches with it, drawing out the syllables resoundingly and putting a strong accent on the final 'bay'. If his Mercedes got stuck in the mud the bearded head would crane out of the window galvanising passers-by to push the automobile out with roars of '*Harambee*', like an old-time bosun urging sailors to haul on a rope. When he was sworn in as Prime Minister in June 1963 he concluded: 'I therefore give you the call—*Harambee!* Let us all work together for our country Kenya.' He even had a meeting of white settlers at Nakuru shouting the slogan back at him just as if they were an African audience.

Within weeks it had become a national craze. No minister could open a conference, no Parliamentary Secretary address a school, no backbencher talk to his constituents, without using the word constantly. Like giving the 'V' sign in Britain during the war, it became the acknowledged way of expressing national solidarity, and, since everyone with the slightest pretensions in public life wanted to make it clear to his superiors that he was behind the Prime Minister, Kenya echoed to the cry. A trade-union leader, calling his members out on a wildcat, unofficial strike, even announced that his union was striking 'in the spirit of *Harambee*'.

This paradoxical declaration is, however, as nothing compared to the absurdities that anyone trying to make a nation out of Kenya has to face. The Kenya that Kenyatta's Government took over on December 12th, 1963, was a classic product of the scramble for Africa, a geographical accident, a country but no country and a fearful challenge.

Its frontiers, as my geography master never tired of describing longitude and latitude, are lines on the map, not, repeat not, gentlemen, lines drawn on the ground. Anyone who did try to draw Kenya's frontiers on the ground would be in for a long and weary job. For the most part they follow no natural feature, no river or escarpment, they accord with no tribal boundary. Lord Lugard wrote of the 1885 Berlin Conference: 'The Powers, in their haste to declare the "spheres of influence" which they claimed, had not in some cases time to go through the formality of making treaties with the natives, and considered it sufficient to notify that they claimed them as hinterlands.' So the Tanganyika-Kenya boundary divides the great Masai tribe, and was only changed to put Kilimanjaro in what was German East Africa as a birthday present from Queen Victoria to the Kaiser.

To the west the frontier is a shade more logical, passing as it does athwart the 14,000 ft. high slopes of Mt. Elgon, although Uganda once administered as far south-east in the Rift as Naivasha, sixty miles from Nairobi.

At the coast there was the complication of the Coastal Strip, that ten-mile-deep fringe of country officially called the Kenya Protectorate which Britain had rented from the Sultan of Zanzibar in 1890 for £10,000 a year and where the only flag allowed to fly from a pole directly placed in the ground was the Sultan's plain red one. Happily one of the Sultan's last sovereign acts, before the Revolution of January 1964 deposed him, was to give the Strip to Kenya. However ridiculous his ownership was in practice, his handing it over was generous, and he was ill-repaid when Kenya refused him asylum, even temporarily, a few weeks later. The official reason given was that his presence there might have caused discontent among his former subjects, which conceivably it might have done, for although they accepted Kenyan rule without trouble one of the major divisions that the spirit of *Harambee* had to heal was the coast's feeling of individuality and separatedness from Kenya.

The rising generation of African historians, researching into the organisation of the tribal societies of the past, quibble at words like 'explorer' and 'discovery'. But even while referring to Livingstone as a mere foreign visitor, they agree that the interior of East Africa was kept in isolation for many centuries by its inaccessibility, until missionaries and explorers, determined upon the diffusion of light abroad and the enlargement of knowledge at home, opened it up to the gaze of Europe in the nineteenth century.

By contrast to such rare and intrepid excursions the coastline was long known to the outside world and settled by Indians, Arabs and Portuguese. It is as idyllic as a travel poster, verged with palms and long white coral beaches, blessed furthermore by two regular monsoons, the south-east and the north-west, on which the Indians came and the trading dhows of Araby still depend. Mombasa was visited in the first century A.D. by the unknown Greek author of the *Periplus of the Erythraeean Sea*, who referred to it as Tonike. Arab colonisation started about the eighth century and led to the tiny sultanates that dotted the littoral at Lamu, Malindi, Kilifi, Mombasa and on down southwards. There had already been Indian settlement. In the century following Vasco da Gama's 1498 voyage down the coast the Portuguese established a control centred on Fort Jesus at Mombasa. This fort was completed in 1592 and finally fell to the Arabs again in 1698. From then until the British came the coast was almost entirely dominated by the Sultan of Zanzibar.

Inland, however, the tropical vegetation gives way to dust and scrub, the level of the country rising dauntingly, up and up 5,000 feet to the level of the great central plateau of the African continent, and beyond that to the Rift Valley and the Highlands. This intervening 200 miles has various names. The Nyika, the thorn country, the Nyiri desert, the Taru desert. After the rains there convolvulus flowers burst out white and purple, grass seeds germinate, the bushes are suddenly green. But most of the year it is a wilderness, and travellers have always hated it. 'Full of wild beasts, such as the rhinoceroses, buffaloes and elephants', Rebmann noted in his diary on May 11th, 1848, and on May 29th: 'The vegetable world of the wilderness seems to have conspired to make the way difficult for us poor wanderers.' Today, whilst the wildlife attracts tourists well enough, the wilderness still conspires against them. Motorists know the greasy, twisting Mombasa road, happily being tarmacked much faster under an African Government than it was under the colonial one, as the slipway to the sea. Although the railway made Mombasa into the gateway of Kenya, the sense of remoteness from the capital remains, reinforced by a hotter, humider climate and a very different human outlook, one both lazier and more humane than Nairobi's.

To the north, Kenyatta faces more active difficulties. The contentious Somali frontier, redrawn in the 1930's between the British and Italians to give Somalia the port of Kisimayo, but still leaving 100,000 Somalis inside Kenya, deserves a chapter to itself later on. The other frontier with Ethiopia, three times laid down yet never ratified, Kenyatta managed to settle early in 1964. The British had found the Ethiopians about as ready to concede land as a dog is to share a bone. 'The Abyssinians,' a colonial official noted in the 1920's, 'are far from docile. Moreover they have rifles and their Government has been admitted to the League of Nations.' In spite of putting Haile Selassie back on the Imperial throne in 1941, the British never achieved final agreement on the Kenya frontier. Joseph Murumbi, Kenyatta's Minister of State, did, however. Not only was the ideal of Pan African unity an aid towards settlement, both countries had raging border disputes with Somalia which inspired agreement on this and on a mutual defence agreement against external aggression.

One compelling reason why African states are so reluctant to alter their boundaries is that it's hard enough to create a sense of collective identity within them as things are. If you let tribal demands influence your frontiers then you unleash a flood of internal demands and risk your country's frail unity collapsing before you can stop it. There are forty-seven tribes in Kenya. Many can be loosely grouped together, like the Tugen, Elgeo, Nandi and others who make up the Kalenjin and who have acted together politically. But in trying to bring them all together in a sense of Kenyan identity the Government faces more than merely preventing the Somalis seceding or the Masai wanting to join Tanganyika. It faces basic disparities between ethnic groups which are bound to remain potentially explosive factors politically for a long time.

The vast majority of Kenya's Africans are Bantu, notably the Kikuyu, who are now nearly a quarter of Kenya's total population; the Kamba; the Giriama of the coast, whose women always wear a short white kilt, or else a thick grass skirt; the Abaluhya near Lake Victoria. There are many others, all loosely related by their languages and by being tillers of the soil rather than herders of cattle. They came to East Africa about 400 years ago, in two major migrations, one from West and Central Africa, the other from the North. It seems to have been a slow drifting movement, for the Kikuyu only crossed the Chania River, twenty miles north of where Nairobi was later built, in 1820. It was also every bit as much as 'colonisation' as the later entry of Europeans, for the true indigenous people, like the Wanderobo, a few of whom still exist as honey-hunters in the forests, were forced back, reduced, and to some extent assimilated by marriage.

The Kikuyu have long been regarded as cunning, guileful and in all ways tricky to deal with. They avoid plain statements, finding a metaphor almost always preferable to a straight declaration. Just before the Emergency Jomo Kenyatta frequently avoided denouncing the Mau Mau by this means. On one famous occasion he said Mau Mau should be sent down to the roots of the mugumo, the sacred fig tree. This could have meant to be buried and done away with, or equally been advice to Mau Mau organisers to go underground.

During the Emergency a lot of old scores were settled under the guise of terrorism, a lot of denunciations of 'terrorists' made not from loyalty to the Government but from the desire to put a rich uncle or cousin out of the way and take over his land. Nor was this merely the way the white administrators saw it. To other tribes the disgusting thing about the Lari massacre, the thing that made Kamba police constables vomit when they reached the scene, was that the bestiality had been inflicted by Kikuyu upon their own tribespeople. Even now, when these horrors are being forgotten, and are best forgotten, the tribe remains a mystery to others. A Baganda friend from Kampala who read the draft of this chapter told me that even after a dozen years working in Nairobi he still couldn't understand the Kikuyu and that while spontaneous gaiety is as much a characteristic of the Bantu as the broad mouth and snub nose, he always found the Kikuyu strangely humourless. There is no doubt that the peculiarities of their character, coupled with their political acumen and dynamic approach towards self-advancement, accounts for much of the other Kenya tribes' fear of Kikuyu domination. Nor does their explanation of their deviousness in past years—namely that it was necessary if the colonialists were to be outwitted—carry complete conviction.

By comparison the Masai and other Nilo-Hamitic tribes have always seemed more noble to the outsider, more upright, more to be respected. The Masai quickly became a legend and the British had a separate treaty with them, one with which not they but the British later played tricks. So high was the repute of the Masai, both as natural gentlemen and as cattle-ranchers, that back in 1903, the year that the first association of colonists was formed, Lenana the Chief Laibon of the Masai was invited to judge at the Nairobi Cattle Show.

Thirty years later a friend of mine, then a young farm manager on an estate near Longonot in the Rift Valley, suffered a theft of cattle by two Masai. He tracked them down and when they tried to spear him shot one dead and wounded the other. Even after telling the police he remained rather worried about possible consequences. What actually happened was that the Laibon of that section of the tribe summoned my friend and congratulated him on dealing out correct summary justice, adding, however, that in future he the Laibon would prefer to do it. They then both ate traditional Masai food, blood and milk mixed and curdled with cow's urine, as a mark of friendship, and my friend departed. The trickiest part of the whole procedure had been forcing himself to swallow the mixture.

Unfortunately the warrior tradition was a bloodthirsty one. The two sports of tribes who live on blood or meat and milk, like the Masai and the Turkana, are cattle-raiding and killing. No young man comes of age properly before he has taken human life, and the more men fall to his spear, the greater he is. The practice is far from dead today, though education, and even more the power of the law, have reduced both it and cattle-raiding to some extent. Both are closely connected with tribal honour and since the Masai have an almost religious belief that all the cattle in the world were originally theirs the raiding is hard to stop. They also have scant respect for Government officers who go about their business in a twentieth-century manner. To the Masai a policeman who evades personal combat when arresting a man is simply a despicable coward. This makes law enforcement, especially by African police of another tribe, an extremely tricky affair.

Although this was all immensely appealing to the British, who have cherished the Masai in their minds as the true noble savage, it is noticeably less fascinating to the Luo and Kikuyu who run K.A.N.U. and govern Kenya today. They can truthfully point to the many things the Bantu and the Hamitic tribes have in common, like the frequent intermarriage between Masai men and Kikuyu women —albeit based on the Kikuyu women's reputation as hard workers. But for all the smoothing over differences that takes place on the surface in public life, underneath their dangers are keenly felt.

Tribalism is Kenya's greatest *bête noire*, if this is the right phrase for the occasion, but the other 'isms' barely lag behind. There are regionalism and white-settlerism, racialism, imperialism and neo-colonialism, though as yet communism is clean of heresy. Catch-words matter a great deal in politics everywhere, Africa being no exception, and so just as the spirit of *Harambee* has to fight the evil 'isms', it is aided by the good '-ations', Africanisation, localisation, even honest-to-goodness blackanisation, while to counter the potential menace of commercialism there is the trusty threat of nationalisation. This last, of course, reveals the fallacy in my obviously superficial division, since socialism is the basic policy of almost all African governments. But it remains curious how the 'isms' have led in acquiring an undesirable connotation.

The first three that I named—tribalism, regionalism and white-settlerism—all contain a potent depth of meaning because they express the forces against which Kenyatta has had to struggle hardest in his drive to create a unified African state and change the concept of a 'white man's country', first propounded by Sir Charles Eliot back in 1903, into the black man's country that it had so long been the aim of the nationalists to achieve. The cry of '*Harambee*' would, Kenyatta hoped, be taken up by Europeans and Asians, while some of his followers indicated that it damn well better be. But basically it was an African word for an African chorus to chant, a call both to unity and work.

Inevitably the British attempt to soften tribal animosities by the policy of regionalism became the target for vilification. K.A.N.U. members, for reasons both genuine and expedient, were quick to set about identifying it with the very virus of tribalism that it was designed to counter.

The idea was simple enough. Kenya was to be divided into six (later seven) regions. Each of these would have its own Regional Assembly, its own civil servants, its own powers and rights guaranteed by the Constitution. The seven were the Coast, the Rift Valley, the Central, the North-East, Nyanza, Western and Eastern. In each there was an effective dominance of certain tribes. The Kikuyu controlled the Central Region, including most of the Aberdares and a certain amount of white farmed land which it quickly became recognised would eventually have to be transferred to Kikuyu ownership. The Nyanza Region round Lake Victoria was Luo. Naturally K.A.N.U., being basically a Luo-Kikuyu combination, with the Embu, Meru and Kamba thrown in, these two regions were solidly pro-Government. Down at the Coast power lay with the Giriama, the Arabs and other supporters of Ronald Ngala's K.A.D.U. The Rift Valley Region, a vastly long area that included the Kalenjin tribes and some Masai, was equally a K.A.D.U. area. The seventh, the North-East, Somali dominated, refused for many months even to elect representatives. It wanted secession from Kenya to the Somali Republic.

Inevitably these nation-wide political groupings overshadowed the other aspects of the regional system. The regions were meant to protect any one tribe from being swamped nationally by others, but although it was immediately noticeable that the Kikuyu of the Central Region were as quick as anyone else to use the rights thus bestowed on them, the cruder generality of certain regions being agin the Government became preponderant. It would have been odd indeed if they hadn't, because behind the system, which K.A.D.U. called 'Majimbo', there lay a short yet emotional history of strife, fought out as much in the foyers of London hotels and in the Colonial Office as in Kenya itself.

The fears of the Masai, Kalenjin, Abaluhya, Giriama and others of being completely swamped by the Luo-Kikuyu combination after Independence were genuine enough. They had come late into the game of modern politics, just as they had lagged in other ways, being slow to welcome education, or to acquire European skills and habits of dressing. They were not sophisticated, quick on the uptake and opportunist like the Kikuyu. Furthermore, they had good reason to think that the vast increase in the size of the Kikuyu tribe, which must now be nearer 2,000,000 than the official 1,500,000, would lead to loss of some of their land. It was no secret that the Kikuyu cast envious eyes on the Mau and Bahati escarpments and on other parts of the Rift Valley. Indeed, once the Central Region was in existence it was remarkable how Kikuyu unemployed applying to the Nakuru Labour Exchange would refuse work on European farms in the Central Region. The whole Central Region was thought of as Kikuyu property now, therefore the place to take a job, and later claim the land, was in the Rift Valley Region. Just how unpleasant tribal clashes might become had been illustrated in 1961 when K.A.N.U. held one of its first mass meetings at Ngong, a few miles outside Nairobi on the edge of the Masai Reserve. It ended with the Masai running for their spears, which they had concealed in bushes not far off, and killing two Kikuyu.

These and other incidents persuaded colonial officials to take seriously the demands of those tribes whose political associations had finally coalesced into K.A.D.U. in 1959. But at the same time the K.A.N.U.-K.A.D.U. relationship was becoming increasingly embittered over the release of Kenyatta. The March 1961 elections were, as I have said, fought as far as Africans were concerned on the Kenyatta issue. The European electors, watching the portly Sir Ferdinand Cavendish Bentinck canvassing from his Land Rover, his election symbol of a rhino painted on its doors, or cursing the supposed infidelity to his fellow whites of Sir Michael Blundell, it might not have seemed so. Air Commodore Howard Williams, Churchillian in appearance, kind, forthright and amusing, marched to the polling booth waving to the African voters and calling out, '*Uhuru na Howard Williams*'. But those same Africans, voting according to the instructions of their parties, thought mainly in terms of Kenyatta's release. When K.A.N.U. gained eighteen seats to K.A.D.U.'s twelve and refused to govern without Kenyatta the situation came to a head.

Sir Patrick Renison, then the Governor, astonished the K.A.N.U. leaders, Oginga Odinga, James Gichuru, Tom Mboya and the others, by insisting that Kenyatta was still an unacceptable risk to security. He called four of them to Government House in answer to their demands, switched on the radio and let them hear his previously recorded broadcast to the country on the subject. They in turn refused to form a government. When eventually K.A.D.U. did so, being given a working majority by the appointment of additional special members to the Legco, it was clear that if the precedents of other African states were any guide, K.A.D.U. were constructing their own coffin. In the meantime they were pledged to create a Regional Constitution before independence.

There is no doubt that Ronald Ngala, the leader of K.A.D.U., co-operated with Sir Patrick Renison because he thought it was the only way to achieve any advance towards independence at all. Memories of the Emergency were then fresh and the powers of the Governor very real. Ngala had been the leader of the African delegation to the Lancaster House Conference of 1960, at which to their intense surprise the Africans got two-thirds of what they asked, and considerably more than they aimed for, from Ian Macleod, including the major agreement that political power would be transferred to African hands. Now here they were with an African majority on the Legco for the first time, and a deadlock with the Governor bogging down progress. So after weeks of rumour-infested negotiation Ngala agreed to lead a government, though he did not have the title of Prime Minister.

Ngala himself is a pleasant person to meet. A small man, soberly dressed, though with a traditional beaded cap on his head, he puffs away at his pipe, ponders, reflects and makes quiet decisions. He was headmaster of a school at the Coast, is a Giriama and, at the time of writing, is still President of the Coast Regional Assembly. Although he lacks the sharp and pointed debating quality of Tom Mboya, with whom he was often to come into conflict over Constitutional points, he speaks with sincerity. Above all, though in fact as concerned for Kenya's independence as any other nationalist, his manner and approach to politics always suggested stability and common sense. His place in Kenya now ought to be that of alternative to Odinga and Mboya in the succession to Kenyatta, since while both these two arouse violent antagonisms, Odinga on account of his communist support and Mboya mainly because he is so self-evidently head and shoulders above most of his colleagues, Ronald Ngala has the qualities of compromise. However, when K.A.N.U. was formed in 1959, and he was nominated as treasurer, he was in London and so disliked the way this office was handed him that he finally declined it.

In Kenya there was great bitterness at K.A.D.U. collaborating with Renison and by-passing the real African majority party, K.A.N.U, even though K.A.D.U. made their co-operation conditional upon the release of Kenyatta 'as soon as possible'. The new Government's rule was bound to prove, and did prove, short-lived. When Kenyatta was reluctantly released, still refusing to commit himself to either party and strongly advocating unity of the two, it looked as though a coalition would be formed. But in mid-October, after five weeks of wrangling, the Constitutional talks that were going on between the two parties broke down and K.A.D.U. came out into the open with their fears of Kikuyu domination, of the quashing of minorities after Independence and of a police state if K.A.N.U. were in power. I happened to sit next to Ngala on a flight from Mombasa to Nairobi during this period and he told me he would not expect to be a free man five years after Independence. Happily his fears have so far proved quite unjustified.

Several occurrences had provoked his disquiet. The Kenya Land Freedom Army, acknowledged to be the new name for the Mau Mau, had erupted into the newspaper headlines. Fifty of them, in a kind of uniform, had actually paraded by Ainsworth Bridge on the way into Nairobi on the day Kenyatta made his triumphal re-entry to the capital. The Land Freedom Army was soon outlawed, and most African leaders denounced it save Kenyatta himself, who according to his associates was still fearful of assassination by his own tribe. Worse still, the proceedings of the 'Gatundu Parliament' came into the open. This was a group of prominent young Kikuyu politicians which met regularly in the evenings at Kenyatta's Gatundu house. Their object was widely believed to be the perpetuation of Kikuyu domination in Kenya politics. As more and more Mau Mau detainees were released it seemed that there might well be a plot to persuade Kenyatta to lead the Kikuyu rather than the nation, and through the Kikuyu to control K.A.N.U. and so in turn the whole of Kenya. The idea of a conspiracy was given further credence when another ex-detainee, Paul Ngei, a Kamba, but an old associate of Kenyatta, called a press conference and declared that he and other members of the old guard of the Emergency—none of them K.A.N.U. committee members—were going to reorganise K.A.N.U. and give its affairs a new dynamism. Ngei had also sat on the platform with Kenyatta at various mass rallies and proclaimed to wildly enthusiastic crowds that all European land would be confiscated and given to Africans at *Uhuru*. None of his statements was contradicted by Kenyatta.

In fact Kenyatta was perforce having to play the game softly and invariably failed to correct anything that anyone else said. The extremist sentiments that he let pass excited comment and flustered K.A.D.U. Meanwhile, on October 8th, the Governor managed to acerbate relations between the two parties further. In the time-honoured tradition of stating the obvious just at the moment when face-saving demands its neglect he made a nation-wide broadcast aimed at K.A.N.U. 'It is the African leaders who have produced this position of standstill which is doing so much harm to the economy and security of their own country. . . . Boycotts and walkouts and smashing of constitutions by refusing to work them may have served their purpose in the past. At this stage I cannot see how they will do anything but delay independence.'

It is easy to attack Colonial Governors for their faults, while skating over their successes. Renison, however, was not the man for this job. He had distinguished himself in British Guiana during a time of unrest, dealing impartially with all concerned. But at this point Kenya needed something more than scrupulous fairness. The African politicians were on the threshold of real power. With a Colonial Secretary who was determined to move the colony to Independence as fast as he could, and was considered by Blundell and others to have deceived them over how soon it could actually be expected, the Governor's task had to include playing up to the tantrums of the emergent African leaders. Yet Renison was not prepared to do this, nor did he apparently feel much sympathy for their aspirations, sincerely felt though they were. His study of past documents evidently convinced him that Kenyatta was an evil man. But from the moment that he declared this publicly he was bound to be publicly humiliated, since the political logic of the Kenya situation was inescapable, if unpleasant—Kenyatta was going to lead the country. Equally unpleasant to an honest man, and equally inescapable, was the fact that once the Lancaster House Conference of 1960 had taken place an increasing part of the Governor's duty would be to prepare the ground for continuing British influence after Independence. This meant humouring the African leadership and being prepared to ditch the settlers if the Conservative Party at home decided their sacrifice was necessary. Whether Renison ever received instructions in these terms I do not know. It is unlikely. Many minor events suggested that he was less than fully in Macleod's confidence. None the less a new image of British authority was needed and Sir Patrick did not fit it.

Despite all this, the coalition Government of K.A.D.U. and K.A.N.U. was formed after the February 1962 talks in London, with a dual Ministerial system that put Kenyatta, who had by then taken the Presidency of K.A.N.U. and been elected to the Legco, side by side with Ngala. The Constitutional talks dragged on with Ngala striving the whole time, by manœuvre and obstruction when necessary, to achieve an entrenchment of the rights of minorities before Independence so that they could not be taken away after it. The struggle, carried through the Conference in London and further fortnightly meetings in Nairobi, held up *Uhuru* for about a year. Finally Renison was replaced by a totally different personality, Malcolm MacDonald, a one-time Labour Colonial Secretary, lately High Commissioner in South-East Asia, and overall a man admirably chosen to speed matters up. MacDonald, silver-haired, gentle, remarkably willing to see someone else's point of view, looked the exact opposite of a filthy colonialist. At the same time he intended to make things move in Nairobi. He immediately convinced the African leaders that his aim was theirs—*Uhuru sasa* (independence now)—while maintaining, beneath a most relaxed charm of manner that even Odinga appreciated, his determination to preserve the rights of minorities in so far as he was able. The smoothness of relationships in Kenya's final handover to African rule owed a great deal to MacDonald, so did the first year of Independence.[1]

Meanwhile Ngala was fighting his battles in London too. He employed a London public-relations company to make his party's views known, the gist of which were contained in a handout issued before the London Constitutional Conference in February 1962:

1. Malcolm MacDonald was Kenya's only Governor-General, from December 12th, 1963–December 12th, 1964. When Kenya became a Republic he was appointed British High Commissioner.

'If the rights of individuals are to be safeguarded, and if there is to be confidence that they will be, Kenya will need in addition (to a stable and competent Central Government) other governing authorities with their own defined rights which do not derive from the Central Government, but are entrenched and written into the Constitution.' And in his opening address to the Conference itself, as well as saying he was determined to achieve Independence quickly, he said: 'We wish to build a country in which dictatorship is impossible and I believe it is only if we manage to do this that we will finally be able to resist the menace of Communism. Already its agents are active in Kenya and in neighbouring territories.'

The truth of this statement was proved conclusively during the Zanzibar Revolution two years later. Logically, even in 1962, one would have expected Ngala's reasoned attitude to the preservation of individual liberty to have won more support in London than it did. When journalists or M.P.s met him in the lobby of his hotel, usually accompanied by the effervescent Masinde Muliro, who one felt must go to bed in his beret cap because he wore it so religiously on all occasions, the sincerity of both men was obvious. Compared with Odinga, flywhisk in hand, creating hell in a London restaurant because people who had booked tables in advance were being given places before him, and claiming this was blatant colour prejudice, Ngala ought to have appealed more to that core of activists who organise British opinion on Africa. Yet, even with the aid of the P.R. men, they were never anywhere near rallying the support that K.A.N.U. found in London.

The reasons for this were several. In the first place K.A.D.U. had the misfortune to have been patronised and adopted by the right wing of the settler politicians in Kenya, even if two years before Michael Blundell's New Kenya Party had hardly seemed that. It was Blundell who had acceded to African majority rule in 1960 and suffered having thirty pieces of silver scornfully thrown at his feet as he descended from the aircraft on his return to Nairobi. But by 1962 Blundell was, compared to Derek Erskine, Marrian and others who had joined K.A.N.U., running a reactionary party. The 'Kept Left' signs in African politics are more mandatory than most people in Britain realise. Furthermore, not a few of the real settler Right Wing, the supporters of Sir Ferdinand Cavendish Bentinck and of the late Group Captain Briggs, had begun to think of Ngala as the 'good African' in whom they might as well put their trust. Little as Ngala was, or wanted to be, a settlers' representative, the role was thrust on him and K.A.N.U. lost no opportunity to spread the idea that the settlers saw in Majimbo a means of preserving their authority over the once white Highlands. This spectre of European support, combined with Ngala's yielding to Renison's persistence and forming a government, was enough to kill his reputation with most influential left-wing Africanists in London. To them non-racialism was a fine principle only so long as it did not involve white participation in Government.

Furthermore Moise Tshombe's secessionist regime in the Congo was then under the heaviest attack. To the *Observer* and other newspapers Ngala began to appear another Tshombe, a man willing to commit the final misdemeanour of co-operating with a white presence in the black continent, and who with his regional plan was at heart seeking the very balkanisation of Africa daily decried by both President Nkrumah and the commentators.

There was another side to it too. As Tom Mboya often remarked, the cost of regionalism would be heavy. Kenya could not afford to pay regional M.P.s as well as national ones, not to mention when there was the additional burden of a Senate. Nor were all the additional civil servants going to be easy to come by, at a time when any able and educated African could take his pick of half a dozen well-paid jobs, and it was even hard to find good enough men to stand as candidates for the Regional Assemblies themselves.

The verbal duels in the Kenya National Assembly (as the Legislative Assembly was now called) between Tom Mboya and the K.A.D.U. members on the subject of regionalism were well worth listening to. They reached their height after Mboya had become Minister of Justice and Constitutional Affairs and before the Independence Conference, in October 1963, authorised changes in the Regional Constitution which sealed the fate of Majimbo. Mboya has a command of English that the majority of British Parliamentarians might envy. His sense of the language's rhythms and the crushing weight that can be given to a telling phrase are allied with a self-confidence—he has never been renowned for his modesty—that gives him an overwhelming, and highly diverting, oratorical power. Added to which a skilled tactician could make adept use of the Constitution's complexities (in which it was second only to the

Cyprus Constitution). Since the 1962 Conference had left undecided the exact distribution of many of the functions of Government between the centre and the regions, there was still ample scope for Parliamentary in-fighting. When not active in the Assembly, Mboya was busy issuing press statements on the 'correct' interpretation of the Constitution. 'There is an impression that the regions are governments,' he said on one occasion. 'I want to make it quite clear that the regions are not governments. We will respect the constitutional position of the regions. But we will not tolerate any attempt by any region, or Regional President, to behave or pretend as though they were governments.'

The behaviour of some of the Regional Assemblies and the K.A.D.U. leaders in them gave Mboya ample justification for laying down the law. In the Rift Valley crowds were frequently told that the region would declare its own independence. William Murgor used to parade on the platform in tribal dress brandishing a whistle, which he declared he would blow on the great day when the Kalenjin tribes rose up against the Government. Even Ronald Ngala became affected by this emotionalism and there was talk of the Coast declaring its independence from Kenya. Every ounce of propaganda that could be made out of regional powers, and certain tribes' willingness to fight to the death for them, was made. At the same time the Government deliberately dallied over handing actual power to the regions. Indeed K.A.N.U. made no secret of its intention of dismantling the system at a later date. One trouble arose out of the percentage of members of the Senate and the Assembly required to vote a change in the Constitution—75 per cent—whilst for changes which affected the entrenched rights of individuals, regions, tribal authorities or districts the figure for the Upper House was 90 per cent. Since the Senate had a higher proportion of K.A.D.U. members than the lower house, it was virtually impossible for changes to be forced through legally if K.A.D.U. did not co-operate.

The battle over regionalism came to a head during the October 1963 Independence Conference in London, when the kinds of bluff that always did characterise such meetings reached unrivalled degrees of both danger and absurdity. It was a matter of who could blackmail the Colonial Secretary most effectively, or, rather, considering Mr. Duncan Sandys' reputation for toughness, thought they could. Suddenly, despite Kenyatta's unrelenting work to restore confidence over the previous four months, the phrase 'civil war' was again on everyone's lips.

First K.A.D.U. members in Kenya led by Daniel Arap Moi suddenly unveiled a plan for a K.A.D.U. Republic that would declare itself independent if Majimbo was altered in London. The concept of a horseshoe-shaped state taking in the Rift Valley, Western Region, North-East Region and the Coast, leaving the K.A.N.U. areas isolated from all except aerial communications, was at once ridiculed in public. One visiting journalist rushed off an article titled '*L'état c'est Moi*', a pun which mercifully his paper did not print. But privately the plan was taken in deadly earnest by the Government, because the Kalenjin tribes were known to be in a state of dangerous unrest, and K.A.D.U. members had plans for sabotaging the railways and telegraphs.

The General Service Unit of the police, its red-bereted riot squad, was immediately distributed round strategic points, the army was put on call and arrangements were made to arrest various K.A.D.U. politicians if necessary. A Government statement reaffirmed 'its stand to deal swiftly with any person spreading ill feeling, alarm or despondency calculated to disrupt the peace of the country'.

New regulations followed, actually drafted before this crisis, making it a punishable offence 'to utter or disseminate . . . any statement, information, report or opinion calculated to cause alarm or apprehension to the public'. A side effect of this was extreme apprehension amongst journalists, who had already suffered a good deal of the backlash from the K.A.N.U.-K.A.D.U. struggle.

In London too the K.A.D.U. plan had its effect. British Parliamentary opinion, as ever more responsive to promises of violence than of moderation, veered sharply in K.A.D.U.'s favour, on the premise that K.A.N.U.'s persecution must have been worse than they realised.

Immediately an emergency meeting of the K.A.N.U. Parliamentary Group in Nairobi, headed by Joseph Murumbi as acting Prime Minister while Kenyatta was away, decided to declare Kenya independent *de facto* on October 20th, the emotionally charged anniversary of the Declaration of the State of Emergency in 1952, if Britain yielded to K.A.D.U. They were helped in their decision by one Minister having sent a telegram to Kenyatta to this effect before their meeting started.

None the less the mood of the Assembly members and Senators was true to this irresponsible resolution. They were seething with impatience to throw the colonialist K.A.D.U., regionalism and all criticism out of the window together. Men I normally knew as sane debaters swore they would leave the Commonwealth, sever all ties with Britain, expel the British Army and British administrators, and seek development aid from the 'socialist countries'. If they were 'unable' to stop the Kikuyu forcibly occupying European farms, what did that matter?

Considering that *Uhuru* had just been brought forward several months to December 12th, this rabid intolerance seemed needless. Had Kenyatta, who was in twice-daily telephone contact with Murumbi, in fact connived at it? Since then other events, like the rapid build-up of anti-European feeling when he was attacked in London the following summer, suggest that he has to exert all his authority to control the backbenchers' outbursts. On the other hand, December 12th had been agreed on by Britain after he, Nyerere and Obote had signed a declaration of intention to federate in June 1963, which specifically said that if Kenya did not achieve independence soon the plans for Federation would be undermined. A year later, with Federation still unaccomplished, Kenyatta told a Nyanza audience in Swahili that this declaration was simply a trick to speed-up *Uhuru*.

At all events, whether Kenyatta was a party to it or not, the threat of unilateral independence on October 20th shook the Colonial Office more than the vision of K.A.D.U.'s Republic. The Conference ended with K.A.N.U. the victors. They had urgently wanted to change the Constitution while Britain and British troops still had responsibility for maintaining law and order. They left London with control of the police and the civil service given to the Central Government. Moreover, although basic changes in human and land right still required the 75 per cent vote in the Assembly and 90 per cent in the Senate, other Constitutional amendments could now be achieved by a two-thirds majority in a national referendum. Such a majority is relatively easily achieved where a strong Central Government is not too squeamish about its methods. Meanwhile Britain politely accepted assurances that implementation of the Regional Constitution, though it could not be completed before December 12th, would be finished afterwards.

No one who knew K.A.N.U. took this as gospel and from then

onwards K.A.D.U.'s members knew they had lost. One by one they crossed the floor. Their chief political adviser, the diminutive and amusing Taita Towett, whose Kalenjin voters had so often been reported as sharpening their spears for action, remarked, 'The only sensible thing is for K.A.D.U. to enter into an agreement with K.A.N.U.' A year later Towett's advice was finally taken.

In the meantime K.A.N.U. leaders began speaking publicly of Kenya becoming a one-party state, though by K.A.D.U.'s collapse, not laws banning opposition such as Ghana and Tanganyika had introduced. When Kenyatta arrived back from the Organisation of African Unity's annual conference in Cairo in July 1964 he announced that all the Heads of Government he had just met had one-party systems and 'from today we shall work towards a one-party system'. No matter that he must have failed to meet the Nigerian, Ugandan, Somali and Sierra Leonean Heads of State. By November so many of K.A.D.U. had changed sides that the party could no longer block amendment of the Constitution. Ngala surrendered gracefully, and was carried shoulder high across the floor of the Assembly while K.A.N.U. cheered and clapped. In what was, for Africa, an almost unique occasion, the opposition pledged itself voluntarily to work with the Government henceforward. In the Government reshuffle that followed Republic Day on December 12th, 1964, Ngala became President of the Maize Marketing Board, the same post given to Paul Ngei when he rejoined the fold and, one hoped, the stepping stone to a Ministry. Kenya indeed needs men of Ngala's calibre in office, not in jail, and altogether it was a gratifyingly peaceful ending to the K.A.N.U.–K.A.D.U. struggle.

So although there are still Regional Assemblies at the time of writing, K.A.D.U. is as dead as settler politics, and Majimbo a burnt-out case. The brief life the two enjoyed revealed how mixed up the motives for opposition can become in Africa today. The fear for individual rights was real, so were the fears of the smaller tribes that they would be dominated by the larger. But on general policy K.A.D.U. had shown few differences from K.A.N.U., both being socialist, and the threats of individual regions to declare themselves independent, their flying their own flags until stopped, and their general attitude showed how right Tom Mboya was when he claimed that 'tribalism is the most dangerous and explosive ground on which to create a basis for a second party'.

Thus regionalism was shown to be directly contrary to the spirit of *Harambee* and sadly, from the point of view of anyone who cherishes freedom of expression, the way was paved for a one-party state in Kenya, the results and implications of which belong to a later chapter. Nor, regrettably, did the decline of K.A.D.U. bring a decline in tribalism. Such strong forces do not collapse overnight. As Rift Valley rebelliousness began to be forgotten, tribalism within K.A.N.U. itself took the centre of the stage instead. The Luo, Kenya's only Nilotic tribe, distinctive in their customs, numbering three-quarters of a million and living highly concentrated on the shores of Lake Victoria, have had little historical contact with the Kikuyu. The Mau Summit and the Rift Valley had kept them apart and so perhaps facilitated their political alliance in K.A.N.U. now. But recently the Luo have become increasingly worried about what their friends were up to; whilst the Zanzibar Revolution and Odinga's well-known communist connections set the Kikuyu in their turn feverishly searching for evidence of Luo plotting. It was incidentally the *Sunday Times* involvement in this, through an article written in London by someone totally ignorant of Luo-Kikuyu rivalry, that led in the end to my own abrupt expulsion from Kenya.

4

The Mau Mau as 'Freedom Fighters'

IT IS AMAZING that the Mau Mau has not counted more in the complicated equation of Kenyan independence. Josiah Kariuki, the present Member of the Assembly for the Aberdares, described in his book *Mau Mau Detainee* how he felt after taking the foul *Batuni* oath: 'My initiation was now complete and I had become a true Kikuyu with no doubts where I stood in the revolt of my tribe.' It having been so avowedly a Kikuyu affair, one might well have expected the ex-detainees and the terrorists still in the forests of the Aberdares and Mt. Kenya to exert an influence in the new Kenya out of all proportion to their numbers, even though their oaths had been perversions of traditional ones.

The prophets of doom, European, Asian and African, forecast disaster at Independence. Not that that was difficult to justify. Various Mau Mau leaders still in the forests had announced that they were intending to come out and assume control of districts near their hideouts. Thus it was assumed that 'Field Marshal' Mwariama would indeed descend from Mt. Kenya and take over Meru, where his name had long been synonymous with intimidation. '*Uhuru na Mwariama*' was a local catchphrase. Together with the emergence of the Mau Mau it was widely thought, not least by police officers, that Kikuyu squatters would move on to all the European-owned Rift Valley farms. When very little of the sort materialised it was not merely another proof that Kenya's disasters were, as usual, being wept over before they had happened, it showed that the existence of an African government made an overwhelming difference to events. The renascent Mau Mau was very astutely handled by Kenyatta, although not altogether successfully.

As 'Freedom Fighters' they were at first welcomed as heroes. Dedan Kimathi and the others who had been executed by the colonial authorities had long been allotted their niches in the mythology of Pan Africanism. Since 1959 they had been hailed at conferences for their part in Africa's freedom struggle, along with the Algerian troops of the F.L.N., the South African revolutionaries like Nelson Mandela and the guerillas in Angola. The shocked reactions of settlers and Nairobi business men to Kariuki's book, in which the Mau Mau's own view of the Emergency was publicly propounded for the first time, surprised nobody and affected practically nobody. It made up a few more white farmers' minds for them, convincing them that all they most hated, and all the British Government had supported them in hating with several thousand troops, was now to be venerated in Kenya and that therefore they should quit. Otherwise it could only be seen as inevitable. Terrorist movements the world over are sanctified afterwards if they win, and vilified if they lose. Even if one still felt that the Corfield Report was right, and the Mau Mau thoroughly atavistic and bestial, well, one's feelings were irrelevant to the new situation, which was that the Mau Mau had, in the end, won. Furthermore, whether known as the Mau Mau, the Land Freedom Army or the Weeping Kamaus, they were now in a position of influence.

The Kikuyu loyalists, about whom so much had been heard a few years ago, had completely vanished from public appearance and by all accounts were now having a rough time of it in private. In Algeria it was the privilege of the harkis who had supported the French to have their noses and ears cut off, if not their throats slit, by the F.L.N. In Kenya the loyalists have been 'donating' towards the upkeep of their former enemies and suffering from much malignant discrimination within such seemingly above-board organisations as peasant farmers' marketing co-operatives.

The real interest of the situation lay not so much in Kariuki's assertion that the 'hard core' Mau Mau were in fact the most disciplined and cleanest fighting of the bands, unlike some murderous thugs who had latched on to a noble movement, but in how the demands of the surprisingly large number of Mau Mau still in the forests were going to be met by the Government.

This bogy had first begun to haunt the country at the time of Kenyatta's release, when ex-detainees were known to be asking for future privilege. Yet, although 90,000 had passed through detention camps, and a bunch of 90,000 embittered men and women could be expected to make its presence felt, they were granted relatively little. The 1963 Elections brought more ex-detainees into the Assembly, but there were still only Bildad Kaggia, Fred Kubai, Josiah Kariuki, Paul Ngei and Achieng Oneko in any prominence, apart from the old man himself.

Additionally the ex-detainees were not necessarily ex-Mau Mau by any means, since scores of political agitators had been rounded up in the 1950's. Oneko, for instance, then Secretary of K.A.U., had been acquitted at the Kapenguria trial, largely as a result of John Stonehouse's evidence. Immediately afterwards he was rearrested and put in detention. The detainees in fact covered a wider tribal spectrum than Mau Mau. As they had not been substantially rewarded there were obvious dangers in giving the forest fighters abundantly more, though enough had to be done to coax them out of hiding. Unless they were rehabilitated quickly these men and women whose lives had become so divorced from the changes in Kenya might easily turn to fighting the new Government just as they had fought the old. The day when a revolutionary takes control of a country is the day when, inevitably, he starts appearing to others as a reactionary, particularly to extremists whose wishes he will be deflected from following by external economic and political factors. Anyone taking over Kenya needed to be friendly with the settlers and the British Army if he wanted continued British financial aid—aid unlikely to be matched by the communist powers since it had already totalled £57,000,000 up to 1964. So the psychological moment for bringing Mau Mau into the fold came exactly at Independence and was bound to be of relatively short duration. In the event the measure of it was provided by 'Field Marshal' Mwariama, who within less than three months found himself jailed five years for intimidation. In May 1964 200 of his Mau Mau fought a battle with police in the Meru area and then retired to the forest.

An Independence Amnesty was actually declared by Kenyatta on November 6th, 1963. It gave a free pardon to political prisoners and to 'persons still hiding in the forests', as well as to various others. Initially no date was set for its acceptance. Indeed it apparently reckoned without the attractions of life as a freebooter, or with the Mau Mau's suspicions of civilisation from which some terrorists had been away for ten years. They had well-established camps, their women with them and were bringing up children. In theory they were still hunted, in practice police only chased them if they saw them and furthermore had for some time been forbidden to fire at them. The forests, where going up a track through the dense bamboo you are always liable to meet a rhino coming thunderously in the opposite direction, are intimidating to strangers but had become of the greatest utility to the Mau Mau.

The eerie dampness of the trees above the belt of bamboo, hung with long grey green strands of old man's beard, the intense cold at night so far above sea-level—the forests range from 8,000 to 13,000 feet up—and the continual presence of elephant and other hostile game were only one side of the story. Ease of trapping buck for skins and food and the absence of rents, taxes, and all the other restraints of village life were the assets, coupled with a fierce pride in this mode of existence. Just as their exploits made others sick, so the terrorists themselves vomited at the smell of soap.

The type of society they evolved varied. In the Aberdare National Park there was still one Mau Mau couple living in 1963. The Game Warden, one of whose scouts was ex-terrorist and extremely familiar with the area, knew this couple's movements well enough. Though living close to Treetops, the famous game-viewing 'hotel in a tree', they were deeply wary of contact with other people, white or black. It didn't need the ten-foot trench that had been dug during the Emergency all round the forest edge near Nyere to keep them out of villages. They were as shy as wild animals, with no apparent intention of either leaving the forest or of attacking anyone; living a life closely similar to that of Kenya's original inhabitants, the Wanderobo.

By contrast Mwariama had over 300 followers, who in August 1963 moved down from the thickest part of the Mt. Kenya jungle to a clearing in a volcanic crater. They had home-made tents, resembling British Army bivouacs, a weird assortment of rifles, spears, axes and pangas, mostly also home-made, and a quasi-military organisation. Some wore bush uniforms with British Army webbing belts and various berets and caps. Mwariama himself, served by a number of 'A.D.C.s', sported a leopard-skin jacket and a bus-conductor's type of shiny peaked hat perched on top of the thick greasy braids of hair, which, together with a rankly pungent smell, are the natural insignia of the forest fighter. Mwariama's army was far from shy. It held the Meru area in terror and its members had only to come from the forest under cover of night to obtain all the food, drink and supplies they wanted. Mwariama had what in another continent would have been called a sweetly set-up protection racket.

It was therefore hardly surprising that the Mau Mau, conscious that they had survived the worst the security forces could do in the Emergency despite expenditure Kenya could never afford again (£64,000,000 1952–60), were canny about accepting any amnesty. Certainly for a month, possibly for much longer, delegates from the gangs came down to Nairobi to see Kenyatta. The secrecy surrounding these visits gradually broke down. Even when wearing normal clothes the emissaries kept their distinctive hairstyle and a group of them disappearing into the new twelve-storey building that houses the Prime Minister's office could mean only one thing. Their demands, one understood, were considerable. Judging from subsequent events, Kenyatta, aided in the lengthy discussions by Mbui Koinange and others, managed to settle with them for land, welfare and public recognition at Independence. It also became clear later that these emissaries had been mere subordinates. The real leaders, the 'Field Marshal' and 'Generals', were too wary to visit the city while the Union Jack still flew.

The day when Mwariama came publicly to Gatundu was a memorable one. The 'Field Marshal' rolled his eyes grotesquely, jumped up and down, clapped Kenyatta to his chest in a great bear hug, a gesture which the Prime Minister's expression suggested he did not entirely like, and generally behaved like an exhibit at Barnum and Bailey's Circus. The B.B.C. filmed this occasion for TV and made a packet from the syndication rights, deservedly, for it was the sort of performance that money cannot normally buy. Mwariama's translated statement that white men and black men were all brothers henceforward carried little conviction.

During the Independence celebrations a clutch of 'Generals' was accommodated in a villa near the Nairobi Club. Shaven and with their hair cut, decked out in clean khaki officer-type uniforms they arrived with all the other guests on the wide lawns of Government House for the Governor's last colonial garden party. To spare the feelings of regular army officers, one of whom had just been promoted from major to colonel so that an African should be in command of at least one battalion of the Kenya Army at *Uhuru*, the

'Generals' wore only strips of green cloth instead of hat badges and red lapel tabs. Indeed as they wandered among the diplomats and politicians who were taking tea, chattering and waiting for Prince Philip to pass round, they looked self-conscious and unimportant. They must in more ways than one have felt like Samson after his locks were shorn. That night, in the stadium, they asked to be introduced to the Prince, but Kenyatta refused to oblige them. When their famous colleague, 'General' China, who had escaped capture and successfully left Kenya, returned from a course of military training in Israel even he had trouble passing the selection board for the Kenya Army on the grounds of fitness and had to sign on as a private soldier. His career would now, one hoped, be a far cry from the deliberately perverted sexual obscenities of the Mau Mau oaths.

In the Westernised society of Nairobi that Kenya's leaders had now adopted the legendary days of the Mau Mau seemed impossibly remote, the 'Generals' a slight embarrassment, and the idea of anyone calling himself 'Kenya Bus' absurd, despite its power symbolism a mere decade earlier. But up at Nyeri, hard under the forests in the heartland of the Kikuyu, things had changed less. When the official surrenders of the Mau Mau to the Government began on December 16th, the Generals having returned briefly to the forest after the Independence celebrations to gather together their men and their belongings, the Kikuyu turned out *en masse* to cheer.

The scene of the surrender was the Ruringu arena outside Nyeri, a bowl-shaped depression in the ground with some simple covered stands at one side and a very small elevated wooden platform. Innumerable rallies had been held here in the past, back in the days when Kenyatta was leading K.A.U. and before. By a coincidence that was something more than strange the morning of December 16th dawned and remained clear over Mt. Kenya. Driving out from Nairobi I first saw the peak, its snow glistening and glaciers crisply defined, from the outskirts of the city. It was still completely visible at lunchtime. This was extremely unusual, since even in the early mornings there are normally wisps of cloud drifting round the mountain and by breakfast-time it is completely hidden. Mt. Kenya is regarded by the Kikuyu as the seat of God, Ngai, and of the spirits. Kenyatta called his book *Facing Mount Kenya* because it was the most evocative title he could choose. When the Kikuyu pray to Ngai they kneel facing towards the mountain. Dedan Kimathi always turned to it when worshipping at his prayer trees. Just as the giant fig that was his favourite prayer tree fell for no observable reason the day after his execution, so now it seemed the mountain was deliberately revealing itself on the day when the Mau Mau were officially welcomed back out of hiding.

Kenyatta made the point to the crowd in the afternoon when he stood on the tiny platform. Before him were at least 40,000 people, perhaps more. Packed densely together, kept in line by K.A.N.U. Youth Wingers, they swayed and surged forward as the old man spoke. 'The rain stopped for *Uhuru*. Today again do you see a drop of rain here?' A deep-throated roar of 'No' came up from the crowd. By this time they were well worked up. Earlier speakers had asked if they would like the bones of Kimathi buried elsewhere and they had cried out 'Yes' and raised their hands in a great rippling wave of movement. To rolls of drums they had been conducted in the familiar patterns of shouting.

'*Kimathi Uhuru!*'

'*Kenyatta Uhuru!*'

'*Mathenge Uhuru!*'

Kimathi's wife, who was alas not the girl Kimathi had with him in the forests at the time of his capture, had appeared on the platform, a hard-faced bulky woman in a simple cotton dress. Someone yelled into the microphone: 'The blood of the men in the forest has been spilt. Those who remain should respect their wives.' Then Mrs. Kimathi herself was leading the crowd in a thrice-repeated chorus of '*Uhuru na Mau Mau*' that made my blood run cold despite the heat and sweat. She began stating the things that the Mau Mau had done that Kenyatta should reward them for, even things that the children had done. 'During the Emergency there were pass books for the Kikuyu, Embu and Meru tribes. The children refused to use them. Kenyatta should remember them.' There was a distinctly threatening ugliness about these speeches that preceded the actual arrival of the forest fighters in the stadium.

Meanwhile African diplomats and politicians sat listening from the security of the covered stand, three Russians or Czechs whitely conspicuous among them. In the compound round the platform journalists, Youth Wing leaders, the 'Generals' in their special uniforms and others milled about confusedly, two being especially worth noticing, an American and Australian.

The American, called Edward Lameka, wore a khaki jacket and forage cap and held above his head a series of clumsy cardboard placards, untidily inscribed with slogans like, 'Oust Britain from colonies' and 'End U.S. tax aid to Britain'. For years he had carried these around the streets of American cities. Now he was a specially invited guest at the Independence celebrations. Unbelievably six weeks later he had apparently overstayed his welcome and been found to be without a return ticket to take him home. By the end of February money was raised for his fare and he was unobtrusively deported.

The Australian, a tall well-built man of thirty-five-odd, was also in uniform, the all-black uniform of the K.A.N.U. Youth Wing's élite. This was Aussie Walker, blond, sunburned, handsome, a local advertising executive and part-time Youth Wing leader, looking exactly like a recruiting poster for Sir Oswald Mosley's Blackshirts, save that his black forage cap bore the K.A.N.U. colours and a black flywhisk swung in his hand. He had a K.A.N.U. flash on each shoulder and, flagrant on his chest there blazed the ribbons of the British war medals he had won in the Pacific fighting, plus two U.N. decorations from Korea. Yet no one seemed to think this incongruous, not even the 'Generals' with whom he was arm in arm. He is married to an African girl and by some curious alchemy, perhaps the same attraction of opposites that makes the coloured man hanker most after blondes, and the quintessentially fair-skinned Scandinavians respond more readily than any other Europeans to African aspirations, he seems closer to the Kenyan leadership than any other white man.

It was Aussie Walker who had been round in the early hours of that morning collecting the Mau Mau from the rendezvous on the edge of the forests, some like uplands, close to Nairobi. The trucks used were those formally given by the United States Government to the Kenya Government a week before, at an impressive ceremony, though hardly more impressive than that to which they now contributed. They were driven in round the back of the arena, terrorists crowding them, waving guns. The Mau Mau wore hides and fur caps, dirty sheepskins and primitive leather sandals. One by one their leaders clambered on to the platform to join Kenyatta, until, what with the Press photographers clinging to its railing on the outside, it looked like collapsing at any moment. To tremendous cheering

Kenyatta examined the weapons. He was handed a gun, its stock crudely carved, its barrel a piece of piping, altogether the kind of weapon of which one could aptly say, adapting the Iron Duke's phrase, 'It may not frighten the enemy but by God it frightens me.' He inspected axes and pangas, admiring them and holding them up for the crowd to see. He was presented with a casket containing Mau Mau insignia and a bottle of ceremonial oil. Two other Ministers on the platform, Dr. Kiano and Dr. Waiyaki, declared that they would adopt two of the children born in the forest and pay for their education. It was announced that everything possible would be done for the forest fighters. But the main theme of Kenyatta's speech was the beating of swords into ploughshares, of using pangas for agricultural purposes only henceforward, to which suitable replies about the Mau Mau becoming good citizens were made.

Every day for more than a week the crowd gathered at Ruringu to applaud more of the returning fighters. Two hundred and fifty had been brought there on the first day. On the third 800 came out. On the fourth, when a further 300 'surrendered', a Government spokesman admitted that young men were leaving their homes and jobs in the Rift Valley to rush off into the forest and re-emerge a day or two later fully qualified for the Government's welfare scheme for ex-terrorists.

None the less, the welcome continued, as eloquently expressed by the recently introduced African columnist of the *Sunday Post*, Joel Maina:

'Their cool, clear and proud eyes, their elegant, nimble and handsome bodies, on most of which spread bridles of three- to four-foot lengths of twelve-year-old hair, and their humble manner in which they surrendered to the one who inspired their cause, now their proud Prime Minister Jomo Kenyatta, the father of the nation, all together, was indeed a unique form of national pride.'

Maina did, however, add a caveat: 'Let us hope that the occasion not be tainted by the presence of some of those habitual criminals who might wish to be associated with these brave men.'

As the weeks wore on it became harder and harder to distinguish between the criminals and the heroes. Although K.A.N.U., the Kikuyu Central Association (still evidently in being twenty years after its proscription), and members of the Mau Mau war councils compiled a list of those who needed help, and resolved that they would all work together with the ex-loyalists and ex-Home Guards in the nation-building, it became clear that quite a number of terrorists were returning to the forests. The attractions of life as a peasant on a small shamba must soon have palled. The Government declared an expiry date for the amnesty. But when it came there were still some unwilling to be absorbed into the new Kenya, while Mwariama, after a period of brief glory in which he addressed rallies in other parts of the country, was sent to jail as I related earlier.

Furthermore, a persistent trickle of reports reached Nairobi about intimidation on the settlement schemes. On the Kinangop plateau, which had been cleared of European farmers in a six-week crash programme just before Independence, primarily to show the African electorate that they really were going to get land fast under a K.A.N.U. Government, the ex-Mau Mau began to take over the smallholdings allotted to ordinary Kikuyu. It was evidently not enough that the Ol Kalou salient was almost completely given over to the ex-Mau Mau; nor that other places were promised, such as the Timau scheme on which Meru forest fighters were supposed to start settling in May 1964. In fact something went awry at Timau. Although in March 1964, 5,000 acres were made available, divided into forty-five separate plots, only five applicants materialised. These paid their deposits and vanished. The following August a shamefaced Parliamentary Secretary had to admit under questioning in the National Assembly that only one single solitary settler had ever actually returned to occupy his allotted farm. Possibly all the others decided to return to the forest.

None the less, the Government has continued with its plans for rehabilitation through settlement. It is the only reasonable way of tackling the problem, especially with unemployment so severe among the landless. The colonial authorities had invariably confiscated the land originally farmed by the 'freedom fighters' and had redistributed it. To retrieve these smallholdings from their new owners, particularly when land consolidation had further changed the old patterns of ownership, would be impossible. And there are ex-terrorists who never possessed any land anyway. To give them all priority in settlement on land which moreover had just been taken back from the European is obviously sensible. Other suggestions put forward, such as sending the Mau Mau as a supplementary army into the North-East to fight the Somali secessionist, recruiting them into the regular army *en bloc*, and so on, sounded attractive in the National Assembly but were politely and understandably rejected.

Whether in the long run the Mau Mau will respond to being treated the same as other new settlers in the matter of paying for that land remains to be seen. When the Minister for Lands and Settlement, J. H. Angaine, handed over plots to the first forty men at Timau he told them emphatically that if they failed to keep up repayments on the loans which had enabled them to buy the farms, at an average price of £250 each, they would be replaced by other people.

This is not precisely what the gangs envisaged as the culmination of their campaign to chase the white man out of Kenya. Some indeed lost no time in establishing themselves in the locations of Nairobi, and with that city's opportunities for crime it will be surprising if they ever go near a shamba again except to collect 'fines', 'subscriptions' and bribes. Others openly fought the authorities. Within six months of *Uhuru* Kenyatta was publicly denouncing Mau Mau activity. When Kenya became a Republic in December 1964 he decreed a second amnesty, and when that produced little response, the police were sent into action. They now had rather less hesitation about shooting and in one engagement, said to mark the very end of the gangs on Mount Kenya, 'Field Marshal' Baimungi, 'General' Chui and two others were shot dead.

However, there remains the exploitation within K.A.N.U. of the Mau Mau's residual political potential. As an organisation it will certainly not be allowed to die. Nor is it any accident that those politicians closest to it are the communist-affiliated and -financed members of 'Red' K.A.N.U. Mau Mau had connections with the communist powers from the beginning. Only the more stupid terrorists stayed in the forests after *uhuru*.

5

Land—African Settlers Replacing Europeans

THE AFRICANISATION of the land, desire for which had been the root cause of all Kikuyu unrest since colonisation, as well as the Mau Mau's main aim, was well under way long before the terrorists came down from the forests to Ruringu to eat roast bullock at the Government's expense and evaluate what the welfare schemes had to offer. Barely a year separated the final closure of the London office providing information for would-be white settlers and the start of the first scheme to put a million acres of the White Highlands back into African hands. By mid-1965 the purchases of land were due to be finalised. The most vital questions settlement officers put centred on the applicant's being genuinely unemployed, genuinely landless and genuinely responsible for a family. Whereas the white settler was given no assisted passage to Kenya and no loans, simply the grant of undeveloped land at a low rental and the implied guarantee of British rule for all time to come, now the black smallholder or yeoman farmer gets a loan of 90 per cent or more towards the cost of land which has already been farmed and fenced, fertilised and proven. Finally, whereas if the white man went bankrupt, that was his loss, now it is unlikely that threats of eviction will actually be carried out even if interest charges are not met.

The Land Settlement programme derives mainly from political needs and little pretence can be made that it is economically anything but extremely hazardous. Through it the Kenya Government has been enabled to show that the Highlands are passing into African ownership, while the Conservative Government in London, which originated the schemes, began the bailing out of a large proportion of the settlers from the consequences of changes in policy, and thus averted dangerous backbench criticism of its dealings with men, especially ex-servicemen, who were encouraged to sink their savings in Kenya farming after the two wars.

Initially the idea was to buy a million acres of mixed-farming land over a period of five years, the first year being 1962–3. The British Government was to pay for the transfer of 1,000,000 acres, while the World Bank and the Commonwealth Development Corporation financed another 150,000. Land chosen had to be suitable for smallholdings and had to help reduce rural unemployment. Each smallholder would get seven acres of good land, or the equivalent thereof, which might be twenty or thirty acres of marginal land. Yeoman farmers would have equivalent to fifty. Care was taken that all tribes affected by European colonisation benefited, although the 'scheduled areas', as the White Highlands were officially known, touched some more than others. Nyanza and the Western Region had few white settlers, the Central Region and the Rift Valley the majority.

When the Boundaries Commission changed the area of the Central Province, now the Central Region, the scheme had to be altered. As all the region was tacitly agreed to be kept for the Kikuyu a further 100,000 acres on the Bahati escarpment now included in the Central Region had to be brought into the scheme. Settlement elsewhere had to be reduced, mainly among the Nandi. Next political pressures on the Kenya Government caused the Kikuyu element of the scheme to be condensed into a period of three years instead of five, so it would be finished by June 1965, and in the end it was done in little over two years. The patchwork of the settlement schemes became more and more intricate both in time and on the map. The pressure of work on the Ministry of Lands and Settlement, and even more on the individual land-settlement officers on the schemes, became worse and worse. At the same time accusations began to build up that the officers were deliberately sabotaging progress, accusations the nastier since a number of settlers had been recruited to help in the programme.

Up on Kipipiri especially things were not going well. It is high, cold, sour land that forty years ago bankrupted its share of white settlers. Being a shelf of the Aberdares and in the Central Region the Kikuyu took it, and they planted their traditional crops of beans and maize, the latter on Settlement Board advice. They also put down potatoes on advice, as a cash crop that ought to fetch ready money in Nairobi. But by bringing in their own potatoes they re-introduced bacterial wilt to Kipi. The reasons why Europeans had taken to growing wheat and pyrethrum were disregarded. Land 9,000 feet above sea-level is not the same as land round Fort Hall, about 6,000 feet up. It was a surprise only to the Kikuyu when the winter of 1962–3, exceptionally bitter, severely affected the maize and beans, while the wilt and a glut of potatoes in Nairobi brought the price right down. Nor is the quality of Kenya potatoes high enough for them to be exported to Europe. The new Kipipiri settlers quickly found themselves *in extremis*, at one point being considered for famine relief.

I used often to stay at a farm in the Rift Valley just below Kipipiri. Two of the labourers employed there had been allocated land on the scheme and when they received their loan of £60 to buy themselves a few cattle came back to ask for some. The lady who owned the farm sold them six at the rock-bottom price of £12 10*s*. each, because she felt so sorry for them. They had been completely unable to get good ones anywhere else. European cattle were then fetching at least £20 a head and there was an estimated overall shortage in Kenya of 18,000 head as a result of settlers selling up before leaving, and all their stock going to the slaughter-houses in a rush. From that day on not a week passed without more Africans coming to ask for cattle. One pair of men, dressed in the usual old overcoats and gnome-like felt hats, had come walking, barefoot of course, for thirty miles. We watched them from the verandah as they trudged across the valley towards us. They had heard that the memsahib had good ngombes for sale, and they each had their money. But the memsahib, who was almost penniless herself and unable to get further credit from the bank, could not afford to sell any more at a loss. The two forlorn Kikuyu turned about and stoically started back on their seemingly hopeless search. The pathos of this incident needs no underlining.

For the settlement officer on Kipipiri it was a nightmare. With conditions so bad, and political pressure so strong to make the scheme work, he had to turn a blind eye to practices for which the former owners of the land would have been prosecuted. On all these schemes the new peasant farmers have been encouraged to run marketing co-operatives for their produce. The handful of cattle that each settler might own produced too little milk for independent selling. On Kipipiri, therefore, a co-operative had been formed. Quite apart from the blatant intimidation within it, control of its committee having passed into the hands of ex-detainees and their sympathisers who did their best to persecute the ex-loyalist members, there was the quality of the milk itself. Dozens of streams flow across the plateau, thick with red earth. Before the milk even reached the co-operative much had been watered down to such an extent that particles of soil were visibly in suspension in it. By the time the co-operative delivered it to the Kenya Co-operative Creameries it was the very negation of all the standards of fitness and cleanliness that the K.C.C. had fought for years to establish, and non-compliance with which would swiftly lose a white farmer his milk quota. But since no one dared refuse to take it, this appalling milk was, and no doubt still is, simply added to the general supply, pasteurised, paid for and forgotten.

The mere process of settlement required great organisation. The most spectacular was the crash programme to complete the installation of 2,500 families on the Kinangops in time for Independence. The order came direct from Kenyatta that it was to be done in six weeks. White farmers who had sown crops of wheat in the expectation of harvesting them before leaving in February or March of 1964 were suddenly asked to move out by the beginning of November, at a week's notice. For a few who had hoped to stay on there this was a blow, so was it for some whose homes had cost far more than the maximum £2,500 compensation paid for a house, a sum kept small because the farm buildings and improvements would be of no use to Kikuyu smallholders. The Kinangops had held a small, thriving community, built on experience similar to Kipipiri's, with its inn, the Brown Trout, the closing sale of which was held in October 1963, its garage, its social life. Suddenly collapse came, presaged by the theft of the recording machine that brought the settlers a touch of England every Sunday by playing the sound of bells from the tower of the small stone church, and which the thieves had used in K.A.N.U.'s local-election campaign a few months earlier. In place of tourists the Brown Trout was full of Government officers poring over maps, planning where new village centres were to go, new roads, new schools, and where exactly the ditches dividing the plots of land would run.

On the 50,000 acres involved there would be one village to every

10,000 acres, or 4,000 people, each village occupying thirty acres. Some of the farmhouses were to be used as social centres, while existing farm schools, usually built by the European farm-owners as an amenity for their labourers, would be allotted ground for expansion. In dividing the area into parts for high-, medium- and low-density settlement careful regard was paid to soil characteristics and to drainage. A thirty-acre equivalent was introduced.

It was impossible to watch the preparations without nostalgia and questioning. On the one hand there was the determination of the Ministry men to make this scheme work. On the other it was heart-rending to see the deep furrows cutting through lawns and flower-beds and fields, marking where one plot would meet another, and to see good wheat rotting. I went up in early December. Heavy rain had prevented the new settlers arriving as planned. Friends' houses lay empty, their gardens gradually going wild. A number of Kikuyu were industriously cutting down the trees in the long windbreaks, which now looked ragged and patchy, like a wood that has been under artillery fire. A few weeks later Kenyatta, visiting the area, waxed openly angry at the hooligan destruction of property left unused, and ordered immediate repair. But he should have known better than anyone how the Kikuyu can scavenge and destroy. While he was in detention his own motor-car left by his house at Gatundu was gutted of seats, instruments, tyres, everything. For several months organised gangs had been attacking Kinangop homesteads apparently as part of ex-detainees' campaign to force white settlers out. Furniture, doors and even windows and roofing vanished when owners were away for a weekend. Nor did the looting and destruction stop after the *wazungu*—the white men—had left. It was in its small way like the Vandals descending on Rome. Between them the Government, the gangs and the smallholders were to obliterate all traces of the colonists, as though the pioneering and the forty years' disciplining of the land had never been. Above all, it was sad to see the old sound husbandry destroyed.

The *East African Standard*, in an article devoted to explaining the virtues of the Kinangop scheme, commented: 'Perhaps it does look a retrograde step to split a hundred-acre field carrying a flourishing crop of wheat into a number of small plots . . . but the onus will be on the new farmers to ensure that they can make an adequate living from their holdings.' This is the optimist's view. The pessimist's is that nothing will ever stop the Kikuyu growing beans and maize, wherever he is and whatever the need for exportable crops. Even after many years' efforts at education in agriculture African peasants are notoriously slow to understand the principles of soil conservation.

Existing Kikuyu farms, in the reserve, can be used to support both arguments. Hideous soil erosion marches alongside meticulous husbandry. I spent an afternoon once with the owner of a six-acre shamba near Kiambu. He grows maize and beans, certainly, but also bananas, potatoes and pineapples. Last year he put in 400 coffee seedlings which then were extremely healthy. I doubt if anyone could use six acres more effectively. The real trouble was that he had three wives and fourteen children, and, whatever miracles he achieved, his six acres just could not produce enough to pay his children's school fees as well as feed them. He was not shown me as an example by anyone else, I met him through giving one of his sons a lift one day, but he was in his way a living proof that the seven-acre plot is out of date in Kenya now, as surely as the fifty-acre mixed farm is unprofitable in Britain. It cannot benefit from any of the economies of large-scale production, which is what Kenya desperately needs if she is to feed, clothe, educate and employ a population increasing at 4 per cent per annum and half of which is now under eighteen years old.

The potential wastefulness of the smallholding schemes had indeed been realised before the Kinangop was taken over. The virtue of co-operatives that would buy and operate existing farms as single units was being canvassed. When Joseph Murumbi, acting for Kenyatta, opened the last Royal Agricultural Show before Independence, incidentally assuring his settler audience that the Government looked forward to the next one, he announced after the 1,000,000 acres were transferred it would not be 'in the best interests of the economy—either from the point of view of production or employment—that large-scale farms should be broken up more than is necessary. Our aim, therefore, will be to provide funds in order to enable mixed farms to change ownership, but to remain as large, economically viable units, to be operated either by experienced African farmers, or as co-operative undertakings, or as companies.'

In fact, as the 1,000,000-acre scheme progressed, the intellectuals in K.A.N.U. were becoming thoroughly worried at the way the country's basic industry was being affected by settlement. The logical way to tackle Kenya's agriculture would have been to extend large-scale European farmers' methods into the native land units—not do the reverse.

Nonetheless the smallholders are repaying 70%–80% of what is due, the World Bank schemes being particularly successful. The whole amount will be recovered by the Kenya Government from the settlers, and Britain may well be asked to reloan it to Kenya, which she will presumably do. Thus what the settlers actually repay will be of acute concern to the Kenyan Government, not to mention that the British loans are at bank rate, and Britain is definitely expecting the interest charges to be paid, even if she never recovers the capital. The actual burden on the African farmer is some 10 per cent per annum of the loan made him, 6½ per cent of which is interest charge and the rest capital repayment. The average cost of settling a high density smallholder has been £475. A yeoman farmer, on fourteen acres or equivalent acreage, needs £920. For the Africans to repay 10 per cent on these sums will be quite an effort, especially when on the Kinangop their deposit was only £10 and when the per capita cash income in Kenya has hitherto averaged only £24 a year. The prospect of failure gave added incentive to the investigation of socialised forms of farming—co-operatives, kibbutz and collective.

On the co-operatively run farms it looks more as though repayments may be kept up, good-quality produce yielded, in fact a successful transfer of ownership made, though after visiting one of the showplaces I realised that some of the estimates were still deceptively hopeful. I went with the Minister of Commerce and Industry, Dr. Kiano, who is a graduate of an American university, a Kikuyu and one of the few Africans who does understand how free-enterprise business works. We were taken by one of the Settlement Board's Chief Officers, Sandy Storer.

The farms, Kobo Rock and Lukenia, had been taken over lock, stock and barrel, or 'walk in, walk out', as auctioneers say. They were near Machakos, in part of the Kamba settlement area. We drove out across the rolling dry grassland of the Athi Plains, past Embakasi airport, its new concrete buildings glittering in the sun, the runway shimmering in the heat. Kobo Rock is in the foothills of the Maur range. It is a typical ranch covering over 30,000 acres, and with its own small river. The Board paid £120,000 for it, including £29,000 for the stock. The sixty Kamba co-operators who now own it subscribed £18,000 as the down-payment—that is, £300 each.

First we met the Settlement Officer, a Czech, once in the R.A.F., next a Kenya farmer and now doing his last job before leaving—a thin, wiry, weatherbeaten man who had charge of Kobo Rock, Lukenia and one other ranch. However, he appeared to have considerable confidence in the African managers of Kobo Rock and Lukenia, both sturdy and impressive men, who ran the farms on the general orders of the committee of each co-operative, of which they are themselves members.

The day-to-day life at Kobo Rock had altered little with the change of proprietor. The labour were paraded as before at 7.15 a.m. every morning. Although some were close relatives of the new owners, they were only being paid the minimum agricultural wage of 2*s*. a day. This came as a slight shock, especially when we learnt that the owners themselves expected to make £75 a year on their investment of £300, and were doing no work at all, apart from giving directives.

It had been easy to get the co-operators to keep their own herds separate from the farm's original cattle, a separation made necessary by the native cattle being small, in poor condition and carriers of East Coast fever through lack of dipping. But the co-operators could not be persuaded to work on the farm themselves. They would accept the principles of ranching, but they wouldn't live there themselves, nor make use of the twenty-acre plot that each member was allotted near the river.

As we talked to them, a bunch of quiet men in slacks and sweaters or tweed coats, shirts open at the neck, it emerged that every single one had an existing business somewhere else. One was a butcher, another ran a garage, and so on. Though they were supposed to belong to one co-operative alone, several hoped to get a share of a new venture next door as well. Although few had raised all their share personally, and Storer reckoned that what with relatives and friends helping subscribe there were probably 250 people involved, it still didn't look much like African socialism. Kiano, who had hitherto kept very quiet, digesting the information given us, agreed with this. But Peter Marrian, then Parliamentary Secretary in the Ministry of Lands and Settlement, though now no longer a member of the Government, who was also with us, didn't like conceding the point at all. He finally remarked that all would be well provided there were also similar schemes that gave the unemployed land. Of course, this raised the question of whether unemployed people would run co-operatives effectively.

Again Kiano was realistic, the mere fact of their being unemployed gave no indication as to whether men would be good co-operators or not. He did however feel that settlers would eventually obey rules if those rules were laid down by their political leaders. They ought also to regard land in a co-operative as just as good security as land held personally. Both these questions are of great concern, because although the initial ten-member committee of a co-operative is carefully chosen by the Ministry, thereafter the running of the farm depends on the owners. If the Committee's composition changes and it refuses to accept advice, or decides to split the farm up into small units, there is little anyone can do to stop them, at least under existing law. The general opinion of Europeans concerned with settlement is that unemployed Africans will make a hash of running large farms and that the great expenditure needed to put them on it will be wasted if there is not constant supervision. Despite Kiano's frankness the Government's outwardly expressed views are rather different. In Kenya today unemployment is a very touchy issue politically.

Finally there was an involved discussion of the likely profitability of Kobo Rock, again a question of future management. These Africans had been led to expect a return of 20 per cent on their invested capital, despite the heavy incidence of loan repayment. This return is as good as the best any European settler ever achieves from cattle. There have only ever been a handful who have attained it, and at the time of Independence there were only three in the country. Up at Rumuruti on Laikipia a well-known ranching company, admittedly highly capitalised, makes only 7 per cent. I happened to have stayed on that ranch in the past and remembered being told how when it was started it could only hold one head of cattle for every thirty-five acres. Thirty years of unremitting labour brought the land to the same capacity as Kobo Rock had now—one beast to ten acres. Nothing but continued managerial efficiency, great efficiency, can keep ranches at this level of production. Nor, as Storer quickly pointed out, is the carrying capacity all—'It's not the number of cattle, it's the weight of beef that counts. Overloading the acreage won't produce a profit.'

Marrian, following both the Government line and no doubt his own views as an experienced farmer up at Mweiga, maintained that most Kenya land is capable of improvement. Kiano sensibly did not commit himself here in what had been an expert's argument between Marrian and Storer. But, as was to be expected, when it came to our leave taking, and a group of the African co-operators were standing round the car saying goodbye, he told them that co-operatives were the answer to Kenya's future as a beef-exporting nation and that they could raise production to hitherto unknown levels. Indeed, if any group of Africans were going to do it, these might. They might not live on the Rock, but they did know something about business as well as about the land. When we drove away Kiano was deeply preoccupied with the problems of making co-operatives work in other places, and with other Africans.

Succeeding months brought various illustrations of this managerial problem. In December a delegation of over 100 large-scale African farmers on the Uasin Gishu plateau came down to Nairobi to warn the Minister of Agriculture that they would be out of business unless more advisory officers were recruited. This was a common complaint. When white settlers came out they usually had experience and the Government advisory service was big enough to cope with those who didn't. Now it was swamped with appeals from new farmers.

The paradox besetting Kenya was evident enough. Before Independence, European agriculture had provided 75 per cent of the country's earnings. Now, just as the African Government's welfare, schools and improvement programmes demanded greater income, the major source of it was liable to be wrecked. K.A.N.U.'s election manifesto had named free schooling as one of its objectives. Yet once in power the party found itself compelled by lack of finance to increase school fees instead of reducing them. This brought widespread uncomprehending indignation from the electorate, many of whom could barely afford to send their children to school before and who now saw secondary schooling as unattainable. K.A.N.U. could not risk undermining their programme, which already depended considerably on international aid. At the same time the 1,000,000-acre settlement scheme simply whetted the appetite for more.

With Independence a new influence came to bear on the land problem. For the first time Russian, Polish, Jugoslav, Chinese and other Communist Bloc diplomats and experts were able to enter

Kenya. At Odinga's invitation they swarmed into Nyanza, producing plans for hydro-electricity and irrigation, filming, getting to know the country. Despite Odinga's long communist connections, and the friendships he had made in Pekin and Moscow he could not, and perhaps never wanted, to commit the communists to Nyanza alone, although any politician seeks to benefit his constituency, and an £8,000,000 communist-financed agricultural scheme was being hatched in western Kenya. Furthermore, no one leader monopolises foreign contacts. Bruce Mackenzie, the South-African-born Minister of Agriculture, was also no stranger to the communist capitals. He had toured Eastern Europe before with James Gichuru, the Finance Minister, investigating aid possibilities.

However, when Kenyatta announced the new plans to settle more than one million Africans on a further two million acres of European-owned mixed farming land, it turned out that despite communist interest in Kenya the first appeal for help was being made to Britain. The difference between this and the original scheme is that the existing European farms will continue to be run as units on a co-operative basis. So large a scheme cannot afford to fail. It will indeed be the largest project of its kind ever attempted on the African Continent. The total cost was estimated in August 1964 at £20 million, but by the time the British Government had sent out a mission to investigate its feasibility, in February 1965, the cost had risen to £30 million.

The Commission, headed by Mr. Maxwell Stamp, had not published any report at the time of writing. But they had embarrassed both the Kenyan and British Governments by telling a Press Conference in Nairobi that 'if the majority of European farmers left now, the economy would be seriously affected'. This was not a palatable remark at a time when the Kenyan National Assembly was being told that 'The Government is proceeding step by step until all land belongs to Africans.'

The subject will undoubtedly continue to be confused until all the land does belong to Africans. The Stamp Commission were considering only mixed farming land. In theory, coffee and tea plantations, ranches, sisal estates and so on were not to be touched, though of course the main concentration of white settlement was in the mixed farming land. In all, Europeans formerly owned 3·2 million acres of the latter. The original million-acre scheme in fact is absorbing nearer

1·3 million acres, though some of it was ranching land. The new 'two million' acres appears to work out at nearer 1·8 million, of which 600,000 acres is to be bought through the Land Bank, itself aided by British loans. Schemes sponsored by the World Bank and the Commonwealth Development Corporation are included in the original 'million'. But the special purchase of 150,000 acres at Ol Kalou and Dundori, where white farming was becoming impossible for political reasons, is not included. Only 200,000 acres, or 200 farms, are expected to stay in European hands, those being Europeans who have taken Kenya citizenship.

The one thing that will distinguish this process from the removal of the *colons* from Algeria will be that whereas Ben Bella expropriated and bankrupted the *colons*, Kenyatta will, with British help, be enabling the white settlers to quit with a certain amount of capital. Not the value of their farms in normal time—which to the settler meant before the Emergency—but five times the annual profit. All the changes of ownership are being done on a willing seller-willing buyer basis, which gives anyone who does want to stay the chance. Additionally a number of 'compassionate' cases are being bought out—old men and women, widows, and others whose farms are not in settlement areas and are otherwise unsaleable.

There was never much doubt about the settlers consenting being bought out, in the majority anyway. Ever since Lancaster House in 1960 they had been complaining that they could not dispose of their property. 'Lord Delamere and I are in complete agreement over this,' Mr. Maconochie Welwood had remarked on one occasion in 1963. 'There must be cheap readily available money to enable companies and others to buy up farms.'

What was almost ignored in this situation was that European farms are by no means the only source of new land for Africans. Granted only one-fifth of Kenya's surface gets the thirty inches of rain that mixed farming requires, and much of that is too steep, cold, stony or badly drained. But that one-fifth is approximately 44,000 square miles and the White Highlands only ever covered 10,200 square miles, a fair proportion of which was range land, not arable. Much land in African occupation is sadly under-developed, if, like some on the Mau escarpment, in use at all. Money spent on buying out Europeans could more logically be spent on drainage and improvement of non-productive areas. Both the British and the Kenyan

Governments have tended to neglect this in their anxiety to meet the political agitation over European ownership. One of the first Russian missions to Kenya was quick to suggest a drainage and irrigation scheme as an aid to development. It appears that it took the Russian experts very little time to evaluate Kenya's limited resources of good land and propose an obvious way of expanding them. Meanwhile, the U.N. Special Fund is working on schemes to develop arid areas, like the Tana River area and Masailand.

It made Kenyatta's declarations to the settlers about his wanting them to stay and farm well look a trifle insincere. In any case not all the settlers had believed him and quite a number of farms, especially round Londiani and Eldoret, had been let slide. Their neglect had already made the Government start taking out management orders and were a constant provocation to landless Africans and agitators. This reinforced Kenyatta's need to satisfy the aspirations of his electorate, which were to own white land, before doing more than pay lip-service to the ideal of a non-racial state. The outcome proves that once again in Africa there is not room for the wealthy minority of another race, just as in Nigeria there are restrictions on Lebanese, and the Arabs have been evicted from Zanzibar, when not slaughtered there. But at least in Kenya the transference of land from white to black hands is being done in a civilised way. If the process gives the communist powers quiet satisfaction at opportunities gained, and Britain an uncomfortably expensive precedent when they come to decolonising Southern Rhodesia, well, that is the way of the world. The next major problem is to ensure that the settlement schemes get the expatriate supervisors they are certain to need if the exercise of transferring the land from white to black hands is not to prove abortive.

Ironically, they will be helped by the African graduates from an agricultural college founded for whites only by an English peer and associated with the Royal Agricultural College at Cirencester. Egerton College, named after the late Lord Egerton of Tatton, stands on 3,700 acres at Njoro, close to the enormous grey stone castle that was his home, and is now one of the country's more pretentious white elephants. The college is the reverse, though it nearly died after Lancaster House when the whole Governing Board resigned on the issue of admitting Africans. Since there were only thirty-seven students then and precious few booked for the future the change had to come. Once made multi-racial, Egerton became revivified, though the output from its two diploma courses sank to six in 1962. A new principal—a jovial, bearded Englishman called Michael Barrett—took it on and has campaigned successfully for funds. It now has a special relationship with West Virginia University, help from U.S.A.I.D. and bursaries for Africans from thirty-two firms and foundations. The autumn intake in 1963 totalled 219 and Barrett had to convert a dining-room into a dormitory with tiered bunks to give them all sleeping space.

Gratifyingly the few Europeans and Asians who were there fitted in remarkably well. When one of the Board remarked at the annual speech day: 'This is a truly Kenyan and national college. A most exciting experiment in non-racial education', one felt for a change that the fine sentiment was the truth. The only jarring moment came at the dinner that night when the Asian president of the junior common room made an attack in his speech on 'hatred, politics and underground movements'. Several Africans walked out, and there was a minute's uproar.

Barrett's hope is that his students will leaven the settlement schemes with some solid academic knowledge, though they are more likely to end up as settlement officers than actual farmers. One of the greatest aversions he has had to fight among his students is that for actually earning a living on the land. Most of them are destined for Government jobs, or work with the companies who have paid their fees.

Various other establishments will help staff the schemes with Africans too. There is a Dairy Training School at Naivasha, supported by U.N.I.C.E.F. and the F.A.O. The school is the hub of a network of 150 co-operative rural milk centres, the overall aim being both to train Africans in hygienic milk-handling and -marketing and to promote the consumption of dairy products among Africans, whose diet invariably lacks protein.

6

The Last of the Happy Valley Crowd

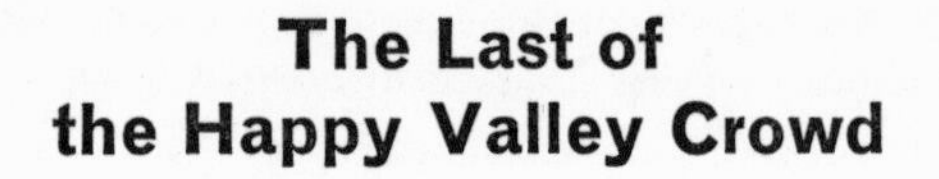

TROPICAL AFRICA has always been harsh, dealing unkindly with man, quickly obliterating human achievement. Its diseases—malaria, dysentery, yaws—can last for life, disabling, sapping the energy, helping to keep the native industrially backward, and, despite the advent of modern medicine, hampering development.

Yet when ideas have been brought they have usually succumbed despite their benefits. It is not only wind and rain let loose with tropical intensity that have made the fifteenth-century ruins of the Arab city of Gedi, on the Kenya coast, seem as old and weathered as Roman relics four times their age. It is lack of human use. The cisterns and bathhouses caved in because the natives never apparently wanted to occupy the city. The parallel with the Saxons neglecting the Roman villas of southern England is evident, but taking place a thousand years later.

There is still no incentive in the African climate, it is a welfare state of its own, keeping the body warm, the stomach just sufficiently supplied from the earth's fruits, and, worst of all, relaxing the brain. The desire for improvement, for growing a surplus above what one needs in order to sell it, is new in Africa, brought by the European and the Asian, and not, I suspect, much welcomed still by the vast majority of Africans, though Independence may be the turning point. I say only 'may' because being willing to accept aircraft, motor-cars, city suits and skyscrapers from other nations, made by other nations, at other nations' expense, is a very different thing from persevering in making them oneself. The foreign-aid programmes are handouts just like the missionaries' bibles and the traders' beads were. They provide what looks like progress but often isn't.

Civilisations have tended to disappear fast in Africa, as Egypt's did. The continent has devoured almost all trace of its own ancient indigenous societies, thus incidentally providing Moscow's African students with a wonderful chance to offer the new states a product more powerful than aid—newly recorded glories of 'original' cultures whose details no one can dispute. The surviving stone walls of Zimbabwe and the superb bronzes of Benin are the exception to the rule, and they lead one most of all to wonder why the societies that created them have disappeared. Nor has the continent been any kinder to the immigrant. Fort Jesus stands at Mombasa still, but the Arab towns of the coastal sultanates are scattered ruins and all that remains of the Portuguese mission stations along the Zambezi is a river-boat song in honour of the Virgin Mary, originally a hymn.

Kenya's white settlers, whatever the social advances brought by *Uhuru*, are destined for a similar oblivion. Sixty years ago the Masai accepted their coming on account of an old legend that an iron snake would bring a conqueror to their lands. When the Uganda railway edged its way across the plains the Masai believed the prophecy fulfilled and came to terms with the European. By the 1920's the welcome of the other tribes was turning to sourness and among the Kikuyu to anti-colonist political organisation as I have described. During the 1939–45 war African soldiers, volunteers in the King's African Rifles, saw in the jungles of Burma that the *wazungu* could be humiliated, wounded, defeated, killed. The British Government's fight against the Mau Mau was the last fling on the military protection of the settler. The 1960 Lancaster House Conference, at which the principles of African majority rule and eventual independence were admitted, spelt the end of white political power. Africa does not cherish the intruder after his strength is gone; whatever his past achievements, it destroys him as inexorably as Egypt destroyed Mark Antony, as swiftly as the 1964 revolution destroyed Arab wealth in Zanzibar.

Hard after Independence, the remaining settlers, still held by their love for Kenya, seem like flies freshly caught in the flow of amber that will eventually preserve them. After *Uhuru* Kenyatta repeatedly pledged himself to safeguard their interests, which through their agricultural production coincided with the country's. So those who elected to stay continue managing their estates, watching the flood of nationalism in the shape of African smallholdings encircle them.

They maintain stoically the daily rituals of what was always a distinctive and self-contained life, the drinks at the Rift Valley and other clubs, the preparation for cattle shows, the racing, the polo and the plain hard work.

But this show in permanence is illusory. Land is at the core of all Kenya Africans' thinking. Its ownership confers self-respect, insures one against old age, feeds the multitude of children that it is good and right for a wife to bear. Land hunger and unemployment will eventually, and sooner rather than later, remove the European. Settlement schemes are buying out the mixed farmers, inevitably the small ranchers and the coffee-planters will go too. No matter how sincerely an African Government tries to defend him, the white settler is a man on whom the vulture has its eye, and the bones of whose society will whiten and crumble with pathetic speed.

However at this moment of writing, the narrow shelf of time on which the author, like a mountaineer, must pause to look round and take stock of the landscape, albeit knowing that later on the view will be more complete, the settler is still an extant species. For six decades, during which he changed appreciably, finally making a great effort to adapt himself to the new environment, it was the settler the world thought of primarily when it thought of Kenya, whether supporting or attacking him. Now he is slipping into history and when, like the Dodo, he is extinct, the memory of all that he was and tried to be, all that he did to make Kenya a country, not just a colony but a real country, will be forgotten. In the words of Kenyatta's own Pan African magazine: 'Colonialism has left Africa in a state of economic devastation. It entered Africa not with the purpose of developing the continent, but of extracting what it could for the development of Western capitalism.' The anti-Colonialist writers who assemble the textbooks of Kenya's history will reiterate this view. Before it becomes unassailable gospel the Kenyan society that the settler made deserves one last brief glance.

The mould cast for the settler character early on was never really broken, an extraordinary combination of aristocratic eccentricity and unremitting hard work, of arrogance and plain speaking, of humour and bloodymindedness, of concern for the individual African's welfare and utter scorn for his collective ambitions, while for the Asian traders there was contempt alone, mixed with determination to create an extension of the English countryside in this climatically superb tract of African highland.

Physically the resemblances between the two areas are striking. Nine thousand feet up on the Mau Summit, where the low cloud and mist hang over the forests and moors until the morning sun disperses them, one can easily imagine oneself in Scotland. Even a couple of thousand feet lower, among the green valleys at the foot of the Aberdares that in their turn are irresistibly akin to Hampshire or Wiltshire, there's enough nip in the air at night for log fires to be welcome. The streams, sometimes clear and tumbling, sometimes more placid between high banks, lay waiting to be stocked with trout. The whole landscape of the Highland bathed in sunlight is as appealing as a tourist advertisement for Britain in June. That the sun can actually burn all the skin off one's forehead in a morning; that after rain the streams run wild, rising six feet in fewer hours, cascading and foaming in an orgy of erosive destruction; that fences rot twice as fast as in Europe and snakes always seem to make their home in the privy; all only served to increase the settlers' affection for this 'other England', their private demi-Paradise. And they themselves, exposed in this deceptive tropical forcing house, became, like the landscape or the fifteen-foot-high groundsel of the mountain slopes, perceptibly larger than life.

They were, of course, not only exposed, they were isolated. Their desire to re-create England in Africa owed much also to the predominance of the English landed gentry, their fathers, uncles and cousins, at the turn of the century. The great estates were both the focal point and the wellhead of the Anglo-Saxon civilisation which the philanthropists had felt it their mission to spread around the world. The Edwardian era that saw, unknowingly, the last flowering of the country houses' rule over Britain was still basically feudal. Long after it was dead its mood continued to dominate Kenya, where owing to the abundance of African labour the cursed servant problem never arose, and which by its remoteness, as much in travelling time as in actual distance, was preserved from the currents of thought and social change at home.

When Delamere bought out a shopkeeper's supply of oranges in Nakuru and urged the crowd to break all the windows of his own hotel with them, or when Colonel Grogan, incensed at the Nairobi Council's continuing failure to tarmac Delamere Avenue in the

1930's, brought a gang of workmen and during the night planted banana trees all the way down the middle of the street's muddy surface, they were behaving exactly as Champion de Crespigny, who used to fight the London cabmen for the fare if he thought it too high, would have done in the nineties and as Christchurch undergraduates still do. Belloc never wrote a truer couplet than:

'The tinkling sound of broken glass
That so delights the upper class.'

The first wave of settlement, before simple patriotism took a substantial number of the men back to Britain to enlist in 1914 for a war that they could very easily have opted out of, had a fair sprinkling of titles. Lord Cranworth at Londiani, the Hon. Berkeley Cole alongside Delamere at Njoro, the Danish Baron Carl von Blixen, whose wife Karen wrote the moving classic *Out of Africa* and gave her name to a district of Nairobi, and many army officers and younger sons of nobility, like the Carnegies on Laikipia.

Clubs were founded almost immediately, and there was even a Hunt at Masara in 1904, the forerunner of others at Limuru, Molo, Sotik and Tantoni, this last surely chosen for the hunting cry sound of its name. Nairobi had its first agricultural show in 1903 and Nakuru in 1909. Cricket and polo became the games, football was unheard of. The more the country was opened up, the more big-game shooting, excitement and the climate attracted men who reinforced this tradition. Large influxes followed both world wars, though after 1945 escape from a Labour Government, austerity and high taxation in Britain was more of a motive than getting rich, for by then the pioneering was over. At one time the colony boasted two dukes and a cricket-team strength of more ordinary peers, not to mention the baronets, knights, retired generals and exiled European princes. In 1961 a Hollywood company filming a wildlife epic had a competition going on between its various departments over which could sign on the highest-ranking local aristocrat. The make-up boys won with a grand duchess.

Right to the end Kenya remained an upper-class colony, from which anyone who fell to the status of a poor white, or landed in jail, was quietly given his passage home. Yet, just as so many English characteristics became heightened, so did the willingness to accept new landowners into the inner circle of Society. If you farmed you were all right. Delamere, finding his Soysambu concession next to one held by a South African transport rider, quickly made a close friend of him. An American retired from being one of Al Capone's gunmen, who bought a farm in the late forties, was equally easily accepted. He fought very usefully alongside other settlers-turned-terrorist-hunters during the Mau Mau and his performances at agricultural shows, when he would stand midway between two targets, draw a gun with each hand and shoot two bulls in opposite directions at once, made him a minor celebrity.

This is why the lament 'There will never be another Kenya' is so correct, why many of the settlers who packed and left for Australia, South Africa, South America and Spain found it hard to acclimatise themselves. It was unique in the British Empire, uniquely English, which again is why so few of the settlers want to return to England itself. The England it was like is no more and, while Canadians, Australians and New Zealanders are apt to regard the Home Country with reverent affection, the white Kenyan is still English enough to despise what England has become—a tight commercial little island with damn all room to swing a cat in, and even the Conservatives as socialist as hell. That's their view, and sitting on the verandah of a farmhouse in the clean sunlight, watching the hawks circle lazily above and the towering white clouds drift over far ranges beside which Snowdon would seem a hillock, one can understand it.

The inspiring size of the Kenyan landscape, so fundamental to the settlers' love of it, is infuriatingly hard to convey to anyone outside. Photographs show what appear to be ordinary valleys and hills, of proportions normal in Europe and pictorially not a patch on Switzerland. But the scale is gargantuan, while the fine weather and extreme clarity of the upland air give a visibility that easily deceives one into thinking the distances less than they are. In the early morning Mt. Kenya is often visible from Nairobi airport, but arriving passengers constantly refuse to accept that such an apparently undramatic pimple of a peak can really be a hundred miles away.

No overnight flight can bridge the gulf of understanding between Europe and Africa. It's just like an American visitor to Britain, whose hostess has proudly shown him her snapshots of the Cheddar Gorge, trying to explain to her the depth of the Grand Canyon. In her heart she doesn't believe it any more than she does her nephew's ridiculous talk about Kenya when he comes home. The tragedy of the British Empire is that the British people never had the imagination to understand or sustain the colonies their kith and kin created, the excitement and love that the Rift Valley set alight in the settlers' hearts. On their side the settlers became more and more removed from British thinking, more and more affected, indeed inflamed, by their new environment.

The traditional approach to the Rift from Nairobi remains with one as unforgettably as Cortéz' first sight of the Pacific from a peak in Darien. After winding up through the densely populated Kikuyu villages outside the city, past the cattle grazing on the road's verges, playing children, women bent double under the weight of great bundles of firewood and looking from behind like a woodpile given unexpected spindly legs by a cartoonist, past the rows of thatched mud huts and the one-storey, corrugated-iron-roofed dukas (Indian-run shops), one comes to a small belt of forest. This is a forest reserve, one of Kenya's many, guarded by a cluster of spotlessly whitewashed huts blessed with elfin tall conical roofs. A sign on the road warns 'No stopping', to deter the Kikuyu boys squatting on the roadside selling fruit, bunches of rhubarb, long and red stalked, cauliflowers, potatoes, even white rabbits held by the ears in straw baskets. As you drive past, these boys leap out on to the road in front of you, like the death wish personified, waving the European vegetables that grow so well here 7,000 feet up on the verge of the Equator.

Then suddenly you are through this thin belt of forest, round a corner, and there 2,000 feet below, sheer down a vast escarpment, is the floor of the Rift. Thirty miles away its further wall rises dark purple against the blue sky, shadowed heavily by the procession of cotton-wool cumulus clouds that drift across its peaks. Nearer, on the valley floor, they make a slow abstract pattern of light and shade, a 1,000-square-mile design, spotted like a gargantuan leopard's back. The Rift is tawny red in the drought, a faint dusty green after the rains, everywhere studded with the darker olive of the thorn trees, seeming no larger from this height than gorse bushes. The scrub appears only as thick grass, very occasionally parted by the line of a fence, while the river-beds, dry most of the year, are marked like hatching on a contour map by the borders of vegetation that spring into life wherever there is moisture in a parched land. Far away a feathery trail of dust betrays a lorry, or perhaps a car, itself too small to be seen, bucking along one of the few dirt roads, while the main tarmac, after curling precariously down the side of the escarpment and diminishing to a mere pencil-line heading north-west, disappears over the shoulder of the 9,000-foot volcano Longonot towards the higher, greener, better-watered ranching lands around Naivasha and Nakuru. Dozens of volcanoes rise in the Rift. Aeons ago they burst fierily through this thinner section of the earth's crust, and now are weathered and breached like old molehills.

The Fever Tree, a species of umbrella thorn, grows particularly finely in the Rift. From a slender trunk, that forks and forks again, its branches spread out to make an almost flat top of foliage, while its lime-yellow bark catches the light like satin, soft and glowing. The early settlers moving upcountry used to outspan their wagons under the Fever Trees at dusk, giving them that name because somehow the idea arose that they were malignant even though hunters make use of them to camp without ill-effect, just as the Masai herdsmen do when they rest their cattle beneath them in the noonday sun.

The settlers always felt themselves drawn to the Masai emotionally, admiring them while despising other tribes, liking to employ Masai cattle herdsmen, while the Masai in turn were decidedly choosy about whom they would consent to work for. For two years in succession, in 1960 and 1961, when there was drought in the Rift, the game died in thousands and so did the Masai's cattle. I remember seeing a herd of Thomson's gazelle near Hell's Gate Gorge at that time. As they started running through what had once been grazing, each animal raised a billowing trail of dust, which crossed and mingled into a grey cloud. The very earth lay bare and rippled by the wind-like sand-dunes. Through this a tall Masai, cloak over his shoulder and spear in hand, drove twenty head of the most emaciated cattle I have ever seen. The white farmer I was with immediately paused to talk and sympathise, not that it did the Masai much good. But it was a mutual acceptance that in nine-tenths of Kenya to sing the cycle of the farmer's year is to sing of drought and locusts, pestilence and pain, precious little else. While usually complaining incessantly, the settlers somehow also rejoiced in Kenya's afflictions. They had made it their country.

In the course of doing so they also created their own Kenya society which only the Boer community up on the Plateau, guided by the

Predikants who had trekked up with its founders in the early 1900's, remained outside, often living in a simplicity parallel to African primitiveness. They did so of their own choice and with reason. They had sought a new land away from British rule—and in 1920 the *rooinecks* officially turned Kenya into a colony.

None the less these Afrikaners played their part in opening up Kenya. It was an intrinsically sad, if locally almost unlamented, occasion when, just before Independence, many returned to the Republic, taking all their belongings, tractors and farm implements south with them on lorries in a reversal of their grandfathers' trek up. Not only dislike of being ruled by Africans drove them away, there was fear of victimisation, a fear which has since proved well founded. The cult of hating everything South African, and especially Afrikaner people, regardless of whether they are opponents of Verwoerd's Government or not, is now so strong among African politicians in independent states as to amount to a religion that is both more unyielding and more violent than apartheid itself. Afrikaners who have applied for Tanganyikan citizenship have been deported instead of being welcomed as converts to liberal thinking, and the same is feared in Kenya when the time to decide on taking out citizenship comes two years after Independence.

It is a typical Kenya paradox, the inevitable exception which proves the rule, that the one white Cabinet Minister in the present Kenya Government should be a former colonel of the South African Air Force, an ebullient, handlebar-moustached farmer called Bruce Mackenzie, who holds the portfolio for agriculture, and who once in a speech appealing for European confidence in Kenyatta's Government told an audience of his fellow settlers that the ruling party's secret service was watching their every move. They did not appreciate this piece of news.

One thing the Boer did have in common with all his fellows was that he had come to Kenya at his own expense, and whether he prospered or whether he went to the wall he expected to do it in an area exclusively white-owned. Britain, quite forgetting the regulations preserving native interests of the 1890's, undertook that it should be so, and on this understanding the settlers sank their capital in Kenya.

Nothing illustrates the fiery individuality of the settler community, and the support their social and governmental connections gave them back in Britain, better than their reaction to the idea of letting Indians into the Highlands, mooted in 1920. Associated with this demand were others—representation on the newly constituted Legislative Council and unrestricted Indian immigration into Kenya. Pressure backed by the Government (albeit British-controlled) of India mounted quickly after the Great War, as nationalists in the sub-continent took up the cudgels for their 'brothers' in Kenya, a practice which incidentally they have now abandoned, despite the rough treatment Africans have given Asians in all the East African territories, not least after the Zanzibar Revolution.

As it became clear the feeling in British Government circles was for giving way to the Indian demands the settlers became more and more impassioned. In January 1922 Churchill, by then Colonial Secretary, told the late Lord Delamere in London, 'We consider that we are pledged by undertakings given in the past to reserve the Highlands of East Africa exclusively for European settlers.' He also said, 'We consider that the interests of the British settlers and the native population alike require that all future immigration of Indians should be strictly regulated.'

By September the 'Wood Winterton agreement' had been formulated, which proposed to enfranchise all British citizens to the point where some 10 per cent of the Indians would have the vote, to abolish segregation, and to leave immigration unrestricted—the reverse of Churchill's promises.

The settlers did not take this lying down. For some months a Vigilance Committee of the Convention of Associations had been organising an emergency military force, checking on supplies, ammunition, petrol, preparing for mobilisation. The influx of ex-soldiers made the colony extraordinarily apt for rebellion. Hardly a European there had not seen military service. Under the direction of retired generals, willing for this great point of principle to forfeit their pensions, yet making their motto 'For King and Kenya', plans were laid to seize the railway and the post offices, to broadcast messages stating the rebel case to Britain and the Dominions, and, most characteristic of all, to kidnap the Governor and hold him at a farm, chosen for the trout-fishing it would offer him during his enforced detention.

Whitehall capitulated—as it often has when menaced—after a combination of misunderstandings made it appear that the settlers had actually seized the colony. There are distinct and amusing parallels between this occasion and the K.A.D.U. and K.A.N.U. threats during the 1963 Conference. But in the end the settlers' action led to the Labour Government's White Paper which declared: 'Primarily Kenya is an African territory, and . . . the interests of the African natives must be paramount.' The arguments put forward about protecting the innocent African from the tainted, corrupted Asiatic prevailed, and forty years later boomeranged on the settlers themselves.

Aided by such events the colony acquired no mean reputation for intemperance. Civil servants were a constant target, understandably considering the absurd development restrictions imposed at the start by the Foreign Office. They were not considered fit for membership of Muthaiga Club, the settlers' most exclusive meeting place and open to practically anyone, of whatever origin, who owned land. An acquaintance of mine, now an old lady, who was the wife of a very senior official in the 1930's, and has never seen the new Kenya, still thinks of it as the place where she was subjected to constant nagging snubs from settlers' wives, one of whom once demanded and obtained the arrest of an African police askari because he had told her, very politely, to move her motor-car as it was causing an obstruction. MacGregor Ross, no doubt feeling the lash of opinion upon himself when he was Director of Works and an 'official' member of the Legislative Council, delineated the borderline of accepted settler conduct with a nice irony. 'It is', he wrote in his book, 'considered debatable behaviour, even apart from legal risks, to beat one's servant, if his skin is white.'

Of actual beating of black men there was always much talk, and, I suspect, little substantiation. Every community has its bad employers as well as its good, but the tales of Afrikaners tying down black women while they raped them smacks too much of deliberate propaganda. What is true is that the white man quickly forgot the Christian principles that first brought his predecessors into the East African interior. The friendship between European and African never flowered. It dwindled and dried up, just as it did in India during the nineteenth century, where my great-great-grandfather's diaries of missionary work in the 1820's reveal a social acceptance of Indians that would have horrified white society there a hundred years later. I can never escape the feeling that this decline dates from the arrival of white women. Certainly in East Africa, where the wives arrived out very early on in the progress of settlement owing to the healthy climate, the 'memsahib', as she is known in both continents, has been the biggest single barrier to understanding between the races. Her racial snobbery and her assumption that all natives are her inferiors, even when not actually her servants, have been a hallmark of British colonisation; unlike the French and Portuguese whose colonies and ex-colonies are very different as a result.

The African was put firmly in his place. A popular Swahili grammar mirrors this prevailing attitude superbly—and quite unconsciously. It is written: 'For the soldier, settler, miner, merchant and their wives—and for all who deal with upcountry natives without the aid of interpreters.' It makes it clear, by omission, that the word 'please' is irrelevant to conversation with Africans, most useful phrases being in the imperative. The exercises are spiced with sentences far more revealing than the author, who intended no social commentary, can have realised. 'Boy, get my bath ready, and don't put in as much hot water as you did yesterday. I like it hot but not too hot.' 'If you want leave to be circumcised I will sign off your registration certificate.' There is even the implicit idea that black skin is unclean *per se*: 'Boy, my razor is spoilt. I know you have used it to shave your head, and my scissors likewise. They are still dirty with your black hairs.' The anticipated reply from an African emerges beautifully from a section on military terms. 'Shoulders back,' cries the (white) officer, 'stick out your chest, raise your chin, straighten your knees! What is the matter with you?' 'Yes, sir,' answers the unhappy askari, 'I try to do my best, but I've lost heart (my spirit is dead).'

Actually the African spirit was so far from dead that it seriously affected settlers' psychology. Laurens van der Post observed in his book *Venture to the Interior* that 'We hear a great deal about the devastating effect that the European has on the native in Africa, but no one has ever stopped to enquire into the effect of the native on the European. There have been murders committed by Europeans in Kenya that have a singularly uninhibited, primitive, almost innocent quality about them. There have been feasts and celebrations inspired not only by Claridges or the Ritz, but also by the Kraals of African royalty.'[1]

Such were those that made the internationally circulated legends of

1. *Venture to the Interior*. Published by the Hogarth Press, London.

the Happy Valley. This stretch of green and pleasant pastureland near the Kinangop plateau, 7,000 feet up, today split up into African smallholdings and its large farmhouses either derelict or used as settlement scheme offices, was inhabited by a handful of socialite farmers. They were well fleeced, several indeed very wealthy, and their collective crazy intemperance became a favourite subject for journalists and novelists.

'Are you married, or do you live in Kenya?' is a saying that seems to have derived from the Happy Valley parties, which added the final ingredient to the settlers' public image—a casualness in sexual relations that readers of the *Daily Mirror* in England could contentedly gasp at, whilst conveniently forgetting the illegitimacy rate in London. What made the Happy Valley so much more intriguing than bed-sitting-room seduction was that the licentiousness was pursued in style, and the rarified air could be blamed for making both men and women unusually randy, even though in Nigeria similar abandoned behaviour used to be accounted for by the appalling humidity at sea-level. I remember vividly as a boy hearing a Kenyan's ex-wife on a visit to England asked if her husband rode well. 'Ride!' she exclaimed contemptuously. 'Ride! He can't even ride a woman, let alone a horse.'

At most the Happy Valley set, including hangers-on, totalled a bare hundred people. There were, however, plenty of other farms where the same rumbustious morals, parties and drinking went on. What is perhaps worthier of note is that when the 1939–45 war began almost all the men immediately rushed back to Britain to fight in it. More than a few joined the R.A.F., several were killed in the Battle of Britain, others died in less famous actions. There have been plenty of more respectable British citizens living abroad, but there have also been plenty who were less willing to return home unquestioningly when their country needed them. The war made an end of the Happy Valley crowd, its last fling being the Erroll murder case in 1940. This sprang from a group of people trying to keep alive a flame that was already dead. Lord Erroll, a handsome bachelor peer, fell in love with the young wife of a baronet, Sir Delves Broughton. One night, driving back from their house out at Karen in the early hours of the morning, Erroll was shot. He was found dead in his car, which had been run into a gravel pit by the road a few miles from the house. The murder was never solved. The Erroll case showed everyone that not merely were the Happy Valley parties now physically over, their spirit was no longer acceptable either.

Although the majority of settlers were and are hardworking farmers, who kept out of politics so totally that their more temperamental neighbours could lead them by the nose all too easily on occasion; although when they prospered they invariably replaced their early wattle houses with stone replicas of the English manor house, mullioned windows, terraces and all; yet the whole community is discernibly odd. It has something about it of Lawrence Durrell's renegade diplomat who put on a dinner-jacket to eat hippo steak in the jungle. Except that the Kenyans do the reverse. They invariably put on pyjamas and dressing-gowns for dinner; indeed one Governor so disliked this practice that he would stay upcountry only on the understanding that his hosts dressed normally in the evening.

Leopard-skin hatbands, snakeskin belts, elephant-ear shoes are perhaps natural responses to environment. But is it really quite normal for a well-known lady to arrive at the theatre in Nairobi wearing a leopard skin made into a coat by cutting a slit in the neck and then worn with the animal's head resting on her breast and its legs, feet and claws dangling behind? Even the colobus monkey cloak of the African elder is more conventionally cut, less outrageously savage. Why do so many settlers, of both sexes, decorate their wrists with the coarse elephant-hair bracelet of the native hunter? After a few months in Kenya one begins to look out for idiosyncrasies as instinctively as if one were gathering the evidence needed to certify a relative.

The altitude is often blamed. If in the Highlands wheat is attacked by so many fatal kinds of blight, what may not happen to people? Perhaps something does, but I am inclined to attribute it more to being on the Equator than to height above sea-level. Tropic latitudes and those between, however deceptively favourable, do impose a strain on Europeans. When combined with all the African influences, and especially the underlying worry of being a handful of whites ruling millions of black men, a handful preserving an alien culture in a continent that has swallowed up so many invaders before, it resulted in hypersensitive settler reactions to anything that threatened, or seemed to threaten, their community. Kenya, if one were to believe them, has been in a constant state of crisis since time began. If it wasn't one thing, it was another. During my first twelve months in the country the following disasters hung over the settlers. First the appalling idea of eventual African rule; then drought; then a moth grub called the army worm which did literally eat up thousands of acres of grazing; then, hard on the drought, catastrophic floods. When I returned briefly in 1962 it was locusts. They lay squashed on the roads, they battered in hundreds against the Nairobi street-lamps. There was also the threat of declining land values and the British Government's refusal to say definitely that it would buy out the settlers before Independence.

On the face of it 1960–3 was thus a period of the greatest imaginable crisis. Yet at the same time world sisal and coffee prices were high, while wheat, cattle and fruit were all in good demand. Friends of mine with a 400-acre farm, 200 acres of it under first-grade coffee, the rest grazing and pyrethrum, took a gross profit well over £15,000 in 1963. Compared to the thirties, when this particular farmer had been a bus inspector, so hard was it to find work at all, the sixties were not so bad. Ah, the thirties! Now they really were disastrous. The depression in Europe drastically cut back demand for primary products and there is no doubt of it the farmers did go through a hard time. Strangely this genuinely tough period is nothing like so vividly remembered as others. The Mau Mau of the fifties stands out, of course. Then back in 1904 there was that idea for bringing the Jews in. And the Great War ruined the decade after that. The fevered plans for rebellion in the 1920's has already been described. That leaves only the forties. Colonel Van der Post records that in the late forties a National Registration Bill had been passed. Afterwards it emerged that Europeans, as well as natives, would have to be fingerprinted under its provisions. An acquaintance told him, excitedly: 'It's just like them, slipping such a fast one on us. But we'll go to London, to Downing Street, to the Privy Council, petition the King, if necessary. But are you sure you didn't read about it at home?' Even as I write this page the President of the Farmers' Union announced that his members were suffering from 'a sort of claustrophobia caused by inability to dispose of their land'.

Crisis, in fact, was and is endemic. In his heart of hearts the settler wouldn't have had it any other way. He likes a bit of drama. Now, however, he is subdued, his spirit as dead as that of the African askari in the Swahili grammar. The following letter which appeared in the *East African Standard* on July 12th, 1963, was typical of many both in content and feeling.

> The alarming increase of crime in the Ol Kalou area is forcing the European farming out of production. Cattle thefts, slashing and maiming of cattle and pigs, robbery with violence, house-breaking and burglary are all too frequent; theft of grain and sheep-stealing are the order of the day.
>
> The land Settlement scheme surrounding us is not immune. Several thefts of produce and machinery parts have been reported from that area, in one case a complete tractor radiator was stolen.
>
> In the interests of brevity, I will enumerate the crimes reported to the police for one day only July 3:
>
> (1) A frail, elderly European lady was attacked. This lady was given a free holiday at the coast by the E.A.R. and H. in recognition of her brave service in a Mau Mau attack on a railway Station in this area during the Emergency.
>
> (2) A Kisii tribesman was killed on Mr. S. E. Botha's farm.
>
> (3) Nine head of cattle stolen from the Hon. R. P. Morgan-Grenville's Simbara Estate.
>
> (4) A cow stolen and slaughtered on Mr. H. R. Munro's farm.
>
> (5) Wheat stolen from Mr. Godfrey Joubert's farm.
>
> (6) Several sheep stolen from Mrs. Ewen's farm.
>
> (7) Maj. Kent's dairy broken into for the third time in a week and cream stolen. Several thefts of gunny bags and produce occurred on the same day, but were not reported to the police. Frustration!
>
> The police in the area have been increased and are doing their best but nothing will stop this growing flood of crime while we have unemployed, landless, hungry people roaming the area, waiting for uhuru and the free land promised to them.
>
> In these circumstances, some of us have decided to sell our loose assets and leave the country before independence.
>
> J. M. KRUGER
> Chairman, Ol Kalou District Association.
> Ol Kalou, July 5, 1963

By Independence about a third of the white farmers had left, the least adaptable and most excitable third. For a time it looked as though the others might survive, provided they kept out of politics and helped the African where possible. Kenyatta had told them himself, at Nakuru, 'Continue to farm your land well and you will get all the encouragement and protection of the Government.' He assured them their children would be treated like other Kenyans. 'What the Government needs is experience and I don't care where it comes from.' The 500 farmers and their wives, visibly convinced of their new Prime Minister's sincerity, cheered him to the echo. They shouted back '*Harambee*' at him just like an African audience would. Perhaps, now that the six decades of fighting Whitehall were irrevocably over, an end might come to the everlasting series of crises. The final and worst of them, African rule, was not going to be so bad, after all.

Alas, once the rejoicings of *Uhuru* were over, which they were in a month, 1964 showed itself in the worst possible light. The army mutiny, albeit suppressed so promptly by British troops, gave a lot of Europeans a nasty fright. But what was worse in practical terms was that the stock thefts and the illegal squatting didn't stop. Early in March Kenyatta ordered a police clearance of squatters of Rift Valley farms. Within a week it was abandoned as a result of outraged protests by the K.A.N.U. backbenchers at such action when unemployment was so rife. Even men completely unaffected by squatters behaved as though they were. With the exception of a small number, mostly young Kenyan-born farmers, who continued to buy land, the morale of the settlers declined. When in August the Minister of Home Affairs signed deportation orders for four Europeans, without reason given, and among those expelled at twenty-four hours' notice was a third-generation Kenyan, Ian Henderson, the depression set in hard. Henderson was, in fact, a police officer, famous for capturing Kimathi in the Emergency, and an obvious target for vindictiveness. But he was also a settler.

Whether or not they are deported, whether Kenyatta keeps his promises or betrays them in practice, the mixed farmer cannot last. The whole trend of the settlement schemes and the Land Bank policy show that. At the same time the Government showed some annoyance at settlers simply giving up the ghost. At the West Kenya Show in April 1964 Bruce Mackenzie declared his Ministry had 'been faced with an increasing number of abandoned and mismanaged farms'. He intended to serve managing orders on these farms in order to lease or sell them so as to put them back in production. He also attacked those who, through lack of confidence, had forsaken normal farming practices. This was indeed a feature of the period after Lancaster House. Settlers have been flogging their land, aiming to earn as much from it as possible, and saving on expenditure by omitting maintenance. They have hardly been encouraged by the Land Bank restricting new loans to farmers who are, or are in the process of becoming, Kenya citizens, or by loans being extremely hacd to get. The only exceptions apply to non-citizens who are introduring some new capital of their own into the country. Taking citizenship is the touchstone of a white man's good intentions, but settlers who doubt their future whether they are citizens or not hardly care to take the risk of losing British nationality, even though special arrangements have now been made by H.M.G. for them to reacquire it if they have to leave Kenya.

Meanwhile to their credit some settlers are making sincere efforts to help the Africans get going as farmers. A few stay on as advisers for a time to advise their successors. A few have split their properties, selling half to their labourers on extended credit. One such is Mr. Lowe, an ardent Oxford Grouper and a very devout man, and therefore something of an exception, who lives up at Subukia. The valleys there, lush, blessed with heavy rainfall and a rich soil, were completely unexploited until after the Great War, when a party of soldier settlers trekked over the escarpment, cutting a road as they went. It took them a month to cover forty miles and since then Subukia has blossomed. But it's much coveted by Africans and when I last drove along that road groups of young Africans scowled at me, some picking up stones menacingly and others dancing an abusive version of the Twist as I passed. Lowe's arrangement, under which his labourers work for him part of the time and he guides their cultivation and arranges the sale of their produce, is taking some of the steam out of the situation.

It is possible that the ranches and the tea and coffee estates will fare better, although coffee, as the most profitable cash crop Kenya has, and one that Africans are growing increasingly, is bound to be the target for take-overs. The export market, mainly to West Germany and Britain, is limited and more coffee is picked than the resultant Government-fixed quota can absorb. It will be remarkable if there are not strong political pressures for African-grown coffee to fill the quota. However, taking note of the best European-owned estates, with their well-weeded lines of sleek dark green bushes, their overhead irrigation equipment and general good management, it is hard to see how Africans will compete in the higher grades, for which there is always demand. The idea that Africans would introduce disease and disruption to the coffee business, which was ostensibly responsible for legislation that for many years prohibited Africans from growing it at all, has now been proven fallacious. Africans can and do grow some of the best coffee in Kenya. But to grow it in quantity requires a capitalisation that is likely to be beyond most of them, unless the Government steps in to loan them money.

Pyrethrum, the daisy-like weed from which a natural insecticide is made, is another matter. Small patches of it are appearing all over Kikuyuland and the Pyrethrum Board dare not refuse to accept the small quantities brought in by Africans, though in theory all growers must have a quota. In 1963 the Board had a stockpile of a year's production unsold. In future years it will inevitably be the European's pyrethrum that is refused, despite it being a business that they founded. The crop is too easy to grow, and too profitable, for it not to pass into African hands soon and the settlers who still have their acreages down to 'py' know it.

That leaves the ranches and the sisal, sugar and tea estates. Increasingly these are company-owned. Often, as the original settlers have lost confidence, Greeks, Italians and local Asians have stepped in and bought them, especially the sisal and sugar interests. Rather to the distress of the Government, more and more Asians are buying land in the scheduled areas now that they are open to all races. Around the time of Independence there was a flutter of Asian speculation in potential sugar land, which immediately brought down official wrath and threats of nationalisation.

The tea companies, Brooke Bond being most prominent, have been more sensible. They run little welfare states of their own up at Kericho, where suddenly one feels one is in Ceylon not Kenya. The neat managers' houses, the club, the offices, the immaculate tea gardens could all be in the valleys round Nuwara Eliya, not in Africa at all. Although the Special Crops Development Authority aims to have 25,000 acres under tea as African smallholdings by 1970, this will not be at the expense of existing plantations. Presumably any future struggles between the tea-owners and the Government will be on the same lines as those in Ceylon. There the game is not to put the indigenous people on to the tea estates as owners but to accuse the companies of every kind of profiteering so that taxes on them can be increased to the point where the estates yield the national exchequer far more than they would if they were nationalised. Happily, however, the Kenya Government has so far given no indication at all of such intentions. Indeed, it is pledged to protect foreign companies and expatriate investment.

Companies are really another story, mainly unrelated to the settlers I have been talking about. Only on the ranches does it seem that the real white Kenyan will survive, and as managers more than anything. Kenya's 1,000,000 head of high-grade cattle earn £6,500,000 a year in exports, and not so many Africans want to supplant Europeans in its organisation. 'This valuable herd,' Mr. Murumbi said at the Royal Show, 'depends for its very existence on strict quarantine and movement control, and on expert diagnostic services and skilled treatment with the most modern drugs by qualified veterinary officers. . . . I know that fears have been expressed about the number of veterinary officers at present serving who will be leaving the country. But a large number of expatriates will remain—and let me assure these once again that they will always be very welcome in Kenya.' The emphasis is strongly on keeping expatriate know-how rather than expatriate ownership.

7

Onward Christian Soldiers (Revised Version)

OF THE four major expatriate activities in Kenya, farming, governing, trading and the Church, only the latter was already doing what the new Government wanted when Kenyatta introduced his new spirit of *Harambee*. With an increasing number of African pastors, and what are now effectively Kenyan organisations, especially the Christian Council of Kenya (Protestant), the Church stands closer to governmental aims than either expatriate advisers or companies do. Not that it is official in any way, but it is tackling tasks of education and welfare in remote areas for which the Government itself lacks the money. While no one would dispute the profound influence that missionaries have exerted on the development of East Africa, the symbol of its continuance is that most priests no longer call themselves missionaries. That stage is past, even though in practice much of their activity resembles that of the C.M.S. fifty years ago. Whereas then it was putting down roots in Kikuyuland, now it is doing so among the Turkana, the Masai, the Suk and other still primitive tribes.

The transformation is the more extraordinary because until recently the missionaries were regarded as a positively subversive influence. It was inevitable that they should have been so originally. Coming hard on the heels of the explorers, often like Krapf, the German-born representative of the C.M.S., being explorers themselves, they were also bringing completely new ideas. By merely preaching Christianity they were undermining the existing tribal society. Trying to replace animist beliefs by a vision of the true, living and charitable God was bound to shatter some most deeply rooted convictions. The elements, the drought and the storm, are particularly savage in Africa. The aim of all primitive African societies has been to control them, whether by outright sacrifice or merely involved ceremonies and witchcraft. Christianity attacked these traditions. Furthermore, missionaries tended to bring with them a Victorian horror of native dancing as immoral and of many tribal customs as evil.

They were also invaders. Krapf confided in his diary: 'A missionary often shares in common the desires and aspirations of a great conqueror.' One doesn't need to have bawled out 'Onward Christian Soldiers' as a schoolboy to realise how necessary an ingredient a certain militancy is to the successful missionary's character. Krapf had come, in the words of the memorial to him on the headland at Mombasa, 'To attempt the conversion of Africa from its eastern shore'. However, he told his young successors when he finally left Africa in 1893, his health broken, 'Do not think that because the East Africans are "Profitable in nothing to God and the world", they ought to be brought under the dominion of some European power.' He was greatly concerned at how the traders and officials, in fact all other Europeans, behaved towards the Africans. He hoped missionaries would 'efface the bad impressions which the conduct of the Portuguese in earlier times had left behind'.

Many others felt the same. The impetus in Britain behind the missionary effort grew, particularly after Livingstone's death had awakened the British public to the idea, as put by the *Daily Telegraph*, that 'the work of England for Africa must henceforth begin in earnest where Livingstone left off'. But with it came trade and Empire. The unquenchable Victorian sense of purpose that motivated the great missionary societies also inspired the trading companies, one of which, the Imperial British East Africa Company, was to have profound effect on Kenya even though it only existed for five years. Once Speke and Burton had revealed the advanced and prosperous kingdom of Buganda, and stimulated a desire to Christianise it, the traders and settlers soon followed along the route to Uganda. They shared the prevailing Victorian self-confidence. Unfortunately, they did not all share Livingstone's feeling that the Africans were 'an imperishable race'. Nor did the politicians who finally divided up the continent at the Berlin Conference of 1884.

To the African mind the abolition of the slave trade soon became obscured as an achievement by the iniquities of subsequent colonisation. Some of the mud stuck to the missionaries, especially as, with the arrival of more Europeans after the turn of the century, they tended to associate as much with settlers as with natives, and started farms as well as schools. When they claimed to act in the spiritual interest of Africans their woolly-headed beneficiaries did not always believe them. There is a cynical Kikuyu proverb that 'A bearded Italian Father is no different from a European'.

This is an undeserved stigma both on today's priests and on the original ones. It is also sad that African nationalism now discounts the efforts against slavery with which the first missionaries were so deeply concerned, not least because there remains at Mombasa a remarkable living testimony to this effort and to the gratitude of Africans for it. This is the settlement of Freretown, created for freed slaves and still occupied and administered by their descendants. Between 1856 and 1873 missionary activity at the coast had concentrated on freed slaves. Krapf had hoped for a settlement at Mombasa, his own mission, the first on this part of the mainland, being only fifteen miles away at Rabai up a long creek which runs into the Mombasa dhow harbour. Eventually Sir Bartle Frere gave nearly 800 acres overlooking the mouth of this creek and it was quickly populated by Africans rescued from Arab slavers. They came from all over East Africa, from what is now Malawi, Zambia, Tanzania, Moçambique and elsewhere. The son of one of them wrote a short but delightful book on how they came there.

Having been caught far inland by Arabs, yoked and marched to the coast, they were loaded on to dhows. When the British warships intercepted them the slaves were asked to tell what evil the Arabs had done to them. 'One stood and showed the captain how his ears were cut in strips, in order to distinguish him. Another showed how a big iron ring had been fastened in his upper lip. . . . When the captain had seen all this he ordered the Arabs to be kept as prisoners and their dhows to be set on fire.' And 'at last these slaves were all brought safely, peacefully, to Mombasa, even to Freretown'.

James Juma Mbotela, the author of this book, made no bones about their gratitude: 'All those who had suffered or been heavy laden with trouble would come to Freretown or Rabai to live in peace and security under the British flag.' Indeed up to 1904 Freretown was larger than Mombasa itself, which was still ruled by a deputy of the Sultan of Zanzibar. It was only the British Navy and the missionaries who protected the freed slaves from the local Arabs.

Mbotela, though an old man now, is still very much alive and a local councillor for the Freretown ward of Mombasa. We spent an afternoon sitting in the cool, dim living-room of his house, drinking orange squash and talking about the past. In the place of honour on a table stood a new transistor radio, a recent present from his 'brother'. He was adopted by an English missionary, Harrison, and taken to England in 1905 as one of the family, educated for a time at a Wandsworth school, and later brought back to follow voluntarily in the Harrisons' footsteps as a mission teacher upcountry. He and the Harrisons' son, who became a District Officer but is now retired, were brought up as brothers and still visit each other.

This adoption came after Mbotela's own father was killed upcountry in an incident that is a Kenya legend. Mission 'boys' were often asked to go with expeditions inland at the turn of the century. In 1904 Mbotela's father went as gunbearer to a trader called Dick. After some skirmishes Dick came to an understanding with the Kikuyu, but almost immediately got involved in one of the many Masai raids on them. He demanded the return of the Kikuyu's stolen cattle at gunpoint. The Masai chief refused, raising his spear, whereupon Dick shot him. Then Dick appears to have gone berserk, and killed a surprising number of Masai before his gun jammed and both he and the unfortunate Mbotela were overwhelmed. Berserk or not, the Masai so admired his bravery that they built a cairn to his memory on the steep slope of the Rift Valley where he finally fell. Every Masai who passed that spot added a stone to it and the mound is still visible, close to the abandoned old road down the escarpment.

Ironically, although his father had died defending the Kikuyu, Mbotela's son Tom, Vice-President of the Kenya African Union when Kenyatta was President, was murdered by the Mau Mau in November 1952. Tom, though a staunch nationalist, had been opposed to violence.

Not that Mbotela complains. Freretown gave him an uncompromisingly strict upbringing. 'The early missionaries,' he remarked philosophically, 'were very strict—one fault and you're out. In other missions they had to warn a man and forgive him.' The freed slave was what we now call a captive audience. Whereas upcountry 'that was different, the missionaries had to deal with independent people'.

The upcountry convert, if disheartened, might suddenly disappear into the bush and forsake religion. At Freretown the absconder was a sure catch for the Arabs, who anyway did their best to tempt and beguile away the mission boys with 'coloured mirrors and coloured beads and highly scented perfumes to smell'. Such things, Mbotela wrote, 'have caused many sons of freed slaves to run away and join Swahili Islams, thinking to gain a life of idleness and endless pleasure. Those that have been caught in this way are now filled with regret.'

The code of Christian living at Freretown was highly disciplined. Outside lay perdition, inside there ruled a somewhat jealous God. Despite the size of the settlement land was seldom given to Africans, though some did save money and buy a plot. Nor were they allowed to run shops, a privilege accorded to some twenty Indians who set up their dukas near the bell-tower at the centre of the settlement. In Mbotela's words, 'The chief preaching was "don't love money".' So the freed slaves were given little opportunity for becoming miniature capitalists. Equally they wore only loin cloths and were allowed no shoes. 'Bishop Tucker he absolutely refused—we were not to wear shoes.' The mission had its own askaris (police) who were quick off the mark. 'If you caught drinking you put in a cell and given the kiboko for that.' Misbehaviour with any of the girls, who were looked after by the missionaries' wives and quartered well away from the men, resulted in immediate expulsion from the settlement. It was only after some years that the missionaries permitted marriages within Freretown.

The day began early, with the ringing of the bell, a six o'clock service and then a roll-call, after which some men went to work on the coconut plantations, some on roads and some on building. A missionary was in charge of each department, one for agriculture, one for carpentry and so on. There was also a Freed Slaves Force, for the defence of Freretown. Its members were equipped with Martini rifles and drilled regularly.

The bell was the centre of Freretown. Round it were a barracks for the Africans, a baraza house, that is, a place for meetings and discussions, and 'a hut for bad people'. These were all of mud with thatched roofs. But the bell hung from a narrow stuccoed arch some twelve feet high, while the church, high and dignified in Gothic style, was also stuccoed. This was finished in 1893 and as a boy Mbotela helped to carry the materials for its construction. It is still spotlessly kept and when we visited it several Freretown women were sweeping out the nave and tidying the vaulted cloister outside, the harsh Equatorial sun casting hard deep shadows under the arches. Inside one might have been in a large English parish church, the white marble font, the dark-stained pews, the whitewashed walls, all assisting in a sudden illusion impaired only by the palm trees waving outside the lancet windows and the boldly inscribed Swahili words over the chancel arch, '*Watamwita Jina Lakwe Immanueli Mngu Pamoja Naswi*'—'And they called Him Immanuel, God with us.'

Unbelievably there are now strong pressures to have this church deconsecrated. Time and greed have overtaken the Freretown in which Mbotela was born. Colonial law and order made it less necessary for the freed slaves to be segregated from others, missionary ideas changed, Mombasa grew into a great port and the land given by Sir Bartle Frere acquired an unexpected value. In 1933 the C.M.S. sold 600 acres to a property company. The church and baraza house were left isolated, whilst the mass of the Freretown people were moved on to a less 'desirable' pocket of land a mile or so distant with room for only about 120 houses. Weeds now grow round the church and the bell arch is in the midst of thick undergrowth, its stucco crumbling. A few yards away lurk the encircling suburban business men's villas that may yet finish off Freretown completely. If, that is, the Freretown people themselves give in. At present they refuse, as they refused to allow the church their fathers built to be deconsecrated. They are trying to prove that the C.M.S. had no right to sell land which was given, as far as they know, for themselves and their heirs for ever. Whilst a settlement of freed slaves is something of an anomaly in a country that has now freed itself from the very same British who freed them, it remains a sad story. The C.M.S. undoubtedly needed funds during the thirties to pursue more urgent work, but this hardly makes it logical to deconsecrate a church which is maintained by such a faithful congregation, and in a predominantly Muslim area at that.

Mbotela went upcountry, as did the missionary movement as a whole. He remembers that among the Kamba 'there were no converts. We taught boys to write on the floor with charcoal until we managed to split some trees and make some sort of a board.' Education has been the great gift of the missions to Kenya and today a good 80 per cent of Kenya's leaders are the product of mission schools, the most famous being the Alliance High School, which is Protestant, and the Mangu College, which is Catholic. But there are many others.

One is the Tumu Tumu Mission, fifteen miles from Nyeri among the ridges of the Kikuyu Reserve and virtually in the shadow of Mt. Kenya. The Church of Scotland settled here in 1908, having first been at Kibwezi near the coast, then at Kikuyu, near Nairobi, and finally here. Tumu Tumu's land was donated by the Government, there being no pressure on land at that time in this area, which was close to the no-man's-land between the Kikuyu and Masai tribes, whereas an American mission acquired their site at Kiambu in exchange for seventy goats. Another mission at Githunguri was given the land by the Thuku family because the missionaries were going to bring education to the area.

The three aims of the Church of Scotland in Kenya have always been evangelical, educational and medical. For a long time Tumu Tumu was the major school in its district. It is still the headquarters of a network of sixty primary and intermediate schools. The Kenya Government now pays the teachers, but the missionary society retains responsibility and there is an agreed timetable of subjects which allows for a period of worship at the start of the morning's work. The missions' policy is to hand over as much as possible to Africans. Indeed, with money short this is just as well. The preponderance of funds subscribed in Britain now goes to inter-church aid and refugee camps, while missions come low on the list.

None the less, Tumu Tumu, having been training Africans as teachers since 1916, managed to build a proper teachers' training college in 1956. Furthermore, as a result of the medical aspect of the mission, they now maintain a hospital with 150 beds and a network of dispensaries in the district. A very moderate fee is charged for treatment, on the principle that 'people appreciate things they pay for'.

These bare facts of its social achievements show how vast has been the contribution of one mission to the Nyeri District. Although international aid schemes are now raising some very magnificent institutes and training centres in East Africa one wonders if they will ever have the spirit necessary to achieve half as much. Expatriate experts come on two- or three-year tours. They demand allowances and housing on a scale the missionaries would never dare dream of, nor probably want in practice. Yet the missionary, staying a lifetime, with leave perhaps every seven years, minutely paid and frugally housed, gives service of a quality money can hardly buy. Furthermore, his skill and education is often quite as good as the experts.

Not that Tumu Tumu is in any way squalid, just simple and unpretentious. The grey stone houses with green painted wooden verandahs cluster among trees below the squat hump of Tumu Tumu Hill. Sitting in a deckchair smoking his evening pipe the missionary teacher whom I visited looked out over the rolling country towards Nyeri, a patchwork of intense cultivation dotted with dark wattle trees and growing hazy in the dusk. Here and there the corrugated-iron roofs of newly built huts glinted. Everywhere the curling smoke of cooking fires was sprawling and blending into the haze. Children's voices singing, the crying of a baby and the lowing of cattle floated up from the village further down the hill. We sat listening as the dusk seeped inexorably down the valleys and the sky darkened. Then the teacher mentioned he had a recording of one of the mission's founders talking about Tumu Tumu as it was fifty years ago, so we went in and sat on his rather battered armchairs to listen to it.

The first mission house was of poles and bamboo. There were no roads, only narrow, winding footpaths and cattle tracks. One rough unmetalled road had been built to Fort Hall, the next Government post on the way to Nairobi, but it was always inches deep in either mud or dust, according to the season. To make a bridge a tree was felled, or else the river was crossed by a crude suspension bridge of strong creepers. The Kikuyu had neither donkeys nor carts and knew nothing of the wheel until the European came and the Indian traders brought ox-carts upcountry.

The Masai were a constant threat, in spite of the strip of grazing land that divided their territory from the Kikuyu's, and women bringing wood from the forests had to be escorted by parties of armed men.

The men themselves wore long skin capes, sometimes made from the brown fur of the tree hyrax, a creature about the size of a rabbit. Everyone dressed in leather clothes, which, if those one still sees give any indication, must have been the same red clay colour as the soil of the reserve. When occasionally one sees a Kikuyu woman dressed like this now she seems a creature of the very earth, more primeval than merely primitive. But in those days the old men were only just beginning to acquire blankets from traders and European clothing was unknown. The society that confronted the newly arrived missionary in the 1900's was, indeed, unaffected by civilisation, though perfectly self-assured in its own ways.

Naturally the missionary, intent upon conversion, sought to penetrate the thoughts behind this primitive façade. He found, as far as he could judge, that the women's minds were almost entirely taken up with their gardens (shambas) and with young children. The Kikuyu woman was, and indeed still is, regarded as meritorious in direct proportion to her capabilities as an agricultural labourer and a bearer of offspring. The young girls spent their time adorning themselves with beads and red ochre and going to dances. The young men did much the same, except that they braided their hair, lengthening it with anything to hand, the wool from a missionary's cast-off sock being particularly prized in this connection. They also covered themselves with red paint. The old men spent the time settling disputes by seemingly endless discussion, or else at lengthy beer parties. In Africa idleness and pombe drinking are the recognised perquisites of old age.

Interwoven with everyday life were innumerable customs connected with God (Ngai) who lived on Mt. Kenya and who had once been seen passing over the Aberdare range to Naivasha in the Rift Valley beyond. Ngai could also be located in certain trees. One which grew on Tumu Tumu itself was known as the Tree of Fat because sheep fat was smeared on its trunk and branches in honour of the God. Mugumo trees, a wild fig tree, were also sacred and later became places of worship for Mau Mau, though the mountain remained the paramount residence of Ngai, which is why Kenyatta's absorbing if atavistic study of Kikuyu custom was called *Facing Mount Kenya*. Actually, Ngai was not exclusive to the Kikuyu. The Baganda, 500 miles away on the far side of Lake Victoria, also believed in Ngai, and so did the Masai. Sometimes the Masai and the Kikuyu thought there were two gods, a white Ngai and a black Ngai. When there was a thunderstorm, as there frequently is here, with vast cumulo-nimbus clouds piling up to 30,000 feet and darkening the whole landscape beneath, it was the two fighting.

The spirits of the dead ranked next to Ngai, being closer to him than mortals. Indeed, the whole universe was full of spirit powers and any accidental offence to them was met with punishment as dire as for any intentional crime. The animist sees the mishaps in life as the penalties of sin in a world where the supernatural is overwhelmingly inimical to the human race. For a Kikuyu to tread on a human bone was as sinful as to commit adultery. Both must be purged by an expensive sacrifice. The similarities to the sternness of the Old Testament are obvious and often the missionary invoked upon the African a God whose wrath was every bit as terrible as Ngai's. Even while I was writing this book a priest in the Congo escaped massacre by shouting at the terrorist about to cut him down, 'Kill me and you will burn for ever in the fires of hell.' The terrorist, horrified, turned and fled.

Some of the Kikuyu ideas provided a good foundation for teaching the Gospels. The idea of uncleanliness could be likened to sin and Jesus to a sheep slaughtered for cleansing men from sin. In their efforts to bring Christianity home to the natives, the missionaries leapt to the laborious task of codifying hitherto unwritten languages. In this Mr. A. Ruffell Barlow, who recorded the account of Tumu Tumu as it used to be, was a pioneer. He wrote a classic *Studies in Kikuyu Grammar and Idiom*. Others translated the Bible into the lingua franca, Swahili, as well as into various of the local languages. Missionaries remained far ahead of both the colony's administrators and its lay teachers in this field. East Africa's schools are permanently in their debt. When in 1963 Julius Nyerere, Tanganyika's President and himself once a mission-school teacher, published Shakespeare's *Julius Caesar* in Swahili he was making a noble and scholarly effort to broaden the foundation they had laid by putting a great secular work alongside the Bible on ordinary Africans' bookshelves.

Witch-doctors, not unnaturally, were far from happy to hear the Psalms, carefully translated so that the strong stresses of spoken Kikuyu fitted the rhythm of the English music, sung by their own 'congregations'. Nor did they appreciate the suggestion that Christ was the Mundu Mugo, the greatest of spirits. They themselves claimed to be intermediaries between mortals and the other world, to have powers delegated from Ngai, and alone to be intimate with the spirits. The European, not having been brought up from birth in the belief that the universe is essentially hostile to man, and observing that Africans are highly impressionable people, has tended to note the state of fear in which the witch-doctor holds a community, and declare with Leys that witch-doctors are 'people of exceptional intelligence who make their living, just as palmists do today, by encouraging superstitions they do not share'. But I know of highly educated Africans who refer to a witch-doctor before making any important decision, which would be unlikely if they as much as suspected that he did not believe in himself. Whether dealing with his many herbal cures, or with blood-letting and grisly ritual; whether squatting, cabalistically adorned, in the dust with the bones before him, or delivering judgement in houses that a London clairvoyant would not despise; whether dedicated wholly to witchcraft, or, as now, perhaps combining it with other business lucratively, the witch-doctor is seen by most Africans as confident in the extra-mortal powers of his prescriptions. To him Christianity was and is both doctrinally wrong and commercially threatening.

In fighting the influence of the Church the witch-doctor could conjure up powerful weapons. If some native ideas could be re-orientated to fit the Gospels, most practices could not. Although these often affected the old most horribly, it was the older generation, as always, who opposed Christianity changing their customs. An old man would only be buried if rich, otherwise his family felt they could not afford to have his hut polluted and made unusable by his dying in it. So when his end was near a little hut of branches would be made for him some way off, and a fire by it. He would be given pombe to get drunk on and then left. After the fire died the waiting hyenas would close in and tear him to pieces. The live babies of sick women would be put out with them likewise. It was a disaster if someone did die inside his hut. A hole had immediately to be made in the back wall so that the hyenas could remove the corpse and fulfil the tradition to some extent.

If these practices seemed detestable, how much worse in the missionaries' eyes were the bride-price system, the circumcision ceremonies, especially for girls, and the deep rituals of initiation. Yet these were central to all the mores of tribal society. In the 1920's the issue of female circumcision came to embody all the African's dislike of European intrusion into his life. African politics were growing fast and the whole question turned into a political one, which then blossomed into ugly violence when two lady missionaries of the Church of Scotland were seized and forcibly circumcised, which caused their deaths.

'When the missionaries first came,' one Cabinet Minister said to me cynically, 'they mixed up religion with hygiene, and it was resented by the majority of people.' One of the easiest mistakes is indeed to assume that because an African doesn't necessarily use soap he is by definition dirty, whereas Africans keep themselves remarkably clean in spite of the difficulties imposed by living in a cramped mud hut. Missionaries also objected to the all-night ngomas, the sometimes frenzied dances that the young so much enjoyed, and very often warning girls to keep away from them on moral grounds resulted only in their keeping away from the mission house instead. When you add to all the other obstacles the fact that the children mostly regarded school and education as a form of game, and that their parents saw no point in it and preferred to have their offspring tending the goats or sheep, it is remarkable that the missions made any progress at all. But they did, triumphantly. Until the early 1930's there were no Government schools in Kenya because the missions made them appear unnecessary and today the Government gives grants-in-aid to many church schools, whose standards are excellent. Today, too, there are large and faithful congregations of African Christians in many parts of Kenya.

No one can say how sincere the conversion of these Africans is. The educational and medical achievements of Christianity are much easier to assess. Will the religious achievements prove a more lasting monument or not? And who can say, critically, that Christianity is only skin deep in Kenya if he himself comes from Great Britain? The wonder is that African converts are so steadfast when faced with the multiplicity of competing sects that Europeans discordantly claim all represent the one true God. Italians of the Consolata Mission, Catholic White Fathers, the Dutch Reformed Church, the Lutheran Church, the American-run Africa Inland Mission, Methodists, Baptists and the Salvation Army are only some of the competitors for the Kenya African's soul.

Then there arises the awful question: Is this true God white or black? At first, since to the African the European appeared as a 'person wonderfully clever and impossible to resist', it could be accepted that the Europeans' God was white. Perhaps, too, the offer of a religion whose God was, at heart, charitable and kind seemed, for those who embraced it, so welcome a contrast to the frequently malignant and always capricious natural forces of animist belief that they didn't bother about the new God's colour. But once it sank in that He was as much the Africans' God as the Europeans', that He was the God of all men, the converts began to ask why He should not be black. The answer must surely be that He is above colour, but may be represented in any colour, even if historically Christ was a Jew and white.

Religious art has attracted talented Africans, and the vitality of their work, as well as the proportion of it to secular painting and sculpture, is remarkable. Happily, some of the best is where it should be—in the churches. In the Catholic Cathedral of St. Teresa at Kisumu hangs a fine small oil of the negro Jesus pointing the path of righteousness to a native child. At Fort Hall in a Protestant cathedral, there is a famous series of murals by a Kikuyu artist, Elimo Njau, showing the Life and Crucifixion of Christ in a local landscape, excitingly reminiscent of Goya. Njau has written verses to go with his bold painting:

> 'Good news.
> Christ has been born on African soil.
> A naked Christ! No robes or decorations on him.
> But his face glows with love like the sun of Africa.
> He brings with him fertility and beauty in the land.'

The Last Supper is in a thatched meeting house with the hills of Kikuyuland rearing behind.

> 'Christ lifts up some millet wine in a gourd.
> He blesses it,
> And it becomes his blood.
> He takes a yam and breaks it into twelve bits.
> And they become his body.
> He gives them all to eat and remember him.
> But they are struck with awe and wonder!
> What is the mystery behind this yam and wine supper?'

Save for Basutoland and Uganda, Kenya has the largest proportion of Christians in ex-British Africa. 10·7 per cent of the population are estimated to be Protestant and 11·4 per cent Catholic. Though noticeably less than in French-speaking countries, where the average percentages are 8·9 and 18·6, it is considerably more significant than the mere numbers suggest. Whereas in Britain countless people, faced with a form to fill in, will call themselves C. of E., often without having been to church since their baptism, in Africa there is little social compulsion to call oneself a Christian. Those who do are usually practising Christians.

One reason for the Kenya Church's strength today is that they long ago realised the need to 'Africanise'. At Tumu Tumu I was told 'our policy is to hand over as much as possible to Africans'. The bald statement sounds like a company director speaking of future intentions to a meeting of shareholders, save that at Tumu Tumu the Church had already been handed over to the local people, and the Minister, the Rt. Rev. C. M. Kareri, a Kikuyu, was Moderator for the whole Church of Scotland in East Africa. He might well have told me in turn, though I hasten to say that he did not, that 'our policy is to retain expatriate assistance for some time to come'. The point is that the church leaders realised in time that, to extend the business metaphor, their shareholders were predominantly Africans and that since they wanted Africans at the top those Africans must be much more than the Men of Straw with which commercial companies later hastily began to decorate their Boards. The Church needed real men. The East African Cardinal Rugambwa of Tanganyika is one such. Another is John Kamau, the General Secretary of the Christian Council of Kenya, a Council which is uniting the various Protestant Churches in the country, Methodist, Anglican and Presbyterian and others.

Kamau, ensconced in his office at Church House, a large modern building in the centre of Nairobi, with a comprehensive C.C.K. bookshop on the ground floor, can look at the Church's position in an independent Kenya with fresh eyes. It is the African church leaders like him who, more than anyone, must establish a *modus vivendi* with the African Government. They are doing it rapidly. In the past, as I remarked at the beginning of this chapter, the missionary seems fated to have been a subversive influence. From an African point of view he became woefully entangled in politics simply by telling congregations to keep out of it. The rising African nationalists deliberately played on the fact that by lecturing against vice and crime the missionary was giving moral support to the colonial government machine. The more the missionaries could be identified with the Government, the more their influence could be undermined. The Mau Mau Emergency was a term of trial for them. In retrospect some wish they had given more positive backing to the African aspirations for self-rule, land and freedom which were enmeshed in that struggle. Those who supported the Tom Mbotelas of the time were, of course, seen as a subversive influence by the Colonial Government, though when the Mau Mau took charge of the nationalist movement it was hard for any Christian not to condemn the nationalism along with the bestial violence, often directed against Christian Africans, which now led it by the nose. However, some missionaries did stand out against the brutality occasionally practised by the security forces against African suspects.

Overall the tortured decade of the fifties was a static period in the Kenya Church's history. While both before and during that time there had been, in John Kamau's words, 'a deliberate attempt to keep people other than Government officers out of the Turkana, Masai and other colonial districts. It was not so much anti-Christian as based on the idea of keeping these areas untouched.'

Though trade may have followed the flag in British Africa, the flag frequently followed the missionaries. Yet paradoxically the administrators invariably mistrusted the priests. There was no possibility of keeping the Church out of the Coast or the Rift Valley or Kikuyuland or Nyanza. It was there before the Government was. But the concept of the noble savage, combined with a not unjustified feeling that priests bring trouble, sustained the colonial administrators in their desire to protect the most primitive tribes from the harsher effects of progress. So where possible the Church was kept out along with traders and settlers.

The African Government of Kenya has no such inhibitions. Its policy is to open up all areas of the country. Without so doing it cannot make one nation of Kenya's disparate peoples. In this the Church's aims dovetail with the Government's. The Church, which no longer considers itself missionary but as established in Kenya, wants to open up the primitive people's minds and, so long as it does not 'misuse its privileges', expects to retain Parliamentary support for its endeavours. It can provide not only schools and teachers for these the remoter parts of Kenya, it can also produce development capital for schemes like the Turkana Fishery on Lake Rudolf, which I shall describe in a moment. The two African pastors at Rudolf, sweating in their shirt-sleeves in the fierce sun to build a schoolhouse of palm logs, are the heirs of Bishop Hannington, who in 1882 'wore slacks and wide-brimmed felt hat' and when he was menaced by a lioness 'took off his hat revealing his bald head, very white in contrast with his sunburnt face, and head down ran towards her roaring and shouting, whereupon the lioness fled in terror'. The spirit is the same, whether today's priests working in the back of beyond are technically called 'missionaries' or not, and whether they are white men or black men.

8

Bringing *Harambee* to the El Molo

SOCIALLY one of the most challenging tasks before the new Kenya Government is bringing the most primitive tribes of the country up to something approaching the level of the Kikuyu, Luo, Kamba, Abaluhua and other leading tribes, and weaning them from the traditional antagonisms and tribal beliefs which reinforce their backwardness. They are people who, while not particularly objecting to being part of Kenya, as Somalis do, barely participate in the life of the state at all. They have little sense of what their elected representation in the Assembly signifies. Education and medicine are only just beginning to impinge on them, sometimes through international aid and missionary effort.

The most curious, unknown and interesting of these are the few remnants of Kenya's truly indigenous inhabitants, the tribes that inhabited East Africa before the Bantu, the Nilotics and Hamites arrived. Though withdrawn, shy, tenacious of their own habits and ways of life, they have escaped total submersion in the ethnic tide of the larger tribes through the undesirability of their habitat. Like rare species, the El Molo have stayed as fishermen on the remote shores of Lake Rudolf, the Waliangulu as elephant-hunters in the desolate scrub bordering on the Tsavo Park, and the Dorobo as honey- and game-hunters in the high forests of the Mau Escarpment.

The Dorobo, or Wandorobo as they are also called, are probably related to the Waliangulu, while both share ancestors with the bushmen of the Kalahari. They are small people, great marksmen with bow and arrow, killing by the use of their own powerful herbal poisons, sticky and dark on the arrow-tip. There is a Masai legend that at the beginning of the world a Dorobo gave birth to a boy and a girl who came forth from his shin bone and became the ancestors of the whole human race. None the less the Dorobo are dwindling, partly through mixing with the stronger races to whom they sell skins and honey. There are now only about 100 pure Dorobo families left. Elspeth Huxley gives a delicate and sensitive picture of a Dorobo hunter in *The Flame Trees of Thika*, a book about her childhood in Kenya. I doubt if it can be bettered.

'He was a small man; not a dwarf exactly, or a pygmy, but one who stood about half way between a pygmy and an ordinary human. His limbs were light in colour and he wore a cloak of bushbuck skin, a little leather cap and earrings, and carried a long bow and a quiver of arrows. . . . From him came a strong, pungent smell, with a hint of rankness, like a waterbuck's; his skin was well greased with fat, his limbs wiry and without padding, like the dikdik's.' The Dorobo, she explains, 'knew all the ways of the forest animals, even of the Bongo, the shyest and most beautiful, and their greatest delight was to feast for three days upon raw elephant'.

The third of these aboriginal tribes, the El Molo, is in many ways the most intriguing, as well as being easier for me to write about, since I have seen them at close quarters on several occasions. There are only ninety-seven El Molo and they live on the inhospitable shore of Lake Rudolf, a part of Kenya where, save for a small tourist fishing camp of thatched huts, civilisation has made no mark and which deserves some preliminary description. Barren, arid and stark are adjectives of flower and fruitfulness by comparison with the nature of Lake Rudolf. It is the northernmost of Kenya's Rift Valley lakes, only 1,230 feet above sea-level, set in a desert of sand and lava rock, fringed by extinct volcanoes, and burning hot.

The explorers—no, forgive me, the foreign travellers—Teleki and von Hohnel had named it, in von Hohnel's words, 'Gratefully remembering the gracious interest in our plans taken from the first by His Royal and Imperial Highness, Prince Rudolf of Austria'. They had heard rumours of these lakes, close to the Abyssinian border, that no European had yet reached, and they approached them by the route up the Rift Valley, utterly unchanged since. 'The scenery became more and more dreary as we advanced. The barren ground was strewn with gleaming, chiefly red and green, volcanic debris, pumicestone, huge blocks of blistered lava, and here and there pieces of petrified wood. There was no regular path, and we had to pick our way carefully amongst the scoriae, some of which was as sharp as knives.' When they finally came in full sight of it their excitement was equalled only by the subsequent disappointment of finding its water brackish and margins devoid of any green thing.

The ancestral home of the El Molo is on the eastern side at the south end of Rudolf's 100-mile length. Their ancestral acres are bare stony ridges rising from the endless miles of a near-black pebbled plain that is strewn with football-sized lumps of pumicestone, rounded by erosion and a tearing wind. This eerie yet strangely beautiful landscape, the embodiment of a Salvador Dali dream, is compounded with tricks of nature that make familiarity with it breed wonder rather than contempt.

The lake has no outlet. Two rivers flow into it from Ethiopia to its north, and Turkwell snakes in halfway down, but nothing goes out. The south end is blocked by a massive natural dam of lava rock and volcanoes, whose half-submerged cones poke up out of the green and brackish water as round as sugar loaves and with their tops cratered like models for a geology lesson. For years no one could understand why the water didn't just pile up and overflow, then someone calculated the evaporation rate. It is eleven feet a year, which over 3,000 square miles of water comes to an enormous volume. While all this ascends into the atmosphere, only six inches a year or less comes down again locally in the form of rain over the same period.

Not content with this lopsided balance sheet, nature additionally funnels a fierce gusting wind over the lake, the result of the difference between the pace at which the land and water cool and heat up. But what is in more temperate climates a soft onshore or offshore breeze is magnified here by the desert surroundings into a forty-knot gale that whips up five-foot waves on the lake waters and has drowned its quota of adventurers, including two of Sir Vivian Fuchs' fellow explorers on their 1934 expedition to the area.

From these dangerous waters the El Molo draw their homeland's only possible harvest—fish. Although their own folk history insists that they have always lived by the lake, they have never evolved a boat. The men go out on rafts of four palm logs tied together with twine, the trees being cut from the only local oasis. On this precarious platform they stand upright, legs apart, their fishing spears balanced in one hand ready to throw. Each fisherman, etched slim and solitary against the expanse of the lake as he gazes into the murky green below, seems a being from the start of time, miraculously able to walk upon the water by an art now lost to mankind, for invariably a slight swell hides his raft from view. He wears only a loincloth and his spear is actually a simple harpoon, an eight-foot shaft with a hollowed end into which fits a short barbed head. A length of twine attached to this barb runs out from his hand when he strikes. Then if the fish tries to run it can be played and held, while the wooden shaft of the spear comes off and floats, waiting to be picked up later. The line is an essential, since the fish are a phenomenon in their own right.

The Nile perch, principal fish of the lake, are monsters, as much giants compared to their English cousins as Kilimanjaro is to the Surrey hills. Two hundred pounds is not an unusual weight, nor four and a half feet an uncommon length. How they came to be in the lake at all is a mystery. Rudolf is unconnected to the Nile, though the fact that the long-beaked ibis, the sacred bird of ancient Egypt, and the Egyptian gull also breed here among the native pelicans and egrets, tends to confirm the theory that millenniums ago a tributary of the Nile did pass this way, though now the two rivers that feed the lake flow in totally the wrong direction, and the Nile itself is 300 miles to the west.

Altogether the Nile perch is the original of the tall story at the Fisherman's Rest. Yet at the same time, indeed perhaps because of this mythical size and the lazy, luxurious living on plankton and smaller fish that enables him to attain it, he would be a sad disappointment to Izaak Walton. He is no fighter. He makes no sport of his passing, no epic Hemingway death like the big-game fish down at the coast, the great marlin and the barracuda beyond the reef. He is a tame inland creature who in his whole cycle never smells the excitement of the sea and when hooked makes only one or two runs and then after a final plunge in the green water gives up his body limply to the gaff. Fortunately he tasted none the worse for his despairing end.

While I was at the Lake an El Molo boy, ten years old, landed a perch of 186 lb. with a line of only 46 lb. breaking strain borrowed from a visitor, much to the fury of his less successful father, who immediately flew into a comically jealous fit of anger at being outpointed.

Although the El Molo dare not venture far out from the shore for fear of their rafts capsizing in a storm, they can still spear perch of a fair size, as well as the small tilapia, tiger fish and others. Sometimes too they kill one of the crocodiles that bask along the lake shore, not so easy as it may sound, since the crocodile looks ungainly but moves with surprising agility. One flick of the tail and he is gone beneath the surface of the water, as likely as not adding a quick snap of the jaws to the movement and taking an unwary spearman with him to the lake-bed which he uses as a larder. The crocodile likes his meat putrid and keeps whatever he has caught for several days before eating it. Not unnaturally, the El Molo are delighted when they catch him instead of *vice versa.*

The effects of this marine diet, one rich in protein but short of calories, has begun to attract the interest of specialists, not least because it is the reverse of the usual African feeding based on maize. Apparently the nearest valid comparison is with the Eskimos. The El Molo have healthy, good eyes and a nil infant mortality rate, but at the same time they are undernourished, lack muscle development and suffer a singular deformation of their bones. The old men's legs are bowed forward in an alarming and unnatural curve, while their chief can only walk at all with the aid of two sticks.

More prosaically, the fish leave their mark on the environment through the El Molo's attitude to garbage, which like most primitive tribes' is unrelievedly medieval. The foreshore by their village has become a mausoleum of fish bones, amongst which a few goats pick their slender way. Indeed, the very location of the village is founded upon a fishy expediency. When I first went there in 1961 it was on one of two small islands a few hundred yards from the shore, halfway to being on a boat, as it were, since it placed them closer to the big fish. Now the village has been moved back to the mainland by the mooring of the tourists' camp launch. Since the visitors frequently donate their catch to the tribe, this means that effectively the El Molo can catch the largest fish without so much as launching a raft. They have had as much as 1,200 lb. of fish from the camp in one day, 12 lb. a head for every man, woman and child. Thus has the corruption of the El Molo begun. When I called on the chief in order to be shown the village I was horrified to find the conversation of this grizzled, bent and wrinkled elder restricted to two crystal-clear demands—first *kibiriti* (matches) and then 'shillingi, shillingi'. This,

I suppose, would be described by proponents of the noble-savage theory as the first stirrings towards a money economy. Alas that it should be the only mark of civilisation. The Kenya Senator who announced that it was Government policy to see that there were no more 'human zoos' in Kenya reckoned without the El Molo's astute willingness to turn themselves into one.

In truth the El Molo show remarkably little of that desire to improve their lot which has so changed the Kikuyu's material circumstances. As with their rafts, so in their houses. These are tiny five-foot-high basket-like huts. Even their owners, who are not large people, have to bend double to enter them and once inside there is barely room to lie down. Collectively they look as bleak as the landscape, a mere encampment rather than a village, with the fishing spears stuck upright in the ground outside the huts and the tribe's few goats penned alongside.

It is hardly surprising that the major cattle-owning tribe to the immediate south, the Samburu, 50,000 strong and proud into the bargain, should despise the El Molo for their ineffectiveness. The local Samburu employ the El Molo to look after some of their cattle, but even though the El Molo have taken to using their language, and the original El Molo tongue is rapidly fading into oblivion, the Samburu apparently regard intermarriage as unthinkable.

All in all, the El Molo are a curiosity. Unexpectedly this precise quality thrust them into much publicised prominence a few months before Kenya's independence. How it came about is a classic *histoire* of political opportunism, a story de Maupassant would have elaborated better than I can, the genesis of a pearl in any language or country, yet as completely African as those Congolese declarations of war by press conference that the world heard so often in 1961.

The Minister of Natural Resources flew up to the lake to be shown a famine-relief scheme among the Turkana on the other side. He stopped at the fishing camp and was also shown the El Molo. Immediately upon his return to Nairobi he called a press conference, not about the Turkana Scheme, which was in fact badly in need of public attention, but about the El Molo. 'I saw,' he announced, 'a desperately sad spectacle of human misery. . . . I spoke to their sickly miserable chief, who said once upon a time they numbered thousands but they were dwindled into insignificance because of chronic malnutrition.' He went on to speak of them dying out. 'I have been sent by them with this message, "Please help us before our days in this country come to a tragic end".' At the same press conference it was stated that the women lacked the strength to bear children and that the men had actually gone so far as clubbing together to buy a young Samburu girl so that they could be sure of having some progeny. At the same time photographs of the starving El Molo were issued. The resultant sob-story was printed not merely in Kenya but around the world. It was indeed a P.R. man's dream, the sort of immediately comprehensible situation that easily wins dramatic treatment over plenty of column inches. From the Minister's point of view it must have seemed a wonderful chance to demonstrate Jomo Kenyatta's new rallying cry of '*Harambee*' (let's pull together). Furthermore, to help the El Molo would need only a small, and therefore easily manageable, pull.

The response was quick. The Catholic Relief Service obtained eighteen tons of food from the United States Agency for International Development. The R.A.F. flew it up. The Christian Council of Kenya got to work. Maize, dried milk and World Health Organisation doctors were made available. The Caltex Oil Company promised a fishing-boat to replace the log rafts.

The doctors were the first to explode the myth. On their return from the lake they announced that far from being unable to bear children, the El Molo women had so many that out of the ninety-seven people no less than forty-six were of school age or under. Their diet was certainly unbalanced and resulted in a calorie deficiency and possible deformation of their bones, but the tribe was far from dying out. Indeed, further research showed that their numbers are increasing. When Sir Vivian Fuchs counted them in 1934 they numbered only eighty-four as against the ninety-seven counted now.

The editorials commenting on this counter-blast dealt charitably with the Minister's inaccuracies—after all, they erred only on the side of good intent. No one thought it wise to add that the photographs issued at the press conference and widely published were not of the El Molo at all. The Government photographer had made a mistake and taken pictures of Samburu children at the oasis.

At much the same time as this furore was being artificially created a debate in the Senate underlined some of the irrational emotions felt by African politicians over bringing primitive tribes into the twentieth century. The debate was on the provision of cattle-dips for the Samburu. In successive breaths the Senator, speaking for the Government, accused the former Colonial Government of deliberately keeping tribes backward to attract tourists, then mentioned that between 1945 and 1961 the sum of £153,000 had been spent on developing organised grazing for the Samburu, and finally declared that it was not the present African Government's policy to provide cattle-dips, which should be done by County Councils. The upshot was agreement that until the Samburu returned to organised grazing, which they had now abandoned, the Government would not advise providing cattle-dips. No motion was passed on how the Samburu should be persuaded to return.

While the Senate has hardly been renowned for the good sense of its debates, this is a fair example of the other side of the El Molo coin. The Samburu change in grazing habits is a fundamental step towards educating them into participating in a modern Kenya. But it's the kind of scheme that is tiresome, time-wasting and productive of virtually no useful publicity either internally or externally. The El Molo, on the other hand, were potential promotion material for the '*Harambee* spirit', and so irresistibly appealing that when it came to the point international or private organisations could be expected to leap forward with most of the necessary—and some unnecessary—aid. While past disregard of the El Molo was no credit to the Colonial Government, there were other tribes much nearer starvation than hey.

9

A Tribe for the Connoisseur

WHEREAS the El Molo are not starving, large numbers of the Turkana, on the other side of Lake Rudolf, are. Alas, for them, they are a connoisseur's tribe. Proud, but the proud go unloved in this world. Wild, but politicians prefer the tame. Numerous, but the census-taker likes his populations accessible. The Turkana man is impressive to meet, his strongly black body slim and athletic, hair elaborately plaited into thick strands and set with white feathers like a coxcomb on top of his head, neck chokered with bead necklaces, and upper arm bound in rings of shining iron wire. He lives in an individual world. Most of the things that comprise it, his belief in evil spirits that dictate social customs, beneficial in practice, his pride, not least his very appearance, are all anathema to the Bantu tribes that now rule Kenya. One might say that the Turkana, like their relatives the Karamajong in Uganda, or their enemies the Dodoth, are an acquired taste. The English administrator who spent his days trying to guide them was a special breed. When he passes, or is 'Africanised', they will very likely find his successor less sympathetic, unless by then they have produced their own officials. Meanwhile changes elsewhere and the unyielding circumstances of their own world have brought many of them to the brink of starvation.

Like the other Nilo-Hamitic tribes the Turkana are cattle people. To them cattle are a man's intermediaries between his own soul and his ancestors', they are to be praised in song and depended on for milk, buying wives and security in old age. The burning-hot north-west corner of Kenya, sandwiched between the 100-mile length of Rudolf and the Uganda and Sudan borders, where they wander grazing their herds, is normally no place for cattle either. As it's too hot for ticks to survive, there is no East Coast fever, nor indeed any of the other diseases that in more promising parts of Kenya decimate a farmer's stock the moment he drops his guard against them. Rinderpest is the only scourge and at last, to the great credit of a single-handed Government veterinary officer called Norman Cowdy, the Turkana have accepted inoculation against it. Primitive peoples are always initially suspicious of the hypodermic syringe. But once the virtue of its magic is acknowledged, the rush for it mounts. I remember a doctor in northern Nigeria telling me that so tremendous had local faith in the hypodermic itself become, as the instrument of healing, that any quack could raise queues of peasants clamouring to pay 5*s*. for an injection and never thinking to ask what was going into their veins—which was plain water. It is somewhat the same with the Turkana. After years of failure by other vets this particular man has gained their confidence and now can barely keep up with the demand for rinderpest inoculations.

Unfortunately no medicine can cure the appalling problem of overgrazing. There are too many cattle, camels, goats and fat-tailed sheep for the scrub, thorn bushes and scanty grass to sustain. A century or less ago the Turkana, a warrior tribe, fought for more grazing when they needed it and were rich in terms of livestock per person. The bride price, which is still adhered to by the old men because it was what they themselves had to pay, reveals their former wealth. Forty head of cattle, plus £100 worth of other goods, is the traditional amount—and a good native beast fetches up to £12 10*s*. But since the old men paid that price to their fathers, long buried beneath rough stone cairns in the wilderness, colonial rule has intervened. It has reduced the natural wastage of men in fighting and cattle-raiding. It has confined the tribe within its district. At the same time colonial medicine has helped increase the Turkana's numbers to the present 150,000.

It has been impossible to keep the herds of cattle increasing comparably. The bachelor who would a marrying go today usually takes his future wife as a concubine and pays for her over many years on the never-never. That this prolonged payment is seldom defaulted upon is due partly to personal honour, partly that if payment is not completed then the children of the liaison revert to the girl's mother.

Thus customs are adjusted to the new situation. But the capacity of the land is less easy to adjust. Attempts to keep the number of livestock rising has led to soil erosion and the other results of overgrazing, which swiftly reduce the capacity of the land. They led to near disaster in 1961. This was a year that will rest in living memory as the worst for many decades. First two rainy seasons virtually failed and drought killed a lot of cattle. After the drought came such exceptionally heavy rains and widespread flooding that even now, two years later, the level of Lake Rudolf is five feet above normal. The grass grew everywhere. In the semi-desert long-dormant seed sprang into life. But the emaciated animals that plunged to eat this manna were unaccustomed to such rich food. At the best of times they eat more of thorn bushes than of grass. They went straight down with scour (animal dysentery), which killed as many as the drought had done before. This compounded disaster cost the Turkana 60 per cent of their livestock. Since they normally eat blood and milk, this meant 60 per cent of both their food supplies and their capital had gone at one blow.

There had long been a famine camp for the Turkana at Lodwar, with 800 to 1,000 tribespeople in it; 1961 multiplied the numbers frighteningly and even two years after the floods, and after strenuous efforts at rehabilitation, there were still four camps in the Turkana District looking after a total of 4,000 men, women and children.

Nor are matters helped by the refusal of rich Turkana to support their poor relations, like the Bantu Africans do. Turkana consider that a man with no livestock has no dignity or standing. Inevitably he becomes an outcast.

Shortly before *Uhuru* I flew with my wife to see the camp at Ferguson's Gulf on Lake Rudolf. It promised a concentration of activity that might epitomise the tensions of progress in the wild. In the camp itself missionaries were making the most of a captive congregation. Half a mile away on the gulf itself a Kenya Government Fisheries Officer was running a scheme to teach the Turkana modern ways of fishing. It had been established mainly with aid from British sources, and was now the subject of take-over bids by both Protestant and Catholic Missionary Societies. In the end the Protestants prevailed.

Flying up the west side of the lake, over sand-dunes out of which jutted rocky humped-back hills reminiscent of prehistoric monsters, then past the meandering green-fringed coil of the Turkwell River, debouching a wide arc of mud into the lake water, we came at length over the gulf. From 5,000 feet it looked like anything but a centre of activity, though its horseshoe shape was prominent enough: a long palm-fringed sand-spit enclosing a sheet of water a mile or so wide. A lazy dirt road, like a scratch on a sand-table, curved up towards it, coming from Lodwar thirty miles away.

This led us to the camp, thatched huts barely distinguishable from sand and palms, with the Turkana milling around a lorry like black ants. After diving down and beating up the area, the customary way of announcing one's arrival anywhere in the bush, we turned and landed on a strip more identifiable by the ring of white stones round its windsock than the margins of its runway. However, it proved well graded and later we learnt that the Oxford Committee for Famine Relief had just spent £1,000 on improving both it and two-thirds of the road to Lodwar.

Robert McConnell, the Fisheries Officer, met us, a thick-set, slightly schoolboyish-looking man in his thirties, with a shock of blond hair over a tanned and freckled face. He wore shorts and a khaki shirt. As he helped us secure the aircraft and cover the windscreen to stop the sun's heat clouding the perspex a few Turkana, spears in hand, wandered up out of curiosity. Their manyatta was a short way off, a cluster of low rounded huts. Their goats grazed on the scrub. They stood idly watching us, weight on one leg and leaning on their spears until we shot off in a cloud of dust to the camp.

The contrast could hardly have been greater. Here was a football pitch with boys in shorts and loincloths racing after the ball, kicking up the dust. Outside properly roofed huts and houses an African pastor, a Kikuyu, who had been here for the past one and a quarter years on behalf of the Christian Council of Kenya, was standing before a half-circle of children teaching them a religious song and beating the rhythm with his outstretched arm. Of 1,214 Turkana in the camp at the time of our visit, 757 were children. The other African priest had organised a school at which they were taught maths, Swahili and English. It was a stout erection of palm logs with a shining corrugated-iron roof and simple palm-log benches inside. A heap of writing slates stood in one corner. On Sundays this building is used as a church. The missionary himself was a studious man wearing glasses and a Homberg hat. Though he was actually in his shirt-sleeves I have retained a strong residual impression of having talked to a black-suited clergyman in an English cathedral close. He was shyly proud of his school-cum-church and at the same time full of plans for building something better. These priests doing the job of missionaries give a lot of impetus to the camp's life in the course of their work to open up the Turkana's minds.

Before the missionaries came in 1916, I was later told, the camp was pathetic. Crossing over to where free maize was being distributed, this was not hard to believe. The women and some old men were queuing for the 20 oz. they get three times a week, on Mondays, Wednesdays and Fridays. Each held a card bearing a date of issue and ruled squares on which a date was stamped every time they drew the maize. This was issued by a man squatting in the shade of a thatch screen who scooped it up with a tin measure from a vast pile before him. The women held out their tins or wooden bowls, and then, firmly grasping the cleft stick in which most secured the precious cards, stumbled off to grind the grain into maize meal and make porridge or bread. In an emergency, after fire or flood or earthquake, the distribution of free food can be an inspiring business. But regular famine relief, day after day, year after year, becomes melancholy and sad, a treading down of the spirit.

The Kenya Government has been perfectly aware of this, albeit following a different train of thought to the missionaries. Although the Turkana rate both maize and fish about equally as a poor second best to blood or milk, there have been fishermen on the lake for many years. They worked from primitive boats and used seine-nets made from dom palm fibre, a material so absorbent that when wet it was a job to haul in the net, let alone any fish caught in it. The resultant catch was not even scratching Lake Rudolf's potential. The Kenya Government's Fisheries Department had already begun considering a scheme to develop a proper fishing industry when the drought and floods made action imperative. The Fisheries Officer came up and began a life straight out of *Boy's Own Paper*, living in a palm-frond hut on the spit of sand that encloses Ferguson's Gulf. His experiments showed that an eight-inch-mesh nylon gill net was right for reaping a harvest of Nile perch and he started training fishermen. But by June 1962 the department had run out of funds, its budget being low, anyway. An appeal was made to Kenya's

National Food Relief Committee and to the District Commissioner at Lodwar. The response was remarkable. The Relief Committee brought an outrigger canoe from the coast and gave the D.C. £200 a month to buy dried fish for distribution to the Turkana famine camps. The British Government gave £1,200 for five canoes, two fibreglass boats, fishing gear and outboard motors. Then Oxfam sent £300 for net-making materials and £1,200 for a twenty-five-foot-long twin-engined catamaran, as well as the £1,000 for the road. Three hundred and fifty fishermen had been trained by September 1963.

The Fisheries Officer took us to meet his fishermen. We crossed the gulf in one of his boats, churning up a wake past palm trees still half submerged from the floods of two years before and crowded with nesting pelicans and cormorants. The sand-spit on the far side bore a small village of dried huts, with one larger reed house for the Fishery Officer and a series of simple wire drying-racks for the fish. Slices of fish up to two feet long and a quarter-inch thick are laid out in the hot sun for five to six days and, once dry, can be kept for a long time without going bad. On behalf of the Lodwar D.C., McConnell paid fifty cents (6*d.*) a pound for the finished product to the fishermen, who sat around on the strand mending nets or weaving new ones. Naturally they bothered to catch only as much as McConnell would buy, which in 1963 came to about 700 tons, as against the 10,000 tons that the available equipment and trained fishermen could take from the lake in a year. However there were another seven men employed full time by the Government to catch fresh fish for the Famine Camp next door.

Finding a market was the snag, and one that was causing a great deal of concern, since the D.C.'s grant for buying the fish was due to run out at the end of the year and there would then be no sale for the fish at all, except to the occasional Indian trader who braved the 250-mile drive from Kitale to buy a few hundred pounds' weight at as low a price as he could negotiate. As a Government body the Fisheries Department was precluded from setting up a commercial organisation. No business men, Asian, European or African, had been interested enough, or had been talked into being interested enough, to start a commercial enterprise based on the Fishery. The bad, untarmacked road to Kitale, the nearest town of any size and the nearest railhead, was a formidable deterrent. Additionally the recent collapse of the trade between Lake Victoria fishermen and the

Congo had led to there being a surplus of fish in Kenya, while 50 per cent of Kenya people won't eat fish at all, anyway.

Not surprisingly the Missionary Societies were eager to leap into this cavernous breach. 'They want the watu held together by an industry so they can preach to them,' commented one European Government official cynically. They themselves, knowing full well they would have to put forward propositions tempting enough to overcome this sort of prejudice, were soon submitting rival bids. The Catholics suggested providing a truly dedicated Father with a Land Rover to help run the Fishery and prepare the way for a Turkana fishing co-operative. Certainly a spot like this needs a dedicated man, which McConnell himself is.

The Protestant C.C.K., however, came up with a three- to four-year scheme in which they were prepared to sink no less than £27,000—an enormous sum compared with anything put in hitherto. They would provide a manager and assistant, a clerk, a lorry, a Land Rover, a decent barge to bring fish from outlying parts of the lake, houses. In fact they had a complete and enterprising plan for which they deserved rather more credit than the Government departments seemed willing to allow them. It would involve campaigning for funds in Britain, Holland and elsewhere, yet, although the C.C.K. would try to organise a sale for the fish in Nairobi, Kitale and other towns, they would make no profit whatever for themselves.

This proposal and the reactions to it were most revealing. The Fisheries Department wanted to keep the overall management in their own hands. Their interest over the long term was in development work, compilation of statistics and so on. They also preferred to have the sale of the fish in the hands of a commercial firm, to which end they were approaching various Asian and European business men. But they were doing so with amazing slowness considering how long the fishing scheme, the D.C. and the famine camps had formed a closed circle of supply and demand which everyone knew would collapse the moment the Famine Relief money ran out. All too many European civil servants, during these last months of colonial rule, were waiting for their compensation and the boat home. Their inertia stultified the efforts of the few energetic men.

More than anything, though, one felt the influence of a long-standing Colonial Government attitude, expressed by the General Secretary of the C.C.K. as 'They're not anti-Christian, but they had the idea of keeping areas like the Turkana, the Masai and other Closed Districts untouched. For years there has been a deliberate attempt to keep out people other than Government officers.' The Closed Districts Ordinance covered many native areas. That it should have been used against missionaries, as it undoubtedly was, is one of the most striking among many paradoxes in East Africa's development. The very colonisation of East Africa arose from the fervent Christian and liberal reactions in Britain to Livingstone's appeals to bring Christianity to Africa. The early missionaries brought schools, crafts and instruction in the ways of Western living. Somehow the administrators who consolidated this start became imbued with the far different concept of preserving the primitive African, of not corrupting him, of allowing him to develop at his own speed. If he was to be prodded into progress, then it should be done only by Government officials, whom the Government could trust.

Only with African-majority Government near, and African influence strong in Government thinking, did this philosophy begin to change. Today, under African rule, the missions can count on Parliamentary support in opening up the minds of the primitive, for the missionary aim coincides with the policy of Kenyatta's Government. In hoping to establish a co-operative venture, to persuade the Turkana, who thus earn money, to spend some of it on their children's school fees, and generally to create a yearning for development, the missionaries will be implementing the Government's self-help programme for Kenya's development. Provided they do not misuse the privilege of access to the Turkana, they expect no Government opposition to the spread of Christianity, and indeed propose a Management Board for the new fishing industry on which the Government would be represented and which would become independent of the Church.

I have gone into details of this scheme because it typifies many. Their results should be a most fruitful, though not necessarily much publicised, aspect of Kenya's post-Independence attempts to develop such resources as the country has. Charity is all too frequently accepted as a permanent solution to problems in African states.

We ended our visit by flying on to Lodwar to see the D.C. It is an outpost that would have delighted P. C. Wren. Like Wajir, it is stiff with the atmosphere of Beau Geste. A thick stone wall surrounds the administrative centre, along the top of which a sentry paces up and down, rifle on his shoulder, head guarded by a first cousin of the kepi, stiff and round and with the same neck flap to keep off the sun that one saw in the Foreign Legion. At intervals he stopped to stand in a fortified sentry-box overlooking most of the boma and also the airstrip that runs straight past below.

The boma is all the area within two miles' radius of the flagstaff, from which on our visit the Union Jack still strained and flapped in the wind, though it was soon to come down for ever. Inside are long neat lines of labourers' huts, a few whitewashed houses, including the one built for Kenyatta during his restriction here from 1953 to 1960, a medical centre, three Indian dukas and a lot of bare stony ground. 'Eight thousand acres of howling desert,' the D.C. commented.

He had spent many years in the Turkana District and he put the Government side of its problems to us succinctly and not without sympathy for the missions' case. 'The Turkana can live on practically nothing—but not on absolutely nothing.' With the aid of a £4,000 grant the D.C. had resettled 1,000 Famine Camp inmates in half a year. When a man had done six months' work in one of the camps he would be given twenty goats, costing the D.C. £1 each. This would re-establish him in the tribe, one curse of the Turkana being, as I explained, that they will not support their poor relations. But the D.C. saw no hope of reducing the camps below 3,000 people. So serious was the overgrazing that there would always be destitution until the Turkana could be persuaded to sell their surplus cattle for cash. Even the goats he bought for distribution were all obtained locally for fear of worsening matters by importing them. The one hope he saw lay in introducing the Israeli-bred white goats from the Negev desert, which grow twice the size on the same amount of food as a local goat, and of planting thousands of the salt bushes they eat there, which in turn can thrive on less than six inches of rain a year. An Israeli expert had come to investigate the possibilities.

Not one of the schemes will solve the Turkana's problems by itself. Each will help, and yet there will still be huge gaps that can only be filled by expenditure the Kenya budget cannot meet. £50,000 is needed to tarmac the worst sections of the Kitale Road. Education demands large sums—plus an illimitable supply of patience persuading the tribesmen to let their children go to school at all. Improvements in primitive areas are always liable to be sub-economic. The acid test of a Government's intentions is whether it continues to put capital into backward areas for the overall good of the community, knowing that the money will never earn a commercially acceptable return. In Kenya it is particularly vital that it should do so because the gap between the advanced and the backward tribes is daily widening in much the same inexorable way as the gap between the developed and the underdeveloped nations of the world widens.

The Kikuyu, through the settlement schemes, through the siting of new industries round Thika and through general Government expenditure, are obtaining a quantity of financial assistance out of all proportion to their numbers.

Due to the logic of one slightly eccentric man's determination, the problems that the Government finds it hard to solve for the Turkana are already being surmounted among the Tugen, a hundred miles further south in the Rift. Down on Lake Baringo a Welshman called David Roberts has started an eminently successful fishery scheme, which he runs in conjunction with a wildlife farm. Baringo is smaller than Rudolf but in barely less desolate surroundings. It is a little higher above sea-level, a trifle less hot, in an area of scrub and stunted trees rather than of actual desert, though not much less intimidating. It is also more accessible. Nakuru is eighty miles off. Whilst this is by dirt road, only the last thirteen or fourteen miles skirting the lake are truly appalling, crossed by innumerable luqqas or river-beds, down which the water thunders when it rains, and which when dry provide the choicest boulders and collapsing banks for the driver to circumnavigate. The day we went up Roberts' African driver had just overturned his only three-ton truck in one.

We knew when we neared Roberts' establishment because a Tugen herdsman stood guarding one of the most oddly assorted flocks I ever expect to see. He was an old man, swathed in a faded red length of cloth which he had knotted over one shoulder like a toga, and he leant on a crooked staff, placidly surveying three ostriches, four zebra and one young bull buffalo, while a short distance away a toto, his assistant, kept an eye on five beautiful glossy-coated eland. They were all quite tame, brought from different parts of Kenya, and now, watched only by the herdsman, his boy and a couple of white herons perched on a fallen tree at the water's edge, they waited unknowing and unconcerned for the day when they would be shipped to zoos in Europe or America.

The house itself was of two storeys in stone with a roof reminiscent of a Swiss chalet. Because of the flooding it stood almost in the water, which lapped around the stone enclosure and covered the original tiny quay to which the fishermen bring their boats. The Tugen and Njemps use log craft that are a degree or two more sophisticated than the El Molo's rafts, but only just. They paddle out into the lake and return, laden with tilapia fish, their gunwales awash—if you can call the ends of several logs 'gunwales'. The tilapia are carried into the house's enclosure and dumped on long concrete tables, round which a number of tribesmen sit on benches busy gutting and filleting. Then the fillets are passed into a packing room, pressed into small aluminium-foil trays and moved on to the freezing chamber. A day or two later, now inside the cardboard boxes that the shop assistants will handle, they are loaded into the truck and driven to Nakuru, either to be sold in the neighbourhood or sent by train to Nairobi. The fishermen get thirty cts. a pound for their catch, Roberts makes a living and everyone's happy.

Lately the demand for Baringo tilapia has risen so much that Roberts, who has just completed a new 'factory' with the aid of a Government grant, is wondering if it wouldn't be possible to start bringing down tilapia from Rudolf somehow. The only people who are worried are the Game Department, who fear Lake Baringo is being over-fished. However, control rests not with them but with the Tugen District Council, who show no such scruple, and perhaps realise how lucky they are that Roberts gets on so uniquely with their people. He has fitted into their tribal life extraordinarily well, no doubt because he is a friendly and unassuming man who has no intention of defrauding them. The one restriction placed on him—that he is not allowed to fish himself but must employ others—is hardly a disability since he devotes as much time as he can to his wildlife collection.

Round the other side of the house from the factory are a series of wire enclosures and cages where he keeps his birds, the wire netting going out into the lake to allow herons, egrets and other waterfowl to paddle about, their wings being clipped. He has flamingoes, pelican, peacocks, fish eagles and many rare species like the tawny feathered Devereaux's eagle. A variety have been bought by the Mount Kenya Safari Club and now wander at large about its grounds, even inspecting visitors by the swimming pool. Roberts' birds are in demand from all over the world. He is also under siege by several well-known publishers who want him to write a book about his life, which would certainly jump straight into the bestseller lists, but he has not yet bothered. A T.V. company have bought the right to film his private paradise. Fame is poised, her trumpet in hand, ready to sweep down upon him at any moment. Meanwhile he and his wife go on quietly bringing up their family of six boys in the house by the lake.

Nearly everyone who comes to Kenya gets the wild into his blood a little. Of the few Euopeans who end up deeply involved in it the majority, the game wardens, the hunters, the naturalists, are surprisingly unassuming about their lives. They are sitting on a publishing goldmine, as Joy Adamson's books about Elsa have revealed, yet on the whole they prefer to leave such outwardly tempting possibilities untouched. Besides, when you're living out in the bush it needs a highly commercialised mind to visualise millions of city-dwellers being enthralled in your day-to-day doings. The very idea seems not merely as remote as New York or London but basically improbable. The realities of suburban life and of the Northern Frontier District are thousands of light years apart, even if nappies do have to be washed in both.

10

Somali Secessionists

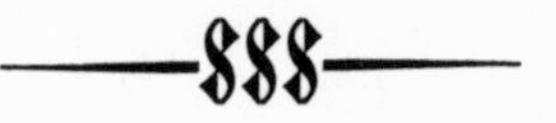

ONE AREA of Kenya where the *Harambee* spirit has made little if any impression, where the missionaries' task is all but hopeless, but which Kenya's leaders do now inspect from time to time, is the North-East, approximately that part of the former Northern Frontier District—the N.F.D.—inhabited by Somalis or related tribes. Its peoples are Muslims who feel they belong not to Kenya but to the Somali Republic. Since before Independence their secessionist movement has verged upon open rebellion, exhausting the temper of Kenyatta's Government by constant attrition from banditry and loss of life. Internationally the dispute with Somalia is one of the most explosive border disputes in the whole continent. It also made Kenya aggravatingly dependent on British military assistance from the very moment of independence.

The N.F.D. is in another world from the rest of Kenya, as my description of the Turkana will, I hope, have suggested. The road to Isiolo, its administrative headquarters, starts out hopefully from Nairobi by winding up through the green patchwork of Kikuyuland, dense with Africans hoeing their shambas or herding cattle along the verges, an area where every valley is watered by a stream. Just before Nyeri the road turns north and brings you into flatter upland, the forested shoulders of Mt. Kenya sloping up into the cloud on your right, the townships deriving their names from the Masai, like Naromoru and Nanyuki. This was a great area of white settlement. Nanyuki itself, where the railway peters out after puffing its laborious way up to 7,000 feet, is still an outback town, albeit dignified by the neat varnished wood road signs and the flower beds that Ray Ryan, owner of the Mt. Kenya Safari Club, has provided to brighten the place up. The Equator allegedly passes across the bar floor of the Silverbeck Hotel, so you can sink your beer in the Southern Hemisphere while your partner drinks in the Northern. The only hint of the N.F.D.'s proximity are the occasional Land Rovers and hunting cars on the way back from safaris, clients and hunter all thick with dust and aching for a cold beer and a bath.

The tarmac runs out before Timau, a ramshackle cluster of houses with a police station and the usual duka. Timau is, however, in the Highlands, witness the abortive settlement scheme for Mau Mau forest fighters there.

Not far past the township you abruptly find yourself at the top of a great escarpment, down which the road stumbles in a series of hairpin bends. The weather will have cleared, for the N.F.D. is invariably as sunsoaked as a travel poster. Stretching away beneath you is a reddish scrub out of which occasional mountains rise. You could now walk had you the stamina, or fly if you had the fuel, but assuredly not drive owing to lack of roads, for a thousand miles through the same kind of semi desert as begins at the bottom of the escarpment. Heading north-north-east you would cut across the south-west corner of Ethiopia after 350 miles or so and again across the Ethiopian border into Somalia after an equally long march through the Ogaden. Eventually, if bandits in one or other of the three countries had not stripped and killed you, you would reach Hargeisa, the principal city of Northern Somalia, formerly British Somaliland, beyond which the land falls sharply down to the even more oppressive and humid heat of the Gulf of Tadjoura on the Red Sea.

The whole way on this march, which can be done because Lord Delamere did it in the reverse direction in 1898, you would be among nomadic peoples in a landscape totally different from the rest of East Africa and compared to which the Masai-inhabited plains of the Serengeti and the Mara River are soft and attractive. At Isiolo, twenty-odd miles from the escarpment, you would have found the first pocket of Somalis living, descendants of Somali soldiers in the King's African Rifles who were given land there many years ago. After passing through the tribal areas of the Muslim Boran round Garba Tula you would have come to where the country of the Somalis begins properly. This is north and east of the Tana River, a serpentine line of water bordered by trees that seem extravagantly green against the surrounding desert and that shelter hippos, crocodile and elephant. From the Tana River to the Gulf of Tadjoura the people all have the same language, the same customs, the same physical toughness and the same aspiration towards unity. They are all Somalis, whether legally living in Kenya, Ethiopia, French Somaliland or the homeland of the Somali Republic itself. When British and Italian Somaliland became independent and joined in one state in 1960 they adopted as their flag a silver star on a light blue ground. The star has five points, one for each of the five Somalilands. Two, ex-British and ex-Italian, are free, the other three await their liberation. That flag is cherished, though not so often displayed for fear of reprisals, in both the Ogaden and the N.F.D.

Since environment helps condition character, the wind-blown, gritty, acerbating nature of the N.F.D. suggests the Somali outlook. Mile upon mile upon mile of stony ground, where the stunted grass is so tough that you can cut your fingers on it and water-holes may be fifty miles apart, make life exceptionally severe even for the habitual nomad. The Somalis' flocks are of camels and goats and fat-tailed sheep. As in the Middle East, the camel has a significance far beyond that of an ordinary farmer's cattle. A Somali herdsman may go three months with no food save camel's milk, which does contain all the essential nutrients of life. His house is a humped tent of skins and rugs supported on a frame of sticks, the whole of which can be collapsed and packed upon the camel's back with the children nestling in the centre, secure against the animal's jolloping, bumping gait. The camel is naturally wealth as well as transport, though its value varies. In the N.F.D. the price is around £25, but at Hargeisa, close to the trade with Aden and the markets of Arabia, as much as £60.

Despite the privations the Somali finds a certain glamour and mystique in his wandering. The colonel in charge of police in Hargeisa once told me that he had been brought up as a camel boy, resented being taken away to be educated and even now had moments when he wished he were back in that life. Coupled with the fortitude it engenders there lurks the strong pride of the Somali race. They are visibly different from the Bantu peoples, with finer features. They carry themselves more upright. Their women dress when they can afford it in gauzy robes of subtle shades, mauves, yellows, purples, magentas and cinnamon colour, catching their hair, which they let grow, in fine net scarves. They look dignified and are justifiably noted for their beauty. The contrast with the Kikuyu women, staggering like beasts of burden under loads of wood, is obvious. The Somalis heartily despise the Bantu and, where Kenya is concerned, generalise by calling them all Kikuyus, or derisively, Kyukes—the same appellation that the white settlers use.

This is not to say that all aspects of the Somali are good. He is also treacherous, thinks nothing of murder and is bloody-minded to a degree. The elders of the N.F.D., ornate in hennaed spade-shaped beards that remind one of the ancient Assyrians, to whom they may well be related, look splendid enough. But any group of the younger Somali politicians in the North-East Region Assembly look more like Ali Baba's thieves than modern Parliamentarians.

These comparisons are relevant. The Somalis came from the Middle East many centuries ago. In Biblical times what is now the Somali Republic was known as the Land of Punt, from which came supplies of frankincense and myrrh. Gradually they have drifted further and further south, overwhelming such resistance as there was in the wilderness that lay before them. The process was finally ended by the British and Italians signing a treaty in 1924 as a result of the secret Anglo-Italian agreement of 1914. This gave Jubaland and the port of Kisimayo, until then in Kenya, to Italian Somaliland. The British also laid down a Somali Galla line, which runs in part along the Tana River and became the official limit of Somali movement south within the colony. But for it they would now be much nearer the escarpment on the inland side and well into the coastal area. Lamu, the dhow-harbour town and former sultanate just inside Kenya near the Somali frontier, is none the less a focal point of Somali trading, while raids by bandits have penetrated nearly as far down as the seaside resort of Malindi, fifty miles south of the Tana's mouth.

Whilst halting Somali advance, the Colonial Government also gave token that Somalis were superior to the other races. They had higher rates of pay officially, were welcomed as N.C.O.s in the King's African Rifles and enjoyed various other minor advantages when they came down 'to Kenya', as they themselves phrase it. But up in the N.F.D. the administration continued to be on the purest *Boy's Own Paper* model long after the processes of British rule had attained a smoother *modus operandi* elsewhere. It was dealing with obstinate tribes. The Boran, Rendille, Gelubba, Orma and

Merille of the N.F.D. have much in common with the Somalis including a distaste for law and order.

There is still a distinctly Beau Geste air about the Government centres of the N.F.D. The police wear legionnaires' hats, exactly like kepis, with flaps to protect the neck hanging down behind. Wajir could be a film set. Its main buildings are all castellated and white-washed, even if the small tower on top of the D.C.'s house is only a bedroom, sited high up to catch every current of air available during the hot nights. The one street is a dusty row of houses and dukas, with a small mosque at one end. Marabou storks, huge, ungainly, scruffy-feathered scavengers, with great powerful beaks, hop about in crowds. For there to be a thousand camels round Wajir's perimeter is nothing, since the place has 600 wells. It also has the Wajir Yacht Club, a white thatched building with a long bar, a model yacht mounted on one wall, a swimming pool and various photographs and relics of celebrities who have blessed its ironic title in beer after their tours of the region. Its pennant is a white camel on a blue ground.

From Wajir, Garissa, Mandera, Marsabit and Isiolo the D.C.s always used to govern with a rough-and-ready justice. I went to stay for a few days at Marsabit with the D.C. before the Somali banditry had started. There were, he explained to me, two types of D.C. The ones who went on safari and the ones who didn't. He did and would disappear for three weeks at a time with a Land Rover and a three-tonner full of armed police. It was possible at any time to meet a band of several hundred Ethiopian marauders trespassing inside Kenya, armed and out for women and stock. Merille from Ethiopia killed 165 Turkana and others in the first nine months of 1963 alone. Equally the D.C. might interrupt the Rendille in full war regalia of feathers, red ochre and spears about to descend on the Samburu. That D.C.s are now called Government Agents makes no difference to the toughness of their jobs.

Under these conditions, even when slightly mollified by the use of Police Air Wing Aircraft for journeying across boulders and lava rock to attend an afternoon's baraza (a gathering with tribesmen for discussion), it was not surprising that the B.O.P. tradition stuck and British officials unswervingly believed that only the British could cope with the N.F.D. It was a place for the élite, a stepping-stone to greater glory. The Regional Office at Garissa, a simple room of hutlike construction, has a formidable array of Governors' photographs hung round its walls. Governors of Kenya, Somaliland, Sudan and elsewhere are commemorated, most of them knighted. At the end of each brief catalogue of achievements runs the inescapable phrase 'District Officer N.F.D.'.

The first African District Officer, a Boran, was ambushed and murdered at Muddo Gashi by Somalis in 1963. But one by one more were appointed, and not only men born in the N.F.D. Today the administration is completely Africanised.

Neither the presence nor the absence of European officers will stop the Somali secessionist movement. Back in 1948 the Somali Youth League, now the main party in the Somali Government, had been proscribed in the N.F.D. for demanding secession. Most ironically it was at that time being encouraged by Kikuyus, while now what worries the nomads of the N.F.D. is having a Kenya African Government. A Colonial Government 'down there in Kenya' had been bad enough, though they didn't mind too much being ordered about by the British, in whom they had an unjustified amount of faith, based on the high personal qualities of the British administrators they knew. But they would not submit to being ruled by 'those Kikuyu'. When the Somali Republic achieved Independence (1960) they became more actively concerned than ever about Somali unity and African-majority rule in Kenya brought their feelings to the boil.

Contrariwise K.A.N.U., K.A.D.U., Paul Ngei's transient African People's Party and everyone else in Kenya politics would not countenance losing such a large chunk of country. Not only would it take a lot of gloss off *Uhuru*, there was always the chance that one of the companies prospecting there might strike oil. Furthermore where the Somalis see themselves as an ethnic group or race which ought by rights to be in one state, the Kenya politicians determinedly view them as a tribe attempting to exploit mere tribalism.

It appears that for a time Britain did consider making over part of the N.F.D. to Somalia. In 1962 Mr. Maudling had appointed a Commission of Enquiry which, after interviewing tribal leaders throughout the area east of Lake Rudolf, concluded that 87 per cent of the tribes throughout favoured secession, while in certain places like Wajir and Garissa the figure was 99 per cent. But early in 1963 the Kenyans let it be known that this would wreck the Constitution newly agreed by Mr. Sandys so painfully and laboriously after he had taken over the Colonial Secretaryship from Mr. Maudling. In addition the N.F.D.'s leaders were not united. Britain therefore carried the Regionalism idea a little further, adding a seventh Region to the existing six by chopping off the predominantly Somali-inhabited North-East from the rest of the old N.F.D. Thereon the Somali Government in Mogadishu unwisely lost its temper and broke off diplomatic relations with Britain, the British Ambassador hurriedly obtaining a Protocol Book from the Consul General in Hargeisa to lend them so that it could be done correctly.

They had some reason for being outraged, Britain having earlier promised to make a decision on the future of the N.F.D. before making any change in the Constitution relating to Kenya. Furthermore they had not unnaturally taken the N.F.D. Commission's report as the strongest possible indication that Britain would permit secession before Kenya's Independence. Instead Sandys indicated that things would have to wait until after the elections in Kenya in May so that Somali leaders could argue out the dispute with Kenyan leaders.

Spontaneous guerilla warfare began. On July 1st the Isiolo D.C., the Boran mentioned earlier, was killed, together with the Senior Chief of the Boran, a noted anti-secessionist. Nor did the Rome Conference in August soften antagonisms. The Somalis were unable to believe that after all Britain's soft soap in the past she could now innocently say, as she did in the Conference communiqué, that since she would only be responsible for Kenya for a few more months 'it would be wrong to take a unilateral decision about the frontiers'. Agreement, Britain declared, 'should be sought by the African Governments concerned working and negotiating within an African framework'. K.A.N.U. was as pleased as punch about this. One reason for their hastening the independence date had been fear that Britain might give way to Somali pressure. They could now continue adamant on the frontier question, though conceding that Somalia had an interest in the future of Somalis residing in Kenya and that if future discussions were fruitless Somalia would be free to bring the matter to the notice of the African States 'within the spirit of the Addis Ababa resolutions'. Although talks did indeed prove fruitless, Somalia has so far failed to get support for her case in the Organisation of African Unity.

After the Rome Conference the momentum of shifta raids began to quicken with the active help of an angry Somali Government. Police posts would be fired on, patrols ambushed, and the raiders slip away into the endless scrub. When chased they often crossed the frontier into the Somali Republic for safety. At the same time the administration was finding it hard to make the ordinary Somalis understand that secession was definitely off. The Kenya Government decided to make a two-pronged attack on the problem before it worsened. It brought troops up to hunt the shifta and with Sandys' encouragement it instituted a development plan for the North-East, as well as making valiant efforts to get elections held for the Regional Assembly and the National Assembly. In May the people had refused to participate in the General Election.

Ironically Kenyatta thus found himself selling regionalism hard to the North-East as an alternative to secession, just when he was preparing to go to London for the Independence Conference and fight against its application to the country as a whole. He would not touch the two Somali Government suggestions of either a joint Somali-Kenyan administration or else a United Nations administration with a referendum at a later date. Instead a thousand leaflets were distributed as part of a drive to explain the people's rights and liberties under the Constitution, including religious freedom; while the powers of a Regional Assembly, if they now chose to elect one, were heavily underlined. Emphasis was put on its control of land, water-supplies, education and health, nearly all of which powers were fated to be lost to Regional Assemblies within eighteen months.

There were promises of increased development too, though by comparison with the millions devoted to settlement schemes, the sum committed was tiny—£50,000 at first. It would go towards improving stock, veterinary services and water-supplies, all of which were indeed close to the nomads' interests as ought education to have been, only seven Somalis having passed the K.A.P.E. exam in '62. Later this plan was increased to an expenditure of £300,000 over five years. At the same time special training schemes were devised to train more Government officers of local origin, although hitherto Somalis who had taken up bursaries usually abandoned their studies after a year or two.

As well as the promises of improvement the twenty or so British senior officials could offer other inducements. The Somali leadership was divided, sometimes chiefs against politicians, sometimes both against each other. Since the chiefs are Government appointed they could be threatened with the loss of both office and of pension rights if they did not co-operate, though this threat was not always effective. In December the Civil Secretary in Garissa, an advocate of the polite blackmailing of chiefs, found himself issuing a statement that 'One of the Shifta leaders has been identified as Maalim Mohamed Stamboul Abdi, a disgrunted chief of the Abdi Wak who was allowed to resign in view of his long service in October 1963, when by rights he ought to have been dismissed'. Evidently it was not only Stamboul Adbi who was disgruntled. So his property, consisting of his pension of £700, his Land Rover, his house, 500 head of cattle, 300 head of sheep and goats and 100 camels, was all seized.

The clear parallel with the Ogaden was at first little heeded. There at this time the Ethiopian Government was needing a complete Division to suppress a Somali revolt. Bands of shifta up to 400 strong were being led by the very men Ethiopia had a year or two before appointed as administrators. However, by December the shifta attacks in the North-East had become so serious that Kenya was forced into more active military action, the second way of attacking the problem. A Defence Pact with Ethiopia, discussed in July, was ratified, though not invoked. This pact is against external aggression, but presumably could be extended to cover the employment of Ethiopian troops in the N.F.D. if both sides felt such a move politic.

The cynic could find amusing parallels between this situation and the rise of the Mau Mau in the previous decade. The colony had been unable to contain the Mau Mau without external assistance. Now independent Kenya asked for it against the shifta. In both cases aid came from the British Army, though this time not with infantry, only with aircraft, sappers, signallers and Medical Corps men. Where the settlers had denounced Kenyatta's links with Moscow, and the fear of communist direction, now Kenyatta's Government was denouncing the Somali Republic's 1963 military aid agreement with Russia. 'The Somali actions do not match with their hypocritical statements and they can do anything because of the money they got from Russia,' cried K.A.N.U.'s Chief Whip. Where white men had been horrified at the Mau Mau's intimidation and atrocities, now a constant flow of Press statements indicated the ex-detainees' own horror at Somali violence. Achieng Oneko was pictured standing anxiously by the hospital bed of a wounded police sergeant-major. The first African officer to fall was immediately commemorated by a new Nairobi name: Lieutenant Tumbo Street, not far as it happens from the new Dedan Kimathi Street. The sacredness of the struggle against alien rule does indeed depend upon which side you happen to belong to. 'We will not give an inch of the country to the Somalis,' Kenyatta declared.

Over the Independence period the Somali Government did announce a cessation of hostile broadcasts—Mogadishu Radio had been busily urging open revolt and accusing Kenyatta of saying: 'I have given orders for the Somalis to be killed *en masse* or arrested.' But by the end of the month the truce was over. A State of Emergency was declared in the North-East Region and the roads closed, incidentally causing the cancellation of a number of tourist safaris. As hunting country the N.F.D. is unique. From then onwards the hunt was to be for shifta, who were sometimes operating from across the Somali border and were receiving training, rifles and ammunition at camps in the Republic. However, it was as hard for Kenya to prove the Somali Government responsible as it had been for Britain to prove that Kenyatta had managed the Mau Mau. A five-mile-wide no-mans-land was established along the frontier and any man seen in it decreed liable to be shot on sight, though the township of Mandera and the trading post at El Wak had perforce to be excluded. Four inspired Members of the National Assembly offered to form a volunteer army to guard the N.F.D., consisting of all Members of Parliament of thirty-five or under, ex-servicemen, ex-Mau Mau, and Youth Wing members of both K.A.N.U. and K.A.D.U. The feelings of other Assembly Members were never frankly recorded and like other offers it was allowed to drop.

Gradually Kenya was beginning to realise that the North-East was likely to be an enduring thorn in their flesh. The shifta raids had a clear pattern. A typical one was made by a gang of fifty on the tribal police at Masabubu, actually in the Coast Region. One of the seven police in the post was killed and four were wounded, plus one wife who died later. When local tribesmen came to the police's help with bows and arrows they were also fired on and 162 rounds were shot off by the police before the raiders moved away, leaving one dead man hastily buried in a shallow grave. A British Army doctor was flown in to patch up the wounded.

In the dry season it is comparatively easy to deal with shifta by cracking down on the water-holes. As in the Ogaden the camel boys are the spare-time bandits and they can be held to ransom for water. When I visited Wajir a tribal police corporal had just carried off such an operation on his own initiative. Indeed he deserved a medal for it. Hearing that a group of nomads with their camels were moving away from the vicinity of a recently discovered hideout, he set off with a fellow African constable. They marched fifty miles across appalling country mainly at night to head off the nomads, arriving first at the water-hole for which the corporal had reckoned they were heading. Squatting by it, rifles across their knees, they held the water-hole for three days until the nomads were forced to capitulate by their camel's urgent need of water.

But in the rains it is another matter. The roads get washed away, so supplies cannot be brought up to the troops except by air. The nomads can go as they please since with restricted communications 49,000 square miles of semi-desert scrub present insuperable problems for a small army, such as Kenya inherited from Britain. There are four battalions, one of which has been in the North-East together with some of the General Service Unit of the police. They become demoralised easily. Before the battalion at Lanet went sour in the mutiny of January 1964 the battalion chasing shifta was already reliably reported to be on the edge itself. Up to the time of writing Kenya's lack of supporting arms has been an important factor in military relations with Britain. The Police Air Wing operates only a handful of Cessna 180s for bush flying. They are superb aircraft but carry only four men. For its spotter work during 1964 the Kenya Army was enjoying the help of British Army Beavers and helicopters, while an R.A.F. Beverley squadron and a twin Pioneer squadron, both based at Eastleigh, were flying continual resupply sorties at a cost to Britain of over £1,000 a day. Without them, and the sappers' roadbuilding, the doctors treating casualties, and signallers working the R.T. networks, the Kenya forces could not have held their own in the N.F.D.

The knowledge that this was so played a part in Mr. Sandys' discussions with Kenyatta over the Kahawa military base in March of that year. While Sandys kept the arrangement to remove all the troops by December 12th, Kenyatta agreed to their returning up to twice a year for training exercises and to the R.A.F. retaining staging rights at Eastleigh. The subsequent exchange of letters between the Governments laid the basis for continuing military co-operation, also earning Kenyatta criticism from K.A.N.U. radicals. At the time of writing it seemed he might well be obliged to ask the R.A.F. to stay for more than just the training of embryo Kenyan and Ugandan air forces, and possibly want to ask the Army Air Corps to remain too. The prevalent African idea that piloting an aircraft is as easy as riding a bicycle will be taking some hard knocks in the future. When the training of Kenyan pilots began decidedly ingenious statements were made about African trainees becoming operational faster than ones in Europe. But the surface winds and thermals in East Africa, especially in the N.F.D., are as savage as the landscape. Records of both military and private flying reveal a steady toll of accidents, which have as yet shown no respect for colour, creed or nationality.

The effect of the seasons on military operations against the shifta have their political consequences too. The Regional Assembly, which at last came into being in January 1964, affirms that it will co-operate with Kenyatta. Whatever their true feelings it is vital for Somali representatives in the North-East to carry on what the French call a *dialogue* with the Kenya Government so as to tide over the dry seasons. Additionally the disagreements among N.F.D. politicians that were a factor in swinging British policy against secession also resulted in some Somalis averring allegiance to Kenya. Finally there is money. Just as organisations in Somalia help finance the N.P.P.P.P., and the Northern Frontier Democratic Party, so K.A.N.U. funds find their way to the anti-secessionist Northern Province United Association. The plethora of parties in the North-East are hardly worth naming, though the N.P.P.P.P. is the strongest. Their titles suggest they represent far more than they actually do. Democratic politics is a new game in the whole N.F.D. That a group of agitators decide to try for personal power by forming a party with a one-room office in a trading post does not mean that they have any support worth speaking of among the vast majority of the population, who seldom see a house at all, being normally on the move with the herds. In many ways the elders and the chiefs are far more truly representative. It is indicative of the unreality of those little offices, small and dark inside and with a crudely but brightly painted signboard hanging on the whitewashed wall above the door, that when the election for the Kenya Parliament was held, also in January 1964, three Senators and three National Assembly members were returned unopposed, while there was no nomination at all for the fourth Assembly seat.

The real decisions are made within the tribes. Nor, I suspect, do the elected representatives behave quite the same in their home areas as they do in Nairobi, any more than Kenya Ministers say the same things in their constituencies as they do in London. When the newly elected Vice-President of the Regional Assembly came down to visit Kenyatta at Gatundu he waved his sheathed simi in the air and declared passionately: 'We do not want guns or any help from the Government. All we want is our Prime Minister's consent so that we can deal with the shiftas in our own way.' If he ever repeated that in the North-East, in Somali, he would be courting assassination, except, of course that it is capable of more than one interpretation.

For a time the Europeans holding key posts in the administration suffered the worst of both worlds. They were asked just before Independence to sign contracts for further periods of service, usually three years. Having done so they could not break them without prejudicing their gratuities and pension rights. The reasons for their retention by the Government were several—lack of N.F.D.-born replacements, unwillingness of other African District Officers to serve in the inhospitable North-East at all, the old myth of the British knowing how to cope being semi-official policy. Equally their accepting to stay was due to loyalty and affection for the area combined with the comforting knowledge that a man in his mid to late thirties increased his tax-free terminal gratuities, colloquially called 'lumpers', by up to £150 a month for every month of those three years.

The penalty proved to be that the expatriate soon became the target not only for the abuse of both sides, but also the gunfire. The shifta threatened them with death and shot at them. The anti-secessionist North-Eastern politicians accused them of sympathising with secession and passing information to the shifta, thereby neatly accounting for their own failure to curb banditry. The Kenya back-benchers claim much the same. Finally the attempts of the expatriates to stop the African security forces indulging in unjustified shooting of Somalis resulted in their actually being fired on by their own side.

It is highly invidious for Colonial Service-trained expatriates to try and play an executive role in an Inter-African war. They are steeped in inhibitions about unnecessary killing, which the Africans find totally irrelevant. Whitehall is always nervous of accusations in the British Press about brutality. But in East Africa the newspapers are too frightened of the Government to make any, and not very much notice would be taken if they did. The British Government encouraged administrators to stay on, apparently failing to understand how untenable their position would become. By Africanising their jobs Kenjatta's Government resolved their dilemma.

Resistance in the North-East is unlikely to collapse, especially if the Government elected in Mogadishu in 1964 for five years fulfils its promises of reducing corruption. Its policy remains to achieve the unity of the Somalis by peaceful means. But, whether with its active encouragement or not, the shifta will continue fighting Kenyan rule because it is unthinkable for them to do otherwise. In the Ogaden their resistance to the Ethiopians has developed into a Jihad and if they die in its furtherance that is simply the will of Allah. The Koran says that if you die fighting for your country you will go to Paradise.

A similar Holy War seems likely to develop in the North-Eastern Region and it will be odd if, despite Kenyatta's published calls for patience, the Kenya Army, once freed from the restraints of British officers, does not adopt Ethiopian tactics for crushing the rebellion. The Ethiopians use tanks, aircraft and artillery mercilessly. As yet Kenya has only foot soldiers. But incidents of uncalled-for slaughter by rifle- and mortar-fire had already begun to appear in mid-1964, one being dismissed by a court as the sort of incident inevitable under a State of Emergency. Kenyatta may persist in his civilised course of developing the region as a means of persuasion. Joseph Murumbi, who was given personal responsibility for the situation in 1964, may exploit existing differences of opinion within the region successfully, though matters will not be made any easier by the further reduction of regional powers under the Republican Constitution introduced at the end of that year. None the less, in combating the shifta Kenyatta is up against precisely the same powerful basic force that brought he himself to power—nationalism. Flaring up during the rains, subsiding during the dry season, the shifta activities look like being a severe drain on both Kenya's budget and its Cabinet's temper for a long time to come.

11

Nairobi—the Alien City

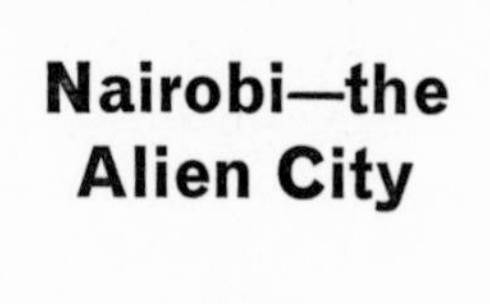

PERSUADING the North-East to play any part in nation-building presents great headaches, and the revenue it produces from taxes doesn't even pay for its administration, let alone its pacification. But at least the system of control inherited from the British is clear-cut, whether in this case it is fully Africanised or not. As when directed ultimately from Whitehall, so now under Kenyatta and his Cabinet. The system of the administration, the army, the police and the prison service help to overcome the disparity of the whole country's component parts. Everyone used to be subject to the jurisdiction of the District Officers and Commissioners, the Provincial Commissioners and finally the Governor. Without the system the Arabs at the Coast, the Kikuyu, the Masai, the Somalis, the Asians and the Europeans would have been as unco-ordinated as the flying specks of dust illuminated by a chance shaft of sunlight. It doesn't matter that with *Uhuru* the nomenclature was changed—Provincial Commissioners becoming Civil Secretaries and so on—or that for a time Regional Assemblies had a degree of power to give them orders. The system still boxes in the fragments of the tribal kaleidoscope that is Kenya.

Socially, however, there is no simple way of putting the African on top, no Africanisation of income, while the politicians find the world of trade and business exasperatingly difficult to manipulate. The Asian community, 200,000 strong, tentacles its way through the life of the nation. Nairobi and Mombasa are European-dominated cities, for all the newly elected African majorities in their City Councils. To some Africans, like the Mayor of Nairobi, Charles Rubia, whose stable personality rapidly made a deep impress on the running of the city, the paradoxes of the social situation are not intolerable. The way to right them is by vast schemes of improvement for the African slum areas and other constructive measures in education, social services, youth work and conditions of employment. Others, alas, tend to rampage when faced with the intangibles of European and Asian economic power. Senator Makasembo, the same hefty Luo backbencher who after *Uhuru* broke the portrait of Queen Victoria in the lake steamship bearing her name, moved in one Senate debate that no European or Asian should be allowed to farm in Kenya and went on to declare that Kenya is the only country in the world whose economy is controlled by foreigners. Although the Government's policy is to encourage private enterprise investment alongside the practice of socialism, not to nationalise business wholesale, Makasembo was expressing an angry disgruntlement that many K.A.N.U. supporters feel. Kenyatta would win thunderous applause in the Assembly if he were to announce plans similar to President Nasser's slashing attacks on foreign business interests in Cairo.

The great dream of Africans in Kenya is to own houses and cars like those of the European. It used to be a standard tactic amongst the less responsible candidates at elections to promise such things to everyone at *Uhuru*. The country went through the same spate of opportunism that afflicted the Congo, with privately organised lotteries for farms, property and women. At 5*s*. a ticket the promoters soon became rich. Nor did they fail to allocate prizes. There was a standard joke in Nairobi about a blonde secretary who decided to quit Kenya and live in England. When she said goodbye to her friends on the staff the office boy came rushing up crying: 'But you can't go, you can't go—I've won you in the lottery.'

Uhuru shattered this illusion for the labourer. It also brought an unexpected series of wails from the Africans who did achieve the supposedly Elysian state of living like a European in Nairobi. The main companies operating there really only began hiring Africans as executives shortly before *Uhuru*, having hitherto left the leadership in this branch of promotion to Shell and one or two other far-sighted firms. Usually these executives received salaries of £1,000 or so a year, seemingly excellent in a place where an African earning £20 a month, as drivers do, thought himself well off. However, one who was working for a British firm wrote an amusing but revealing letter to the local newspaper about his struggles. He had rented one of those pleasant stone-built houses set in a large garden that characterise Nairobi's once exclusively European suburbs, immediately finding he needed a cook houseboy because his wife couldn't manage everything. So his food bills rocketed. Not only was the boy unwilling to cook anything except European food for his master, he stole from him just as he would from a European. Again, as the *bwana mkubwa*, the big boss, the executive discovered a shamba boy essential for tending the garden, and a large dog to guard the place, since burglars are among the least racially conscious craftsmen in the world, with no prejudice against stealing from a fellow African. And so it went on. The letter ended by saying that the net result of getting a white man's job was that he needed more money than ever. Were all these much envied standards of living worth the bother? He might well have added that he also had to re-educate his wife to new ways of behaviour when personally he was content with African customs and traditions. He was floundering between two worlds.

These are common complaints in Nairobi today. The African civil servant wants to send his children to a better school, taking advantage of the opening to all races of various European establishments like the Delamere Girls' School and the Duke of York's School for Boys, both run on the lines of English public schools. But civil servants can't afford it unless they're in the top grades. Nairobi is in many ways as expensive a city to live in as London, partly because the expatriate civil servants and the expatriate business men have long been receiving generous 'inducements' and allowances. Contrary to the practice in some other ex-colonies, Kenya is not giving home-grown men the same allowances. Why should she when there was a £3,000,000 gap in the Development Budget for 1964–5 anticipated, and the register of unemployment was running at 205,000 (August 1964).

At the same time *Uhuru* puts prices up. Embassy staffs are willing to pay rents way above the norm—the Chinese are paying £200 a month for one house and most diplomats will pay £70 or £80 for property that two years before Independence fetched £50. Inevitably major companies have to keep pace if, as many do, they employ staff recruited abroad. Furthermore, whilst some white Kenya residents find Nairobi as bitterly expensive as the African executive does, the uncertainties attending the transfer of power raised the profit levels demanded by most business people. They would not commit capital to a venture unless it yielded about twice what it would in Britain, often far more. On the Nairobi stock exchange the price of local brewery shares is such that they give an 18 per cent dividend. The house I rented was valued at £5,000 and I had to pay £55 a month (£660 a year) for it.

Independence may have removed the legal barriers of colour, with regulations forbidding landlords to turn down African or Asian tenants, yet it's still difficult for the African and European ways of life to come to terms. Nor, incidently, is the upper class of African showing much interest in multi-racial living, a point I shall return to. Nairobi illustrates how irreconcilable varying racial groups are by nature, as well as being the focal point of a national test case in their collaboration.

One trouble about Nairobi is its very opulence. It is a luxurious, polyglot city, completely unrelated to the simple life of the bush around it. Squalor and splendour exist side by side in a South American profusion. It was created by Europeans, by the adventurers and the speculators, and latterly by more solid citizens, some simply the gamblers grown older, plus many industrious Asians. The only truly African parts of it are the slums and shanty towns that the City Council is systematically destroying. It's an emergent Johannesburg, Salisbury or Abidjan not recognisably in the same continent as more truly African cities like Ibadan, Accra and Dar-es-Salaam.

The city began as a camp on the Uganda railway, which at the turn of the century had made its laborious way 300 miles from the coast as far as the Kikuyu Highlands and the Great Rift Valley. As the engineers paused to gather together resources for the next stage, Nairobi was born. Colonel Meinertzhagen recorded in his diary in 1902: 'The only shop is a small tin hut which sells everything from cartridges at eightpence each and beer at 5*s.* a bottle to sardines, jam, tinned food, etc. It is run by two bearded brothers called Stewart. . . . The only hotel here is a wood and tin shanty sometimes known as Wood's Hotel and sometimes as the Victoria Hotel. It stands in the only "street", known as Victoria Street. Mr. Jeevanjee,' Meinertzhagen added, noting another essential of expatriate life, 'has a soda-water factory.'

Although by 1906 it had 'trebled itself in size', Nairobi remained like a frontier town in a Western for many years, with wide muddy streets for the ox-wagons, and one-storey bars, banks and hotels.

Settlers came to farm on the land near the railway. The Indians originally brought to work on the track went into trade, the Gujeratis and Hindus to shopkeeping, the Sikhs to building and furniture-making. Some are still on their original sites, like the British Furniture House, presided over by a venerable Sikh, turbaned and with a long white beard flowing down over his suit. The Norfolk Hotel is little changed. It was the Mecca of all who came up on the railway, arriving, because the tracks were unballasted, shrouded in dust, and longing for any kind of bath. It was from the Norfolk Bar that intending settlers would be led forth by speculators to inspect 'A land going for a song'. The hotel's atmosphere is virtually unchanged today, indeed a Canadian professor I know objected to staying there because of its colonial aura. It is also still the rendezvous for hunters and their safari clients.

Theodore Roosevelt, archetype of the rich visitor and originator of the great American sporting connection with Kenya, used to set out on safari from the Norfolk, a crocodile of a hundred native porters in blue sweaters trailing behind his immediate entourage of professional white hunters, each porter wearing his boots hung by their laces round his neck for fear of damaging such valuable by-products of big-game shooting. The area really was teeming in game then. Lion could be shot from the verandah of the Nairobi Club and the Athi Plains swarmed with wildlife. If one thinks the Nairobi National Park amazing today for the facility with which one can see animals only ten minutes' drive away from the city, it is salutary to look at Meinertzhagen's diary again, even if his capacity for quick adding up of numbers does stretch the imagination. 'Counted the game on the south side of the railway between Athi River Station and Nairobi. It amounted to 5 rhinos, 18 giraffe, 760 wildebeeste, 4,006 zebra, 845 Coke's hartebeeste, 324 Grant's gazelle, 142 Thomson's gazelle, 46 impala, 24 ostrich, 7 great bustard and 16 baboon.' That was all seen while travelling fifteen miles, albeit with a grandstand view. You have to go to the Serengeti to spot such numbers of game nowadays.

Soon wooden one-storey verandahed offices gave way to three-storey stone ones, then to semi-skyscaper concrete blocks that soar white and dazzling as a mirage out of the surrounding African plains. So fast has been the change that you can see all three incongruously alongside each other. The avenues are now adorned with statues and planted with blue flowering jacaranda trees or great sweeping stretches of bougainvillaea. In the suburbs, growing now eight and more miles from the centre, and still occasionally visited by the lions whose home it was before, the traditional Cotswold house and the white stuccoed Spanish villa replace the old corrugated-roof bungalows. Occasionally, as in the new cathedral, massive beside the diminutive spire of a pioneer church, or in the oriental inspiration of the Ministry of Justice offices, there is a bloom of exciting modern architecture, as though the British designers had been liberated from their inhibitions by the Equatorial sun.

Occasionally, too, the prosperous is o'ertopped by the fantastic, Sunset Boulevard struggling to be reborn in another continent. In Muthaiga, the snobbiest suburb, now dotted with consulates, Jean Pierre Pichaud built his Petit Trianon. It was an exquisitely finished replica and at the height of the opulence he had inherited from an elderly friend Pichaud would fly a three-piece orchestra out from Paris to play at his parties there. He became honorary Vice-Consul for France. Then suddenly the foreclosure began. The coffee estate on which it all depended had to be sold to pay debts and the elegant house went too at a savage loss. It is now, very suitably, an art gallery. Pichaud ran a night club for a time until that too tottered, whereupon he flitted with the cutlery and some other valuables to Usumbura in Burundi. There he bought a small, chic bar from a Belgian, obliged travellers by changing money at black-market rates and still chattered away as though he were on the Riviera instead of in a one-horse capital at the head of a lonely African lake. There, finally, as the Belgian colons packed and departed for home, he committed suicide, still barely middle-aged.

Derek Erskine, wholesale grocer and sometime K.A.N.U. Chief Whip, lately knighted for his services to Kenya, built himself a vast house in Riverside after the war with a swimming pool on the first floor and the only drawing-room in Nairobi large enough to take a hunt ball apart from State House (formerly Government House). He maintains, smiling impishly at one past the moustache of a cavalry officer—which he once was—that 'the United Kingdom is unsuitable for white settlement, my dear fellow'. But he is trying to sell or let the mansion. With a fifteen-acre garden guarded by a high wall it would, he suggests, be ideal for a communist embassy. 'They could train a whole army in here and nobody would know.'

Eccentricity the Africans don't mind, perhaps enjoy. Kenyatta is said to have seen a newspaper picture of Derek Erskine, riding to hounds, top-hatted, and brought it to show his Cabinet with the words: 'That's what we want here—an aristocratic tradition.' In any case, Erskine long championed the Africans when they were underdogs, and amongst many other things, including unremitting work for Africans' sporting training, founded the United Kenya Club, the first multi-racial club. Originally it had the simplest of premises near the railway station, but now occupies a specially built residential clubhouse which many M.P.s use as their quarters during sittings of the Assembly. Its existence has helped outbalance the dogged conservatism of the Nairobi Club, which with a last convulsive struggle forced itself to become officially open to all races just before *Uhuru*.

In one way the clubs send the African right up in the air with fury, because they seem to be veritable castles of white privilege. Practically every Minister in the Cabinet has portentously and publicly warned them of dire chastisement if they do not admit Africans. The other side of it is, of course, that Africans rarely want to be admitted save for the sake of visibly breaking down the barriers. To them the clubs seem inexpressibly dull. Africans like clubs, all right. If you go to the Africa Club in Jeevanjee Gardens you see their version. It has a high subscription, a strict rule against talking politics, though that's still discussed, no colour bar and its members are the educated African élite. But as one remarked to me: 'We don't like to be too formal. When you come in and find a friend here you slap him on the shoulder and offer him a drink. No one's afraid to talk. Listen—it's six times as noisy as it would be in the Nairobi Club.' After the Dar-es-Salaam Club was nationalised it turned swiftly into something quite like the Africa Club. The same may yet happen to Nairobi and Muthaiga, though fortunately for them neither is in such a provocatively conspicuous place—the Dar Club is on the harbour front among the Government offices—nor is Kenya's leadership so wild for nationalisation yet.

Thus it is not only the cost of living in Nairobi that makes things hard for the African coming up in society, the white milieu does too. The European community continues much as before *Uhuru* and, though mainly English, is quite unlike any community in Britain. For one thing there are no ordinary white workers. Kenya has rarely if ever had white bus drivers and artisans, and none at all for some years. The whites are solid middle class, largely business and professional men, who invariably have far less understanding of the African than the settler. Many are not interested in trying to comprehend the native ways of life and thought.

The city families of white Nairobi are often as staggeringly aloof from what is going on around them as it is possible to be. The wives are the worst. Their husbands do meet educated Africans in the course of their work, and appreciate their good humour and friendliness. But the wives appear to think they are in a rather superior Wimbledon, graced by the sun and the proximity of exciting wild animals, but unhappily full of black men. These latter, they think, are a menace to one's children—but given close supervision they can be allowed to work for one in the house. That the wage for a cook houseboy should have gone up recently from around £8 to around £9 a month plus a room is thought intolerable. Now it may sound as though I am inventing this. But I am not. Once I tried to get a job for a very reliable African who had worked for me in the past and was now unemployed. The woman who took him on quibbled at paying £8 10*s*. a month, makes him start at five in the morning and for a day off gives him from midday to six on Sundays—if she has no guests requiring lunch. A change comes over our compatriots on contract in the tropics. If the altitude has affected the settlers they are at least respectful of their African employees' needs, whereas the newcomer, and I have noticed this in South Africa too, derives an immediate and disgusting sense of superiority based on having servants, leisure and overseas allowances which add up to a standard of living Britain only provides for the very rich. I remember one wife telling me that she counts the lumps of sugar in the sugar-bowl to see if her houseboy is stealing. She didn't think it ironic that she did this while her husband was giving large loans for more fortunate Africans to start in business. 'You can't trust them an inch,' she declared, 'not an inch.' The houseboy's feelings may be imagined. Who would blame him if he did steal?

The few racial bridge-builders cantilevering out friendship from the European residents' side are unlikely to succeed at all dramatically. Sometimes, like the Capricorn Africa Society, they have been a trifle too patronising, inclined to say of men now Ministers, 'Dear Tom' or 'Dear Julius,' or whoever it happened to be, 'he *is* so clever.' The time quickly came when the clever boy was speaking to the

United Nations and taking home £400 a month in salary so no longer needed the paternal encouragement which, for a year or two, had been useful. Now the educated African, so reluctantly admitted to white tea parties, is tending to withdraw into his own circles, which are, after all, the circles of real power. Occasionally something does spark from the new to the old. Unbelievably the gossip column of the *Sunday Post* newspaper appears to have done this. Its dated style has never changed, nor has its name, 'Miranda's Merrier Moments'. Yet to the surprise of no one more than the editor it is now scrutinised as avidly by African and Asian ladies as it always was by setters' wives. Miranda's description of the *Uhuru* Race Meeting will illustrate the quality of this minor racial miracle:

> The sun really shone for the *Uhuru* Meeting at Nairobi's Ngong Racecourse, and a happy Prime Minister was greeted on his arrival by the Jockey Club's Chief Steward, Sir Charles Markham. Sir Charles and Mr. Kenyatta made their way between lanes of enthusiastic spectators, pausing *en route* to speak to some of the Jockey Club's Officials.
>
> Later in the afternoon the Prime Minister presented some trophies, notably, of course, the very handsome *Uhuru* Cup which went to a delighted Lady Delamere, looking lovely for the occasion in a suit of black and white and an altogether gorgeous white hat.
>
> Lord Delamere was there, too, of course, and prominent personalities included the Minister for Finance, Mr. James Gichuru; Woolworth's Mr. R. Patel was racing—as indeed were Mr. and Mrs. Bob Harries, seen talking to Mrs. Humphrey Slade; Mr. and Mrs. Osmann of the Sudan Embassy; Mr. Bashir Mauladad; also Mr. and Mrs. Clive Salter. Dr. Aziz Khan and Dr. and Mrs. Sethi . . .

The Africans who feature in Miranda's small if now elastic-sided world are those who have reached the top, usually directly or indirectly through politics. Posts on the statutory Marketing Boards, in the direction of the radio and T.V., in fact at the Board level of all Government-controlled or-influenced organisations, are now basically political appointments, as are the Ambassadorships abroad. The speed of change has been such that very few Africans could be expected to qualify for them save through political experience or political suitability. They have moved overnight into the *dolce vita* that goes with power. Directorships are pressed on them by companies anxious to present an Africanised appearance. They can travel abroad as much as they want to—it needs only a word to a diplomat from the country of their choice and they're off at that country's expense. The world is at their feet, both East and West courting their influence.

At home the gap between them and their constituents widens rapidly. After the June 1963 elections no less than 102 out of the National Assembly's members obtained credit from a finance house for new cars, mostly Mercedes, and this in spite of the fact that many already had cars of other makes. Those who have Nairobi houses usually keep their telephone numbers secret and put no nameboards at the end of their drives. If they do then hordes of relations and beggars from their own tribe will descend on them, demanding the traditional hospitality of a life that has nothing in common with the city. A lot is talked about the detribalised poor African in Nairobi and his misdemeanours, little about the detribalised top strata. Not every leader follows Kenyatta's example by spending part of every week at home among his own people.

Parties, some public and therefore a duty, more private and pleasurable, occupy a surprising amount of time. So do girls and intrigue. Africans see nothing shameful in this, there is no ghost of Mrs Grundy ever at their shoulders. They make no secret of liking whisky, women and plotting. As in every other aspect of leadership, there are the handful who have learnt, or know instinctively, that Government is carried on by drafting documents and endless negotiation. The rest are amazingly fey and reckless. A European who was a Parliamentarian once let his hair down to me about policy meetings. 'We argue for eight hours,' he said, 'getting nowhere. Then they realise it's nearly evening and in the last quarter of an hour a rush of decisions are made just because they all want to get away. Invariably they turn to me as they leave. "Oh," they say, "could you get all that down on paper now?" So I spend the evening hard at it while they drink. Trying to work with Africans is infuriating.' For obvious reasons I have left out this man's name. In time the communist delegations, now at the stage of drinks and secretive discussions with Africans, will encounter the same exasperating preference for talk rather than action.

It is amusing to note how each 'foreign power' has its own preferred hotel and will shun those frequented by the others. Thus the Chinese latched on early to the New Stanley, normally doing everything in their rooms, including eating, and the Russian Satellite Group to the New Avenue. This doesn't stop the Americans using both, but it tends to keep the Egyptians in the Ambassadeur. A great deal of politicking goes on in Nairobi, as it will in any capital, only less inhibitedly. Africans lack inhibitions about blowing the gaffe if they think their listeners are worth impressing. Nor is there much shame attached to womanising, though the politician who was caught one night with a prostitute during a police round-up did seem somewhat embarrassed. Africans throughout the continent regard sex as an amenity and Governments often provide girls for important visitors during conferences. Politics may be an overwhelming preoccupation, by comparison with which the arts receive only the most perfunctory acknowledgement, except for traditional tribal dancing, and economics scarcely more, but the political merry-go-round does revolve with a pulsating swing.

Money, not to be confused with economic questions except in the last resort, also ranks high as a matter for concern. Corruption and graft are the bugbears of Africa. Happily in the Kenya civil service and the police there is hardly any. But in politics and business it's spreading, though much less than in some countries. One of the less well known of Kenya's politicians, getting a salary of around £2,500 a year, told a mutual friend that he expected to salt away £20,000 in the next two years. 'But,' protested the friend, 'what about your socialist principles?' 'Well,' he said, 'well . . . anyway, it's nothing to what the others are making.' Such are the rewards of office, and they accentuate the absurd contrast between the high life of the city and the day-to-day existence of the ordinary African population, living in mud huts on tiny plots of land.

But where are the Africans in this? They are, of course, still the servants and boot-blacks, the labourers and the newspaper-sellers. A few Members of Parliament and others prominent in the restaurants don't make Nairobi an African city. It remains an alien dream realised in the wonderful climate that a 5,000-foot altitude on the Equator provides, and it has attracted thousands more Africans than it can afford to put to work, in spite of its wealth. Round its perimeter are the African locations, some rebuilt by the City Council and given Biblical names like Afafa Jericho, are clean. Kariokor, a name corrupted from the British Army's Carrier Corps of the Great War which had a barracks here, has been rebuilt. Before, it was a slum, a shanty town of shacks and filthy huts, without sanitation. Others are being pulled down, like the jembe-roofed huts of South Eastleigh. A jembe is a tin of any kind, such as a five-gallon petrol can. When beaten flat jembes can serve as a patchwork roofing material. So severe is Nairobi's overcrowding that there is or was a car park in the very centre where whole families live in the bodies of abandoned vehicles.

The City Council finds squatters putting up illegal shanties almost as fast as it tears them down. In mid-1963 there were over a thousand of them 'housing' 5,000 Africans. It was a Cabinet decision, not just a city one, to stop any more being erected, so great is the problem of coping with the steady influx into Nairobi. In 1963 when the population was already 266,000 planning was still based on an estimate of 270,000 in 1975. But at least after 1948 there had been some planning where there was none before and a Master Plan did exist, although it has now had to be revised. Up to and including the Great War the city had grown haphazardly, and, for all its suburban delights, often viciously. Slums within sight of the vast open space of the Athi Plains are an unnecessarily bad anachronism. Even until the 1950's there was a shanty town near the bazaar in central Nairobi. It was a literal den of thieves, pimps, prostitutes and illicit liquor-stills. So many terrorists based themselves there that during the Emergency it was systematically dynamited out of existence, hidden explosives and ammunition popping off in a constant unofficial fusillade.

Pumwani, Pangani, the River Road area and many other parts are still as vice-ridden. When five major shanty towns were pulled down in Mbiyu village at Eastleigh more than a thousand gallons of Nubian gin were unearthed, hidden in oil drums under piles of sisal in the bush nearby. Prostitution is so prevalent that one of Kenyatta's Government's first actions was to set up a Ministerial Committee to examine the underlying causes of it. The girls one sees strutting in incredibly short skirts along some main streets, standing by service station forecourts or sitting over a drink of Fanta in the cheap Sombrero Night Club languidly watching 'The Authentic Strip Act of the Devil and the Virgin Never Before Presented in East

Africa', are just a small outward manifestation of a business that stretches deeply back into the earth-floored bars and packing-case homes of the shanty suburbs, where a girl costs 10*s*. and V.D. is rife.

The pickpockets and beggars of the city are organised from these locations on lines that Fagin would thoroughly approve. The old man one encounters in Kenyatta Avenue, dressed in rags and sacking, his straggly beard and rheumy eyes so pathetic, hobbling up and down with the aid of a stick and thrusting out a cardboard box for alms as you pass, is in fact brought in by car every day to work. There is a hunchback dwarf, legless into the bargain, who sits supported on two crutches at his shoe-cleaning box by the New Stanley Hotel. Ordinary, what one might call freelance, beggars have admitted to making 30*s*. a day, even though one never sees an African drop as much as a ten-cent piece in their hats. They depend on tourists and European and Asian residents' consciences. How indeed can one fail to give a shilling or a fifty-cent piece to the grotesquely deformed boy who crawls on all fours outside the Post Office at night? His legs stick out askew, probably from untreated polio, condemning him to move like an animal for the rest of his life. '*Asante Bwana*,' he says, '*Asante Sana*, *Bwana*', and forces his head back to smile awkwardly up at one. The Mayor is trying to end begging, which has swollen in its proportions greatly under African rule, but as he says getting cripples off the streets is not the end of it. Begging is their only means of livelihood whether they are exploited by criminals or not. Completely new social services are needed for their rehabilitation. It can no longer be left to a few voluntary organisations and to the Church.

It is with some justification that Tom Mboya said of Pumwani's inhabitants: 'They have experienced the misery and squalidness of under-privileged groups in towns all over the world. Their plights have been worse because of the attitudes and policies of former Governments and the prevailing conditions. For many years their domicile in the towns was accepted only on sufferance. Their homes were only of "temporary standards" although they had to last for generations. Health and other facilities were minimal. . . . Colonialism was not only a matter of political domination. It also involved economic exploitation and social inequality.' Community Centres, like St. John's at Pumwani, have done much to alleviate individual miseries. But the noble new concrete office blocks and hotels, sun-louvred and photogenic, do not alone make a city. Order has to emerge from disorder throughout. One of the saddest aspects of Nairobi is how the racial divisions have also been the divisions in the standards of living. As late as 1958 Tom Mboya himself still lived in a tiny Pumwani house without running water or electricity although he was a famous trade-union leader.

The stresses between the different racial communities are potentially highly explosive, and are reinforced by the natural antagonisms of the poor for the rich. Unfortunately for them, it is the Asians who constitute the immediate barrier to African advancement. They are the artisan class who hold the jobs that Africans covet, they own the small businesses and fill the lower ranks of the civil service. They are the bank clerks and cashiers, the grade of secretaries next most desired after Europeans, the shop assistants and garage-reception staff. In every way they stand between the African and the next step up. The dream exploited by the pre-*Uhuru* lotteries may have been of European houses and offices, but in real everyday life these are still too remote. It's the Asian flats that rise between the European suburbs and the African locations, hideously designed in neo-modern styles and painted in greens, pinks, yellows and blues, in fact looking for all the world as if they had been modelled from blocks of Neapolitan ice-cream, but none the less desirable to Africans.

The Asians live mostly in the cities: Nairobi and Mombasa. They keep strongly to their own sects, Sikhs and Hindus, Muslims, Goan Catholics, Ismaelites owing allegiance to the Aga Khan and many others. Mosques are dotted about the city, minarets poke up behind the public library, Hindu temples, as crisply ornamented as wedding cakes, are improbably next door to the rough, tough area of River Road. The Aga Khan Hospital, Aga Khan schools, the Patel Club, the Goan Club, witness to the social exclusiveness of tight-knit communities. They have been warned that they must open their doors. 'To call yourselves the Indian Chamber of Commerce,' declared Dr. Kiano on one occasion, 'is to separate yourselves on racial grounds.' But it is in their nature to cherish their own institutions, to defend the Hindustani broadcasts and the Asian newspapers. Even when printed in English the announcements of their cinemas have a flavour definitely their own, invariably emphasising a sugar-box version of modern love against old-style prearranged marriage:

> Now showing to entertained crowds
> The sweetest love-birds on the screen
> RAJ KAPOOR and SADHANA
> together for the first time in the
> MERRIEST MARITAL MIRTHQUAKE

Even in the English-language newspapers the Asian columnists hammer away at showing African current events in Asian light, with unending references to what the Mahatma would have done in such a case, and how Panditchi's example ought to be taken to heart in another. In the words of one of them, N. S. Toofan, who writes for the *Sunday Nation*, 'The Asian community is a microcosm of the whole of India and Pakistan.' It is also extraordinarily introverted.

Admittedly their fine schools and hospitals, usually built by subscription within their own communities and so most understandably felt to be their own, have been opened to Africans, but in spirit the Asians are the least assimilable people in the world. For a woman to marry out of her caste is to court ostracism, to marry an African quite unthinkable. To Africans now obsessed with breaking down racial superiority this would be bad enough. But small business is largely in Asian hands. The little shopkeepers, the duka wallahs, as they're called, have long dominated Kenya retail trading. A duka sells absolutely everything: soap, cheap cotton frocks, bedsteads, posho (ground maize), flea powder, Coca-Cola. In the Northern Frontier it may be the only recognisable building for 100 miles. Around the Nairobi Bazaar the duka wallah's names are a sing song, Khimji Bhimji, Kurji Karsanji, Shah Mulji Meghji, and their bargaining is likewise. 'I am telling you these are very good Indian sheets, very *best* Indian sheets. Forty-four shillings. I am making no profit, no profit at all on these sheets, it is sale you see. Well, forty shillings. Only could I be doing this for you sir. . . .' And so on. The Africans trying to go into trade demand of their leaders, 'How can we compete with these astute and slippery Asians?' In Uganda it has been done in the past by boycott and violence. In Tanganyika the Government is backing co-operatives that will put many Asians out of business. The Asians in Kenya are likely to suffer similar attacks on their livelihood, if not on their persons. One of the first actions of the army mutineers in Dar-es-Salaam was to spend a morning looting Asian shops and killing their owners. In Nairobi a single incident of an Asian driver knocking over an African has been known to set a street ablaze with violence and end with sixty parked cars damaged, overturned or on fire.

One reason for African hatred of the Asian trader is that the latter has not only been sharp, he has shown more forethought than his customers. Time and again the duka wallah upcountry has bought maize or beans off Africans who later in the year find they have miscalculated, are reaching the bottom of their store-bins long before the next harvest, and must buy back maize. They then object to the higher prices that shortage and the trader's normal profit impose. Asians have never been allowed to own dukas in the reserves (so called because they were reserved from foreigners for the protection of African interests). Now those with dukas in the scheduled areas are feeling the pinch. As settlement schemes enclose them, their business droops. I remember interviewing one trader at Naromoru. He was so frightened of being seen talking to a reporter that he took me into the back of his store, which was the usual one-storey, corrugated-roof affair with a relatively impressive painted brick front and a dingy rear. We sat on sacks of posho in a room where his daughters also slept. He was a thin, wearied man, a Gujerati, who had been scared stiff during the Emergency. 'What other Asian would have been coming to help me if I am crying out in the night? No one at all, I tell you.' Now it was the K.A.N.U. Youth Wing intimidating him. His turnover had dropped to half of what it had been and for fear of theft he no longer stocked large quantities of anything. With Africans opening their own dukas on the settlement scheme with the aid of Government loans it looked as though he couldn't last long. His one belief and hope was that they would be so inefficient that they would go broke or else put up their prices above his. 'We don't mind if they starting dukas,' he explained. 'They all coming in slowly, slowly but they don't know how the business run you see. I mean one thing they all got on their mind is that Asians cheating them but in five years then they know how much expense you get on the shop.'

In Nairobi the same is happening to a certain extent. In River Road you can see where African ownership is gradually creeping inwards towards the city. Every now and then the 'difficulties' for an Asian become too great and a one-room shop is cleared of its multitudinous variety of cotton goods, frying pans, nails, paints, hurricane lamps, cheap wooden beds with 'springs' made from strips of tyre rubber, and so on. Instead an African starts selling posho, greasy stewed mutton, sickly lemonade and probably pombe or Nubian gin from behind the rough wooden counter. Up goes the sign 'Uhuru Bar', inexpertly lettered. Another River Road property has changed hands, the Asians have retreated another five yards.

None the less, the supreme Asian characteristic is willingness to suffer in order to survive. As the doyen of the Sikh community said memorably to me, 'We are prepared to undergo that humiliation that accompanies Independence—a humiliation the European will not stand for.' They are the Jews of East Africa. But for them there is no Israel. Anything is better than going back to the overcrowding and poverty of India, while Hindus and Sikhs feel that Pakistan is closed to them. Meanwhile in both Nairobi and Mombasa they are taking over the upper end of the shopkeeping profession. One by one the luxury European shops close down or sell out, like one by the New Stanley Hotel selling leopard-skin handbags and other curios. In a few months its takings dropped from £200 a week to £30. An Asian bought it. Its standards will drop a little and its prices drop considerably. But no doubt it will prosper because the tourist business is booming, only Germans on package tours won't pay as much as settlers used to when they came to town to see their coffee auctioned and thought they'd take home a decent present for their wives.

The worst point of conflict with African interests arises from Asian predominance in the lower ranks of the civil service. This resulted from better education and ability, and was given impetus by the original Asian arrivals' strong desire to see their progeny in secure and respectable employment. In 1962 an Asian held the third highest office in the whole Kenya administration, and Asians felt justifiably that they formed the backbone of the civil service. Alas, since 1963 they have found themselves merely at the receiving end of a crash programme of Africanisation. For instance when I went to open a new telephone account in June 1963 the Telephone sales department was headed by an Englishwoman and mainly staffed by

Asians. The following April every single desk was occupied by an African. When a row broke over future conditions of service in the East African Common Services Organisation the two thousand Asians employed in the Income Tax, Motor Licensing, Civil Aviation and other offices there decided to resign in protest. They thought the threat of E.A.C.S.O. being dislocated would succeed. It didn't. A thousand realised their mistake earlier enough to retract. The other thousand were flabbergasted to have their resignations accepted by the Ghanaian Secretary General. A great deal of weeping and gnashing of teeth followed but in the end a series of Air India flights took the unhappy ex-civil servants away, lucky only in that they did receive small pensions or gratuities and could afford to go to Bombay or Delhi and look for Government work there.

The lesson that Africans cannot be so easily blackmailed as the British proved a sharp and bitter one to learn. Indeed the non-designated civil servants—those not designated as expatriates as the majority of Europeans were, sometimes in spite of being Kenya residents—are in a sad case. They had no option to go at Independence nor did Britain ever subscribe for a compensation scheme for them as she did for the designated officers. They face the certainty of being replaced in the future and thus finding themselves unemployed, albeit with pensions, though these are reduced if they do not complete the full length of service that Africanisation itself prevents them completing. Equally the civil service is closed to their children, for whom it would have been a major outlet of employment. The Asian population is expanding. Every Asian-owned car one sees is crammed to bursting with children. They may become Kenya citizens, they may have lived in Kenya four generations. But current policy, as a Recruiting Officer said of vacancies advertised in the papers, 'is not localisation. It is definitely Africanisation.' Even more frankly the General Secretary of the Kenya Federation of Labour, Senator Lubembe, has called for faster 'Blackanisation'. Yet in theory, under the Bill of Rights, all Kenya citizens should be equal. An Order in Council of 1958 stated, 'A person shall not . . . by reason that he is of a particular race . . . be subjected to disabilities . . . with respect to employment.' But in Tanganyika President Nyerere's statement, made two years after Independence, that all Tanganyika citizens must be equally eligible for jobs regardless of race met with the deepest antagonism in Kenya, where trade unionists, fearing a precedent was being set for them, issued howls of protest at the suggestion.

Nor has the belated part that Asians took in the African political struggle earned much reward. It always did look rather like jumping on the bandwagon at the last moment. For me it was epitomised by a book called *Struggle for Release Jomo and his Colleagues*, a remarkable selection of *cris de cœurs* ranging from eulogies by Odinga and by Professor Potekhin, the Russian Africanist, to a single scrawled sentence from Dr. Banda saying: 'I want Jomo out as quickly as possible.' It was compiled by a Mr. Ambu. H. Patel and published on Independence Day. This book is a strange mixture of genuine sincerity and blatant emphasis on the Asian efforts to aid Kenyatta, some from well-known communists. The photograph of the members of the 'Release Jomo and his Colleagues Committee', of which Patel himself was Hon. Secretary, shows no Africans, simply nine other Asians, which is odd. A page-long caption explains: 'But for their support the Movement could not have made much progress. Before during and after Emergency, throughout those long years of stress, these young Indians and their numerous friends stood by the Compiler and provided him the necessary volunteers, transport, clothes for the needy, funds for work. . . .' At the end of the book there is a Swahili poem extolling Kenyatta and the Mau Mau, which proves predictably to be 'Composed on Indian tune by Ambu. H. Patel'. Mr. Patel also describes himself, at length, saying: 'I have lived, worked and breathed every moment of the day for Baba's release and Kenya's Freedom. I have adopted Jomo Kenyatta as my Baba [Father] and all other Africans as my brothers and sisters.'

Alas, to most Africans things look different. The Asian shops may now all display colour pictures of the Prime Minister in their windows, but the rush to salute him at his release, when traders gave him more than three times as much new furniture as his Gatundu house could hold and the most colourful triumphal decorations in Nairobi were the Asian-erected ones in Bazaar Street, carried little conviction. A very few Asians, like the trade unionist Makhan Singh, or Pio de Gama Pinto, whose wife is Oneko's private secretary, and the lawyer Fitz de Souza, are accepted as having played an active part in anti-colonialist politics. The rest are regarded as having sat on the fence until the outcome of the battle was certain. 180,000 have now registered as British citizens. Indeed, just before Independence a thousand Asians a day were applying for British passports whilst still entitled to them as colonial subjects, so showing a lack of confidence in Kenya which again enraged the Africans. Ships to India are permanently booked full. Granted there are two Asians in the Government, but as the families move out on the sunlit weekend evenings from their overcrowded flats to sit jostling and laughing together on the grass in the public parks, they must be anxiously wondering how they are going to survive. As masons and carpenters they have literally built Nairobi. Their fathers were welcomed, indeed often brought here, by the British. Their skills as mechanics, carpenters, plumbers, electricians, in every trade in fact, are skills few Africans possess. Without them Nairobi would come to a standstill.

But the bitter experience of other African countries is that for all the talk of Afro-Asian solidarity, the two races mistrust and dislike each other. If the unemployed of Nairobi's African slums, and ex-detainees of the Mau Mau Emergency, take it out on anyone, it is likely to be on the Asians. If they opt for Kenya citizenship two years after Independence, when each man's decision has finally to be made, they will in theory be equal to Africans in all respects. In practice they are bound to be discriminated against, a fact recognised in the Indian Government's cautious willingness to have them back, if all else fails, while their great virtue of being able to make business almost out of thin air will be quoted inevitably as proof that Africa need not care for them.

12

'Blackanisation'

THE AFRICAN impatience for control often seems exaggerated to outsiders. Why this passion for Africanising everything? Why do white residents who are deported have to be ordered out at twenty-four hours' notice, instead of being given a week or two to pack and depart? Africans throughout the Continent live for the *moment*, seeing neither the future with foreboding nor the past with much regret. This is the secret both of their happiness and their instability. It explains the apparent dichotomy between their adoring grand gestures made *now*, and yet frequently proving unable to plan ahead successfully, or even to apply plans made for them by outside experts.

Thus the East African leaders discussed Federation at P.A.F.M.E.C.A.[1] meetings from 1960 to 1963 without even managing to draw up a draft Constitution. Suddenly on June 5th, 1963, Kenyatta, Obote and Nyerere met in Nairobi and signed a Declaration of Intention to Federate. Tom Mboya flew to London almost immediately after this and persuaded Britain to bring forward Kenya's Independence date from around April/May 1964 to December 12th, 1963, the three African leaders having stated that any delay would hamper the achievement of Federation. Britain allowed herself to fall for this blatant gimmick, partly because earlier Independence would mean Kenya could take her seat in the United Nations in 1963, instead of having to wait for the last quarter of 1964, and partly because the Federation ideal was believed in London to be genuine. So it was to many East Africans too. But although by October 1963 a Constitution had been drawn up the leaders could not agree on it. A year later Kenyatta revealed at a rally in Nyanza how Nyerere and Obote

1. Pan African Freedom Movement for East and Central Africa.

had agreed to make the grand gesture simply so that the British could be manœuvred into granting Kenya Independence earlier. It was an empty declaration, a classic example of African living for the moment, which ironically was later taken up by K.A.N.U.'s extremists as a stick with which to beat Kenyatta himself.

None the less the passionate, emotional yearning to be self ruling sooner was a genuine sentiment, not springing from any personal longing for power. It had been well and fervently expressed in P.A.F.M.E.C.A.'s Freedom Charter back in 1958. 'Every hour that passes under imperialism takes in its train a measure of our freedom and a portion of our noble heritage as Africans, the true and just and rightful masters of Africa's destiny. Every hour that passes means one more hour of subjection, degradation, exploitation, and humiliation by imperialists, white supremacists, and foreign self-seekers.'

Hence the mania for Africanisation. Hence the endless political debates, which rage through cocktail parties and dinners, are harked back to in the corners of hotel lounges, and are marginally exposed during interviews with journalists, leaving an impression that politics is everything in Kenya today. It seems impossible that the settlers, whatever Churchill may have felt about their wrangling back in 1907, could ever have talked politics as solidly and constantly as the African leaders now do. Oginga Odinga, the Republic's Vice-President[1] is even apt to telephone his associates and order them round for discussion at five in the morning, which to anyone who's been out on the tiles the evening before is more like the middle of the night.

Whether to satisfy private or public ambitions the politicians are all trying to discover how to control the machine of State they've acquired. Everyone wants to know how to make the African personality felt in Kenya. For the sake of international respect and the survival of the domestic economy the ideal of a non-racial society is paid much more than mere lip-service. But the hot, deep-down urge is to force this former 'White Man's Country' into a mould that is demonstrably African dominated, or in Senator Lubembe's phrase, 'blackanised'.

Fortunately the tiered structure of the administration could be Africanised straightforwardly. Members of the National Assembly might be woefully unaware of the reasons for not interrupting their

1. Odinga moved from the Ministry of Home Affairs to the Vice-Presidency when Kenya became a Republic on December 12th, 1964.

own leaders in the middle of policy speeches and look upon the Speaker and the Mace as an anachronism imported from Westminster, but then politicians are liable to be thrown in at the deep end in any country. What mattered more was that by Independence Day there were some really experienced and competent Africans in the top echelons of the civil service. Charles Njonjo, now Attorney-General, a sober-suited lawyer with a touch of elegance; Duncan Ndegwa, now Permanent Secretary in the Prime Minister's office and effective Head of the Civil Service; Robert Ouko, now Permanent Secretary dealing with Foreign Affairs; such men, to name only three, had all been in highly responsible positions for several years. Admittedly there were not many at the top and, when the inevitable campaign came to Africanise all the Permanent Secretaries' posts, others of lesser calibre had to be promoted. But if the Ministry of Finance, for instance, still badly needed its expatriate Permanent Secretary, Mr. Butter, at least the civil service had a core of Africans who were first-class men by any standards. This was just as well, since the rush to Africanise, coupled with certain Ministers' determination to appoint the men they favoured, was to strain the standards of administration. Whereas Ghana had Africanised from the bottom up over a period of four years, Kenya, following Tanganyika's example, seemed impatient to Africanise the whole bang shoot in about six months.

Britain had prepared only for the Ghanaian precedent, not the Tanganyikan. The Institute of Administration at Kabete, occupying the buildings of the former Jeane's School, began running a variety of courses, including the obvious six months' one for District Officers. Here again the calibre of African passing out has been gratifyingly high. The snag is that the Institute started too late in the cycle of events. The brevity of the transitional period from expatriate to African running of the State left ample opportunity for blunder, incompetence and intrigue. The blame, however, lay further back—in the lack of educational facilities. More was left to the mission establishments—like Mangu and the Alliance High School—than they could fulfil. The Colonial Government did too little, with the result that Africans were being trained for responsibility who not always had the right basic educational and intellectual qualification. At Egerton College the African students sitting drinking beer in their short black academic gowns on that sunny Prize Day had seemed genial enough, but all the prizes save one had gone to the handful of European and Asian students. The American lecturer I stayed with told me that while three of his students had reached the seventh Mau Mau oath, their examination performance was pathetic, one even being unable to do long division. He had found himself compelled to mark them on common sense instead of knowledge of animal husbandry, and he was appalled at the standards of entry the college had to accept. 'You want more than just warm bodies,' he said. The men from these first courses would get the top jobs and 'when better men come through later these ones will see them as a threat and thwart their careers'.

This applies all the way through the Africanisation programme. There is no escaping it. Later the students coming back from abroad, or graduating from the University of East Africa (the amalgamation of Makerere in Uganda, the Royal College in Nairobi and a new college in Dar-es-Salaam), will be available. But no one can wait for them. Delay is rarely acceptable politically. Furthermore the Kenya Government made a major error in thinking that expatriates would stay on until the exact moment when they were to be replaced. A myth had grown up that the Colonial Service men were such fifteenth-rate material, and so unlikely to find subsequent work in Britain, that they could be treated with disdain and still have to remain at Kenya's beck and call. This myth not only revealed an interesting African view of the European as being a servant the moment he ceased to be a master, it was almost completely unfounded.

Expatriate civil servants were sought after by the Commonwealth Relations Office and Foreign Office to fill diplomatic posts in Africa; by companies taking the plunge in to the potentially profitable post-Independence African market; even by the United Nations. They were actually men with far more ability than their new bosses had ever cared to realise. Nor did the term of compensation encourage them to stay. The British Government was financing a scheme that gave men suffering most—those in the middle thirties to middle forties who were within sight of the top and now had to start again—both a moderate pension and a substantial tax-free gratuity. An ex-school friend of mine aged thirty-three, a District Officer, was expecting £300–£400 a year pension and £8,000 compensation. Only the old who got more pension and much less gratuity had any incentive to continue for the sake of keeping a high salary for a few more years. Had Kenya's Ministers made more sincere noises about needing their services more might have stayed. As it was, antagonism drove them away, along with the vets, the doctors and dentists and nurses and other professional people. A doctor at Nakuru who generously treated any poor person for 5*s*., and who asked these patients to enter by a separate door, for the sake of identification, was publicly vilified for racial discrimination because most of the 5*s*. patients were African. Forty per cent of the Government's vets left in a year; one hospital had to advertise in London for nurses; suddenly a town like Nyeri found itself with only one doctor, an Asian, and fifty years' progress dropped away as the only alternative source of medical attention became the missions, as it had been in 1910. The process of rebuilding staffs will be slow.

This decamping of professional people went right down to the secretary level. When a new Government Secretarial College giving free training to all races to help the Kenyanisation programme was opened by Joseph Murumbi he declared openly: 'Kenya desperately needs more typists and clerks to replace the European and Asian secretarial workers who are leaving the country.' The college was an admirable start, but it could only dilute the penalty being paid in both commercial and Governmental offices for Africanisation—switchboard delays, corrupted messages and painfully slow paperwork.

That Kenya had a far larger and more sophisticated Government machine than an African country of its size can afford is indisputable. As a white colony it was generously staffed. Consequently its services were good, just as East Africa as a whole had the most efficient Civil Aviation network in the African Continent. A decline was inevitable. What matters is whether it will be below the lower standard that an African-ruled Kenya considers acceptable. Perhaps with Russian, American and British aid it will not. But the bugbear of having recruited so many low-grade Africans into middle-strata posts will remain with the country a long time.

So may the undercurrents of tribal animosity that appeared even before *Uhuru* in the administration. Both Kikuyu and Luo politicians were tempted to finds jobs for their friends. Such patronage had the additional merit of helping them construct private tribal intelligence networks, a game in which returning students from the 'East' help. In Nairobi a list of Home Affairs Ministry staff reveals how Odinga accumulated Luo's beneath him, no doubt because he felt he could trust them. Equally the Kikuyu Ministers formed a close-knit group, including Dr. Kiano, Dr. Mungai Njoroge (Minister of Defence), Mbui Koinange (Minister of State) and Mwai Kibaki, a highly intelligent young Parliamentary Secretary. The roots of K.A.N.U. unity, always fragile, though now receiving much loving attention, were further struck at by the formation of K.E.M.E.M.A. This 'Kikuyu, Embu and Meru Elected Members Association' linked the politicians of the Mau Mau tribes, aggravating Luo fears.

Here I should explain the Luo position in national politics. The two dominant figures are Tom Mboya and Oginga Odinga, with Achieng Oneko running third from Odinga's stable. There are good reasons for Odinga and Mboya being at loggerheads much of the time. Odinga is the older by twenty years, a veteran Luo politician and immensely popular in Nyanza where he founded the powerful Luo Thrift and Trading Corporation. He is colourful. For a year or two he used to appear against the formal backdrop of the Assembly in what he called Luo traditional dress, a variable mixture of skins, fur hats, red, white and blue painted leggings and so on. His attitude was tribal and atavistic. Since then he has changed to simple Chinese-style suits with tunics and trousers of coarse woven linen. He is said by his friends to be direct and honest, certainly he shows no embarrassment at allegations that he receives Chinese money. He has even asked an audience rhetorically if they had ever seen him in possession of any yen. He is also shrewd. He has adopted the title Jaramogi which harks back to a famous Luo warrior and indicates headship of the tribe. Oneko calls himself Ramogi, next title down the scale, thus leaving little for Mboya. When Kenyatta dies Odinga will be an obvious candidate for the Presidency, if, that is, the Kikuyu will stand for having a Luo Head of State. His money has been invaluable to K.A.N.U. in both the 1961 and 1963 Election campaigns, and his personal group of politicians includes the former Kikuyu detainees Bildad Kaggia and Fred Kubai, as well as influential men in the trade unions. Finally he has sent hundreds of students East and opened the doors for communist schemes of development in Kenya.

Mboya, now thirty-four, having been born on Rusinga Island in Lake Victoria, is claimed by Odinga's supporters to be less than a true Luo, and has always stood for election in a Nairobi constituency.

As a trade unionist he received substantial help from the American Labour Movement and has an appreciation of and grasp of economics, gained through experience not formal education, that would have taken him to the top anywhere. He dresses like a successful executive, not flashily but well. He is one of the few Kenyans with whom a European can feel at once that he is talking on the same wavelength. Though somewhat vain, Mboya knows instinctively what makes the Western world go round. He organised the Kenya Federation of Labour brilliantly. In spite of having made enemies both there and in his subsequent political life he is so able that it would be a foolish Government that let him drop.

Around Independence the Luo-Kikuyu rift appeared to be widening, one measure of it being an evident *rapprochement* between Mboya and Odinga. Just as rumours were flying round of two improbable-sounding organisations, LUTO (Luo Takeover) and KUTO (Kikuyu Takeover), the Government found itself with an army mutiny on its hands, its share of East Africa's January tumult. It was only six weeks since *Uhuru* and a month since the Declaration of a State of Emergency in the North-East Region.

One of Kenyatta's first acts, after calling in the British troops as Obote had done the day before in Uganda, was to forbid any Minister to see the mutineers, a significant order. Odinga is alleged to have been stopped by police on his way up to Lanet Barracks near Nakuru, where a number of privates and N.C.O.s had raided the armoury and tried to seize the camp. The mutiny was quickly put down by 3 R.H.A. while other British units covered the Langata camp outside Nairobi, there being indications that the revolt might have spread.

Various reasons were advanced for the affair. It had derived inspiration from the Tanganyika Rifles mutiny at the beginning of the week (January 19–26th). Army pay was low in all three countries and the Tanganyikan dissatisfaction with the rate of Africanisation of the officer corps may have been reflected in Kenya, even though Kenya now had an African lieutenant-colonel and several majors, while Tanganyika still had nothing African above a captain. Then there was the flaming example of the Zanzibar Revolution of January 12th and possibly some deliberate interterritorial organisation.

Meanwhile the first reactions revolved around the terrible loss of face involved in recalling the colonial power six weeks after Independence. This was felt in spite of the tact and lack of bloodshed with which British troops had acted. The newspaper photographs of men of the Kenya Army, dishevelled, hands resting on their heads, being marched along to detention by armed British soldiers represented unspeakable humiliation. Down at Dar-es-Salaam a Tanganyikan official had stood outside the Colito Barracks while Royal Marines disarmed the Tanganyikan Army and as Press photographers came out he confiscated their film of the event. The Ministry of Information in Kenya would, I think, have given a great deal to prevent photographs of the round-up at Lanet reaching the outside world.

Immediate advantage was taken of the mood by the left wing, as though wringing the last drop of profit from the frustrated mutiny. Word flew round that British troops must now leave the country, it being conveniently forgotten that they were there by agreement until December. I have a vivid memory of one left-wing Briton who was closely in touch with Oneko sitting at a table in the open air outside the New Stanley and declaring that Kenya would not stand for having British military police strutting about the streets of the capital. That none were visible and British troops were wisely being kept in their barracks was irrelevant. The hurt that national pride had suffered was being exploited to the full by the politicians whose views he was repeating.

It was a genuine hurt. For even a fraction of the army to turn against the Government was a bitter blow.

It seemed only yesterday that in the Independence Stadium, under the batteries of spotlights, a contingent in the red fezzes of the King's African Rifles had marched and counter-marched before the vast crowd and then handed over the battalion standards to another contingent dressed in the dark green peaked hats and tunic uniforms of the new Kenya Army. The askaris' short sleeveless zouave jackets had gone for ever, thrown out of the window with colonialism, and on the dais with Kenyatta had stood the first African to be promoted lieutenant-colonel in service dress and shining Sam Browne. Now, suddenly, that army's loyalty to its country had broken down. Naturally the left wing claimed that this was because the remaining white officers had trained it in colonialist ways of thought.

If anything the climacteric last two weeks of January were a moment of truth for East Africa's elected leaders because they saw acutely that one man one vote was no guarantee against subversion. Parliamentary democracy had put them in power, but now the British were gone it could not stop them being overthrown by a determined minority. No one seriously doubted that the minority might make another attempt, or that they were communist-backed. The events revealed a devastating and totally unexpected disloyalty to the architects of *Uhuru*.

Knowledge of the Zanzibar Revolution had flashed round the mainland territories as an inspiring example of what the African Revolution could achieve. 'When they pipe in Zanzibar people dance on the lakes,' used to be the saying. It is still true. In Nairobi the K.A.N.U. Youth Wing celebrated the Zanzibar 'Field Marshal' Okello's exploits as prefiguring the triumph of socialism in Kenya. Within a week the mainland mutinies had followed and as a result of Nyerere hesitating to ask for aid Dar-es-Salaam had been at the mercy of the mutineers for five days. The territories had indeed quivered to Zanzibar's tune. I was lucky enough to go to the island for the *Sunday Times* immediately after the Revolution, flying myself across the forty miles of clear blue Indian Ocean in a light aircraft.

The Revolution in Zanzibar was led by young communist-trained trade unionists and Youth Wingers, the precise equivalent both of the K.A.N.U. Youth Wing and the bands of jeunesse who roam and terrorise the eastern Congo, save that the Zanzibaris were more educated and more organised. Not that it took much organisation to overthrow the Sultan's regime in the absence of any army and the absence of British intervention. Once John Okello, by birth a Ugandan but for several years previously a painter in Zanzibar, had rallied the group trying to storm the police armoury, and taken it, the issue was decided. There were several mainlanders among his lieutenants. One I met came from Mombasa and told me of his training in Cuba, to which he had returned for a three months' refresher course shortly before the Revolution. Babu had said the Government of the Zanzibar National Party would be overthrown shortly after their *Uhuru* on December 10th, 1963. John Okello brought it about, and afterwards openly declared that the Zanzibaris could not be trusted to run their own uprising.

The 'Field Marshal' was previously unheard of in East Africa. He emerged meteorically, carving a flaming swathe through the front pages of the world's newspapers, before being doused by Babu and Zanzibar's President Karume. He was, or I should say still is, because he is busy somewhere, in Accra or Cairo perhaps, a revolutionary evangelist of African nationalism. The things that seemed horrific and absurd about him to the Western world struck a deep chord among his contemporaries in Kenya. To them his broadcasts on the Zanzibar radio threatening hundreds of years' imprisonment to opponents of the Revolution, and describing exotic forms of capital punishment, made sense. They were exactly what they wanted to do to the colonialists and to the Asians. Okello's war was emphatically against the Arabs, the first colonisers of the East African coast. Later on, he said, he was going to lead the liberation movements against the whites of South Africa. Again if this sounded ill in the ears of the educated South Africans who run the A.N.C. office in Dar, and are quite content with their existing leadership, it sounded splendid to the Youth Wingers of Nairobi.

I spent a morning with Okello, being led to his office in the radio station through crowds of Zanzibaris and up stairs littered with loot from shops. He was extremely black-skinned, as most of the Luo and related tribes are—he is an Acholi or a Langa. He wore a captured police officer's hat, decorated with a band of yellow and green revolutionary colours, and made elaborate preparations before posing for my camera. A Bren gun was placed on the desk before him, he grasped a pistol in his right hand and placed his left on a large bible. Then sitting bolt upright, and staring like a Napoleon into the middle distance, he was ready. Setting this *mise en scène* actually took twenty minutes, while a rather dishevelled guard lay in the doorway with another Bren gun. But it wasn't all vanity. He felt himself to be the leader not merely of the Zanzibar Revolution but of the African Revolution. The picture that the world would see of him had to be right. The bible emphasised his Christianity and the armament his mastery of war.

He spoke through an interpreter, since although he knew some English he disliked revealing its limitations. It emerged that he was not intelligent but very single-minded. The wildness, the savagery, the Messianic sense of being chosen, were there too. He was in the direct line of African terrorist prophets. On his two visits to Kenya, one before and one after his removal from Zanzibar, where he had become an embarrassment not least to Babu's private army, his language became mixed with the leavings from a feast of communist jargon. But his real cause was Africa.

Okello's impact in Kenya was unmistakable. I think his example, showing that you could have an army without all that colonial inheritance of rules and discipline and white officers, had helped bring about the mutiny. There was also a more sinister side to his Kenyan relationships. Not only were a number of his lieutenants in the Revolution visibly Kenyan, it was believed that he had strong connections with Oginga Odinga and Achieng Oneko, both of whom are Luos and tribally related to him. The *Sunday Times* published an allegation, not in fact sent by me, that Okello had been telephoned by Odinga and Oneko three times on the day before the revolution. Some measure of the suspicions in Kenya that there was a Luo plot to overthrow not merely Zanzibar's Government but Kenya's as well, may be gained from Oneko's immediate issue of a statement that he and Odinga were suing the *Sunday Times* for £100,000 libel damages each. Oneko himself told me at the time that he was very worried about accusations by other K.A.N.U. members. Certainly Kikuyu suspicion of Luo motives was then at its height. The libel case against the *Sunday Times* has never even progressed as far as a writ, let alone been brought to court.

Okello was eventually declared a prohibited immigrant in Kenya, though not before he had spent a week in the purest cloak-and-dagger style in Nairobi. He had been whisked away from the foot of the aircraft steps when he arrived, and excused all formalities, the control of which rests with Odinga's Ministry of Home Affairs. Thereafter no one could find him, neither the journalists of Nairobi and the foreign Press, who were out after him in force, nor even several Kikuyu Kenya Ministers. He was thought to be in one of Odinga's houses—Odinga has spent some of his Chinese-donated funds on buying Nairobi residences for his friends—but calls on various suburbs produced no 'Field Marshal'. Then suddenly he was spirited up from nowhere for a press conference. Although he was in no way an official Government guest it was Oneko's Ministry of Information which rang journalists and summoned them. It was no surprise that during his next visit he was expelled, nor that he then drove to the Uganda frontier in a brand-new Peugeot obtained in Nairobi.

January's upheavals made everyone take a close look at the system of control that Kenyatta had inherited from the last Governor, who incidentally now found himself as Governor-General deprived of access to most official sources of information. The Colonial system was simple—army, police and, above all, the colonial administrative system. Different elements of the Kenya community viewed these in diametrically different ways. The white business men and settlers saw the continuance of old traditions as a potential safeguard to life and property, if not as good as the presence of the British Army, or the R.A.F. and Navy, whose jet aircraft and ships seemed to be making a remarkable number of visits to Kenya in 1964.

The whites had one thing in common with 'white' K.A.N.U. (the Western-orientated wing of the party). Both were horrified that the British-trained Kenya Army could ever mutiny. How clearly I remember the lofty tones with which my friends discussed the Congo in 1960 and 1961, sitting in the open-air café at the New Stanley, condemning the Belgians and saying, 'It could never happen here.' I said the same myself. The Congolese Army mutiny was the root cause of four years' chaos in the Congo. Once an army has mutinied it will never again be effective unless it is completely purged and reformed. Neither the British nor the politicians who had not so long ago had cause to fear and respect the Kenya askaris ever imagined the same could happen in East Africa, and especially not when those askaris came under African leadership in their own states.

The communist-orientated 'Red' K.A.N.U. took the opposite view. The army had too long imbibed British ways. Its Sandhurst- and Mons-trained young officers gave scant welcome to the variety of K.A.N.U.-backed 'military' men seeking to join. For two or three years before Independence 'students' had been going to China, Russia, Egypt, Israel and the satellite countries for military training. Just as 'General China', who after Mau Mau had been in Israel, received a far from effusive welcome when he wanted to become a Kenya Army officer, so there were bound to be difficulties in absorbing the others. The obvious way to place them and reap the rewards of having political influence in the army leadership was to change the outlook and structure of the army.

This may explain why the Israeli-trained officers took so active a part in the Tanganyikan Army mutiny. It would be completely illogical for Israel to promote sabotage of Governments like Nyerere's which are giving them both the diplomatic recognition and the commercial opportunities they need to counter Arab influence in Africa. But Israeli training, like Communist training, evidently instils a keen sense of political purpose, adding to the other pressures that make a young army politically orientated. The danger is then that the army starts seeing itself as a better arbiter of the peoples' will than either the Government or the ballot box.

There must at the time of writing be several hundred Kenyans undergoing military training in communist countries. It costs nothing to send them and the lengths to which it is worth going to get them there were well illustrated by an incident that took place three months before Independence. Fifty genuine students were going to Bulgaria by arrangement with the Ministry of Education. Actually the scholarships had been secured originally by Odinga and the Bulgarians appear to have made a clerical error in informing the Ministry at all, because when the time came both he and the Ministry had a set of students ready. At 7 a.m. on the morning of departure Odinga came out to Nairobi airport with his fifty-five students, turned the Ministry's ones away and had their baggage unloaded from the plane. He then wrote out 'passports' for his fifty-five on pieces of paper and, with the connivance of the Bulgarians, they were airborne before the Ministry offices opened that day. Odinga made no secret of their being sent for military training. Nor is it any secret among Kenyans that education is often used to repay electoral allegiances and cultivate support. The row that broke that day in the National Assembly made headlines but could not bring back the plane. Subsequently relevant legislation was amended so that all students have to pass through the Education Ministry. The Bulgarian batch were explained as an unfortunate continuance of the practices K.A.N.U. had to adopt in former times to evade Colonial Office restrictions.

It is a major question whether Kenyatta will continue to oppose the dilution of the army with such material. The agreements with Britain, under which Britain continues to train the Kenya Army, suggest that he fully realises the dangers, though the fiercest pressure on him to accept communist-trained soldiers will only arise two or three years after Independence when large numbers will be back and possibly be unemployed. By that time, however, the army will be very fully Africanised. Until 1961 there were no African officers. At the end of that year eight effendis (a rank similar to the Viceroy's Commissioned Officer in the Indian Army) were promoted to lieutenant and photographed proudly standing in their new service dress with the Governor on the lawn outside Government House. From then on progress was fast and by *Uhuru* there were over 100 African officers, including the one colonel and several majors.

Since the mutiny this rate of Africanisation has, if anything, been stepped up, while the Junior Leaders' Company, giving secondary education alongside training for posts as N.C.O.s, produces replacements for the British sergeants. The role of the British will become advisory and in August 1964 it was promised that the G.O.C., at that time Major-General Freeland, would be replaced by an African as soon as one with enough experience was available. The mutiny also caused an immediate review of pay and substantial increases were announced soon afterwards. By these measures it is hoped to preserve the army as a non-political force that the Government can rely on. Equally, everything is done to prevent its tribal composition becoming a contentious issue. At Independence its 6,000 men were approximately one-third Kamba and one-third Kalenjin, with 60 per cent of the officers Kamba. The Kikuyu, owing to none being recruited during the Emergency, were in a small minority. They had never been a tribe who particularly favoured the army, though a large number of the circumcision group of 1940 had volunteered during the war, come out skilled in fighting and, whether fortuitously or not, ended up aligned with the Mau Mau as the notorious 'forty group'. Now more Kikuyu are being recruited, which will be one way of taking steam out of the Youth Wing and unemployment. The territorial unit, the Kenya Regiment, formerly white-dominated, had been disbanded. Rather late in the day it had opened itself to all races and met with a good response from Africans and Asians, but its campaign record against the Mau Mau hardly stood it in much stead, nor did its settler tradition.

The army was always a predominantly black/white affair, with virtually no Asian element. There are a few Asian officers, recipients of Queen's commissions since 1957. But they have severe doubts as to whether the new Kenya Army holds any future for them, although they are not the stumbling block to African promotion that Asians are in the lower echelons of the civil service and to some extent in the police. One frequently sees Sikh police officers in Nairobi, the badge of the force pinned at the front of their immaculate white turbans. The threat to their livelihood is harsh—efficient and impressive though they may be. As soon as Africans are qualified for their jobs, and probably before, they will be cast out on pension along with the Customs officers and Post Office clerks, the railwaymen and Council officials. It will be quite extraordinary if despite Kenyatta's declarations about Kenya being the very model of a multi-racial state the Asians retain office for as much as another decade, especially in the police.

The Kenya Police, like the Nigerian Police, are one of the finest of Britain's pro-consular legacies to Africa. The African constables that I have come across have been invariably helpful, humorous and strict, whether telling me the way, pinching me for a parking offence—they have a truly British enthusiasm for parking fines in Nairobi—or removing a dead-drunk old African from the gutter. They are always smartly turned out in uniforms that are not basically impressive—grey shorts and shirt, leather belt, boots and thick stockings, plum-coloured steel helmet. The helmet they wear all the time, an indication of the violence a constable can often expect to meet, and at night they often patrol four together plus an alsatian dog.

Europeans living in Kenya have grown accustomed to high standards in the police and take it for granted that if you dial 999 on the telephone a dark blue police car, usually an English Ford, will come screaming round in a matter of minutes, and that country constables will bicycle round periodically to check that all is well on the farms. Unless they take unusual interest they are only marginally aware of the vast amount of patient research mixed with real risk that goes into counteracting crime in the African areas and in the crowded African locations of Nairobi. It is easy to forget those policemen who have been speared or shot pursuing both fanatics and ordinary murderers. The virtues of the Kenya Police only hit you in the eye if you travel elsewhere in Africa, in the Congo or any of the former French countries, where the gendarmerie lounge around waving sub-machine guns, taking graft and generally behaving—in my experience, anyway—like the worst sort of film portrayal of the worst sort of American cop. Then it is that you appreciate how miraculously the natural vagaries of the African temperament have been subdued and disciplined among their counterparts in Kenya.

There are also some remarkable ancillary services. Apart from the tribal police serving all over the country, distinguishable by their wearing thick maroon sweaters instead of a shirt, the belt over the sweater, there is the General Service Unit and the Police Air Wing. The G.S.U. I have mentioned earlier. It is a para-military unit, based at a camp near Nairobi airport, its men dressed in khaki fatigues and boots and gaiters and red paratroop berets. Now increasingly African-officered, the G.S.U. is a tough organisation, armed, used against demonstrators, shifta and in any other situation where the police are liable to find themselves fighting. The Police Air Wing oyerates four-seater Cessnas from Wilson airport at Nairobi, with British pilots who have police rank but usually only limited police training. As well as being used to control crowds, chase cattle-thieves, report on tribal raids and so on, they ferry Kenya Ministers frequently and for this have acquired a twin-engine executive transport, a Cessna 310. They are in fact used as a private Government air service. As yet no campaign has been mounted for Africanisation of the Air Wing.

From the moment Kenyatta took office as Prime Minister control of the police became a controversial issue. Instead of allowing that function to the Minister of Home Affairs, which had been the practice, he retained it himself, as he retained Foreign Affairs and Defence. This was an obvious blow to Odinga, although too much can be made of the fluctuating relationship between the two men.

Since the police force is one of the keys to Kenya, Africanisation of its top echelon was an immediate target. At *Uhuru* the Inspector-General, Sir Richard Catling, widely acknowledged to be highly efficient, had been asked to stay. Especially after the army mutiny, it must have mattered a great deal to the Prime Minister that the police chief should be reliable. Needless to say, a tremendous campaign was mounted within K.A.N.U. for Catling's dismissal. Its left-wing members were active in circulating every form of libel against him, albeit on very predictable lines—he was an imperialist stooge acting for the British, he was playing up invented disloyalties by Ministers in his reports to Kenyatta and so on. When the third Briton deported after *Uhuru*, myself being the second, proved to be an Assistant Commissioner of Police, Mr. Leslie Pridgeon, it was no surprise that the action was accompanied by a chorus of demands for Catling's removal too, especially since he went to the airport to see Pridgeon off. A few months later his resignation was announced and he left Kenya at the end of 1964.

As Minister of Home Affairs it was Odinga who signed the order declaring Pridgeon a prohibited immigrant for 'reasons of national security'. That was in June 1964. In August four more Britons were removed, prominent among them the newly retired thirty-seven-year-old Assistant Commissioner of the Special Branch, Ian Henderson. This was announced as a Cabinet decision. It also created a considerable stir since Henderson was a third-generation Kenyan, and was famous for his work against the Mau Mau. He won the George Medal twice for operations in the forests, captured Dedan Kimathi and later wrote a bestseller about the hunt. Henderson was pretty likely to have headed any black list in a country which now considered Kimathi a hero of the Revolution. At the same time he was very able, and must have known a very great deal not only about the Mau Mau but also about current Kenyan affairs. The Special Branch had been given an African chief at once and many of its European officers had left even before *Uhuru*. That it was felt necessary to deport Henderson indicated how dangerous Odinga and others must have considered his presence, even allowing that it is virtually impossible to overstate the fear of politicians in emergent African countries that their white civil servants are duping them. When not only Russia, but China, the satellites and Israel are all training African 'students' in the techniques of espionage and subversion, control of the Special Branch and of any Intelligence Service that may be created weighs heavily in the struggle for power. Inevitably Independence brings with it a highly fluid situation. The old colonially imposed balance of political power is gone, and the new African internal balance is being created. Whoever gains an ascendancy over the Security forces during this post-Independence period, buying allegiance where he cannot get his own men appointed, gains mightily. The standard of impartiality and loyalty to the Government with which Britain imbued Kenya's Army and Police are undergoing considerable strain.

13

The Power Struggle

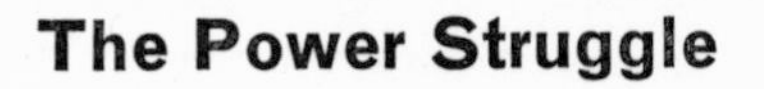

THE POWER STRUGGLE in Kenya is deceptive and hard to analyse. To crystallise it in terms of the relationship between Kenyatta and Odinga is a dangerous oversimplification, if not an outright false one. Odinga's fight is not so much against Kenyatta as against the Western influence in Kenya, the pressures of which are as yet the most insistent upon the President.

Odinga has never made any bones about who is the boss, while Kenyatta frequently reminds audiences of their old friendship and how Odinga was the first to campaign for his release from detention. Jomo even danced a celebratory jig with him at one K.A.N.U. rally. He has allowed Odinga to handle important negotiations with the communist powers, from whom Kenya is now deriving substantial economic aid and a very large number of scholarships for students—there will be soon over a thousand students in Russia alone. There is no evidence to prove that Kenyatta does not still cherish sympathies dating from his pre-war days in Moscow. But even if he is simply, as he says, a neutralist, it could be a long time before he needed to curb Odinga's introduction of communist influence. Neutralism in the African view implies taking as much from East as from West, only very seldom refraining from accepting eithers' gifts. It will be years before the existing Western entrenchment in Kenya is equalled by the communists'—teachers, business men, experts, farmers, householders, and personal friends. So long as Odinga's main concern remains how to improve the lot of Africans there is likely to be less deep dispute between him and Kenyatta than the Western Press, supposing Kenyatta to be basically attached to the Western camp, believes, as his appointment to the Vice-Presidency showed.

During his four decades of political life Kenyatta has so steeped himself in the practice of making men do what he wants that he can now draw the best from every member of his Cabinet. Thus though some of them are young and still lightweights, and one at least holds office more as a reward for past devotion than for present capacity, Odinga is not the only one who is capable of disagreeing with Kenyatta nor the only one with power in his own right. Not so long ago Tom Mboya was being advised by his friends to quit politics and join the United Nations. He is now a key figure, so is Joe Murumbi, a burly, cultivated half Goan, half Masai who was almost unknown to ordinary Kenya voters before his return from a self-imposed exile, but is now the Minister of Foreign Affairs, where his ability and drive have contributed greatly to the stable and favourable image that Kenya enjoys in the rest of Africa.

The essential point is that bit by bit Kenyatta has so moulded matters that what is done is usually what he wants done. His retaining control of the police, and his announcing that from August 1964 all deportation orders, hitherto signed by Odinga, would now be personally authorised by him, show that he is prepared to keep Odinga in line. Equally he took the trade union's *Uhuru* bonus dispute out of the hands of the Minister of Labour, E. N. Mwendwa, and settled it himself. But no one sees the latter as indicating a split between him and Mwendwa. When Lawrence Sagini's somewhat nebulous pre-*Uhuru* agreement with Nationalist China was dropped the incident was not shouted about as revealing a rift between Sagini and Kenyatta.

Within the Kenya Cabinet there are various groupings, as there are liable to be in any Cabinet. The doctrine of Cabinet responsibility took time to sink in, especially since of the sixteen members only nine had held Government political office of any kind before, namely Kenyatta himself, Kiano, Mboya, Gichuru, McKenzie, Sagini, Angaine, Mwendwa and Mwanyumba. Whilst one can still discern the white K.A.N.U. and red K.A.N.U. clearly, the split that ravaged the party in 1961 and 1962 has been smoothed over in the Cabinet. Whereas in 1961 Odinga and Mboya were each issuing Press statements denouncing the other now the conflicts are tempered by office and it has become increasingly clear that K.A.N.U. and the Government have only one boss, Jomo.

Having acknowledged this one can the more clearly examine the other major influences the Government has to control, and in which individual politicians are certainly involved. The simile of a Prime Minister sitting on the lid of a boiling pot is hackneyed, but apposite.

First there are the significant expatriate-run organisations which the Government either feels it must control, or which a group of politicians feel ought to be State-run, or that the public demands should be Africanised. As well as the administration, the army and police, there are the Post Office, railways, electricity and other semi-Governmental organisations, the all-important Press and radio, the manufacturing, the business and finally the tourism and national parks.

Secondly there are elements loud in the campaign against European control, but a growing problem to the Government. Briefly these are the trade unions, the Government's own backbenchers, K.A.N.U.'s own Youth Wing, and the rising numbers of unemployed and school-leavers.

Foreign Powers intertwine their designs with both sets of factors. The British, pouring in money, trying to make the commonwealth mean something, hope to keep Kenya on an even pro-British keel after having launched her. The Israelis are penetrating business and hoping to keep the Arabs out. The Egyptians are playing on Pan Africanism to forestall the Israelis. The Americans are filling the vacuum left by British in teachers, experts and development generally. The communist powers, divided into Russia and her satellites, and China with North Korea and North Vietnam, seem out to increase the vacuum and also to prevent the Americans filling it. All have their eye on something, all make their alliances in the unions, the Youth Wing, business, the Press and the Cabinet.

Numerous links exist between Kenya, Tanganyika, Uganda and Zanzibar, created by the British, cemented by their reinforcing each others' struggles for Independence and underlined by the discussion of East African Federation. Extending outwards from East Africa are the less concrete alliances that were implied in the now all-but-defunct Pan African Freedom Movement of East, Central and Southern Africa. Zambia, especially under the leadership of Kenneth Kaunda, tends to look north. Ethiopia and Somalia have a concern already described.

Finally there are barely veiled activities by Ghana in support of Nkrumah's concept of African unity, which East African Federation would run contrary to, and on behalf of the All-African Trade Union Federation, which is trying to oust the I.C.F.T.U. from Kenya. One way and another a newly Independent State has more to occupy its mind with in external affairs than simply deciding how to cast its precious United Nations vote on critical occasions. African politics are keen, active and internecine.

None the less, Kenya's leaders have been most urgently concerned about creating an African state out of a white-dominated colony. Having seen the Africanisation of the land and the Government services under way, the next target was inevitably the broadcasting and the Press, both of which were predominantly under expatriate control. Broadcasting is felt by most African Governments to be so important a media of communication that it must be state controlled and reflect Government policies. The majority of Africans are not reached by any newspaper at all, even local newsheets, and so the radio has greatly enhanced potential. Often the Government gives grants for social centres and meeting places to have wireless sets.

Kenya has quite a sophisticated radio and television network. The original Kenya Broadcasting Service had been created with extensive B.B.C. help and was wedded to impartiality, albeit employing staff who were often paid by the colonial Government. In 1962 this became the Kenya Broadcasting Corporation and a few months before *Uhuru* an experienced American, George Cahan, was appointed Director-General, the idea being that he should train an African to succeed him as well as soften the colonial aura of K.B.C. At this time K.B.C. was broadcasting three full services, English, Hindustani and Swahili, while its vernacular services reached the country's remotest areas. It was a commercial radio system, the main income being derived from advertising in the English and Asian services. Despite this the Corporation had to be given an £165,000 subvention by the Government in 1963 to keep going, principally because of losses on the vernacular programme.

The Television service, blessed with studios as good as those of Norway, Denmark or Sweden, had started in 1962. Its scope was limited by the costs of T.V. sets and its main revenue also came from advertising on the European and Asian Services. In November 1963 only fifty-eight Africans held T.V. licences, though there were 180 community sets, some donated by K.B.C. and some by the West German Government. The T.V. service was owned by a consortium of commercial companies, the Thomson Organisation have the major holding, and the total financial commitment being about £232,000.

Although Cahan Africanised so fast that soon after *Uhuru* only six executive jobs, including his own, were held by Europeans, a vehement series of rows shattered K.B.C.'s peace. Two Africans who had been accused of embezzling funds and previously had been dismissed suddenly had the charges against them dropped by the Attorney-General and K.B.C. was ordered by the Minister of Information, Oneko, to reinstate them. A wave of veiled intimidation swept through the studios and offices, the upshot being that even the key man, the English Operations Executive scheduled to keep the K.B.C. running efficiently during the start of the new African Director-General's reign, quit a few weeks after signing a fresh contract. Various of the newsroom staff were identifiably K.A.N.U. agents. As a resident foreign correspondent friends still at K.B.C. used to warn me when another was appointed. This, one recognised, was part of the Africanisation process. But it still pointed the contrasts Africa affords. A thousand miles further south the attempts by the Southern Rhodesian Government to exert pressure on the liberally minded white-run television produced world-wide reactions. *The Times* even wrote an editorial on the iniquity of it. But the destruction of the K.B.C.'s impartiality in Kenya merited no such clamour until the issue of censorship arose.

Before the State finally took over K.B.C. there was resistance to political control both from Cahan and the Board, on which several Africans sat, including Charles Rubia. Eventually an African Director-General designate was appointed who was not a politician. Advertisements for this £3,000-a-year post had stated frankly that 'previous experience in broadcasting is desirable but not essential'. They also introduced a new phrase into the terminology of Africanisation, 'Candidates must be manifestly of East African origin.' There had recently been a local outcry against the employment of West Africans directed at Mr. Adu, the Ghanaian Secretary General of the Common Services Organisation, who hit back by telling East Africans publicly that they were lucky to get West African help, and subsequently left to join the United Nations.

Meanwhile a battle had raged over the content of the programmes. In July Oneko had said: 'The Asians of this country must be able to speak either English or Swahili. . . . It is the intention of the Government to reduce tribal languages, and it is not going to happen with the Asian language only, but with all the other languages as well.' This would, for instance, hit the Kimvita service, which is all that 50 per cent of the Coast people understand. Oneko also delivered a definitive verdict on K.B.C.—its purpose was to bring about national unity, to explain economic policies, to exploit and conserve economic resources and to inspire the people with a spirit of self respect. It had the right to ignore irresponsible opposition to the Government. Naturally K.A.D.U. reacted, urging the Government to follow the example of the B.B.C., and be impartial.

Such advice was the opposite of the Government's intention. After *Uhuru* the relay of B.B.C. news was discontinued and the output was largely pre-processed by a newly established Kenya News Agency. The result was that news bulletins fluctuated from eight minutes to fifteen and assumed an amateurishness of editing that only untrained Africans could have achieved. Long and turgid Ministerial speeches were reported verbatim, interspersed with brief items on fighting in the Congo, or Vietnam or Cyprus. The old professionalism had vanished.

In October 1963 a Commission had been appointed to enquire into the K.B.C.'s finances. Its members, two African, one Asian and one European, took scant evidence from either the contractors or anyone working in broadcasting. Its report was highly critical of K.B.C. generally, from the degree of Africanisation of the newsroom to the actual losses. On the basis of this report the Government took over K.B.C. and it is now called the Voice of Kenya.

These moves to end expatriate influence and ownership, which also extended to Swahili papers staffed by Africans like Baraza and Taifa Leo, were accompanied by a definite campaign against both the local Press and against foreign correspondents based in Kenya. *Pan Africa*, a magazine owned by Kenyatta, Odinga and Murumbi, yet edited by an Englishman called Rogers, took a prominent part in this. It was, however, no surprise, having happened already in Tanganyika.

Whereas before Independence African leaders have used the Press extensively to air their grievances and owe a vast debt to publicity, especially in the U.S.A. and Britain, after Independence they develop an apparently pathological hatred for reporting at home or abroad that does not follow their Governmental line. Perhaps it's due to fear, or underlying lack of self-confidence. Even Richard Kisch, who was closer to the Ministry of Information than any other foreign writer, ended up by being told to leave for 'misreporting' a speech of Kenyatta's. Odinga can work himself into a fine fury over the 'hysterical and highly emotional reactions of the British Press' to his expulsions of British subjects. President Nyerere, who has in the past himself written for the *Observer* when he wanted to put his case against South Africa, and who has been magnificently treated by the B.B.C., suddenly expelled the B.B.C. correspondent in Dar-es-Salaam for sending an alleged report which the B.B.C. Director-General immediately confirmed had never been received nor broadcast. Even in the stress of the mutiny period this kind of action makes former assertions about wanting a free Press ring nastily hollow.

'Irresponsibility' in reporting was the cry raised in Kenya to justify curbing the Press. The major Kenya English language newspapers speedily adopted an attitude to the new African Government that was co-operative to the point of cringing, particularly the *Daily Nation*, part owned by the Aga Khan and part by the Thomson Organisation. The *Nation* and the *Sunday Nation* were a venture into tabloid journalism introduced at the end of the 1950's to take advantage of the *East African Standard*'s conservatism and to break its monopoly. Yet the *Standard*, which has a sedate, somewhat *New York Times*-like appearance, and the *Kenya Weekly News*, a commendable *Spectator*-pattern magazine run from Nakuru, have decided that sometimes they must make a stand for what they believe in. The *Standard* had even suffered being publicly reprimanded by the Ministry of Information for printing a Minister's speech precisely as he made it. The fault lay in their not correcting mistakes made by the Minister before publishing his remarks. On this occasion, despite the flood of demands for accurate reporting with which newspapermen had recently been assailed, and the obvious comment that evidently one reason why the Government wanted control of the Press was that it couldn't trust Ministers not to make fools of themselves, the *Standard* kept its temper. But when an undercover attempt at Press censorship was made by the Ministry it acted.

The censorship battle illustrated how easily liberty can be undermined in a newly independent country. Both in Tanganyika and Uganda Press censorship has been imposed for very brief periods by clear and unequivocal decree. In both countries it raised protests from Africans, who saw that although restraints on what was still basically a foreign Press might appear not to affect themselves, in the end it would. Similar protestations had begun to appear even before Independence in Kenya, sparked off by the decree in October 1963 which had made it a punishable offence 'to utter or disseminate . . . any statement, information, report or opinion calculated to cause alarm or apprehension to the public'. Oneko had stood up in the Assembly and assured the House that 'The new regulations were not intended to curb the activities of the free Press but they are supposed to guard against irresponsible and destructive statements by irresponsible leaders'.

None the less thereafter apprehension among journalists became lively, especially when every declaration on Press freedom made by Oneko ended with a rider on irresponsible behaviour. An African writing to the *Standard* said: 'The question posed today in free Africa is whether the African nationalists' Governments recognise the role of the Press as it is in free Europe?' He went on to mention that the Pan African Union of Journalists was pressing to preserve freedom of the Press and ended on a fighting note: 'The Press in free Africa neither objects to criticism nor wishes to be immune from it any more than any other national institution, save it cannot put up with the unfair share of misunderstanding, vilification and abuse, nor tolerate the unfair imposition of legislation by statutory body of the Government, which only expose it to arbitrary measures of suppression.' The nearest Oneko had ever approached to meeting such criticism was in saying: 'The Press is a national institution and as such it should be so manned and directed as to serve the true national interests.'

Since Jomo Kenyatta was already on record against censorship full use was made of the Kenya News Agency in a devious way. The Agency was equipped with Russian and Czech teleprinter equipment and with communist-trained African staff. It had two functions. One was to distribute news and Government handouts within Kenya; the second the more long-term role of sending approved news out from Kenya. With considerable naivete various politicians expressed the hope that the latter would prevent 'misreporting' by foreign correspondents, as though national newspapers in the rest of the world would prefer a Government agency's reports to their own sources, even if their normal correspondents were banned.

The first aim was easily fulfilled. The Government concluded a contract with Reuters under which it received Reuter's News Service as the sole agent for Kenya. It also took Tass. It then resold these to newspapers and to the K.B.C., as it then was. Although in theory the newspapers could refuse the arrangement, in practice it was difficult. Incredible debates took place in the Senate with members suggesting that it was subversive for an independent organisation to receive an outside wire service. Even the International Press Institute had its Reuter service taken away, though because all the students were African this was delayed until the end of the current course to avoid embarrassment. Needless to say the items that filtered through the Kenya News Agency were very different from the full Reuters service. The tape would carry anything up to four hours of Soviet policy speeches before a single Western item appeared and there was a constant delay of two or three hours on all news, a very serious delay for daily papers. What did come through was clearly only what the K.N.A. thought ought to be printed.

At the same time notices purporting to come from a senior official of the Ministery were pasted up in the K.B.C. offices and in the Kenya News Agency. They drew attention to Kenya's policy of non-alignment and stated that items from Tass and Reuters must be judged in the light of that policy. Anything that might conflict with it should be cleared with the Minister. The staff were instructed to be objective and truthful and not to distribute any news which might be subversive, seditious or libellous, or which was antagonistic to the Government of any African country or might estrange Kenya's friendly relations with any other nation, or which was unfair to any section of Kenya's population.

This directive, so artfully confusing propaganda with genuine news, would for instance have prevented publication in Kenya of the International Commission of Jurists' censure of Nkrumah for dismissing the Ghanaian Chief Justice, or of U.N. speeches that opposed African aims. Its possibilities were endless. Sure enough the K.B.C. rapidly reached the point of taking Tass's blatantly propagandist version of talks between President Johnson and Sir Alec Douglas Home, and of the Cyprus dispute. Western aid to

Kenya was played down to the ultimate by mentioning the schemes but not the donor. The newspapers of course did not have to play ball as slavishly as the K.B.C. newsroom staff, although they felt obliged to give prominent showing to all Government pronouncements.

The moment to question this growing interference with that very freedom to which the Kenya Government had constantly committed itself in public came on March 6th. Kenyatta was holding a press conference. Since the main purpose was to announce defence agreements with Britain the room was crowded both with journalists and diplomats. Arriving, one noticed at once how fortified his offices had become. Railings and sentries had sprung up everywhere, while each floor had its guardian reception desk and barrier. However, we were welcomed. Kenyatta was in good form, well dressed with a corner of white handkerchief showing from the breast pocket of his blue suit, vigorous, confident. After he had given a brief discourse on defence he asked for questions. An English reporter of the *Standard* asked if it was Government policy to permit the censorship of news through the Agency. Kenyatta, blinking under the floodlamps of the TV and film companies, launched into a lengthy answer about 'We are not likely to make any censorship at all, but we would like to ask the Press to be considerate because members of the Press can be destructive and at the same time they can be constructive.' Oneko, thin, tall and neat, sat smiling at one side. It was clear that the Prime Minister had not appreciated the significance of the question at all. The reporter rose again to his feet and pressed it home, relating the circumstances. Kenyatta blinked and a flicker of surprise passed over his face. 'If this happened,' he said, 'it may be the policy of different news agencies but the Kenya Government is not—I mean is not—directing any censorship in the Press.' The next day the notices vanished.

Before the year was out the Kenya News Agency had brought censorship into the open. It withheld all the Reuter reports of the Belgian paratroop move to rescue the European hostages from Stanleyville at the end of November—and the reason given was that Kenyatta himself wanted to approve the news before it was issued. A few days later Oneko defended his Government's policy of censorship in the National Assembly. *Inter alia* it had suited the Kenya Government to suppress details of the atrocities committed by the Congolese rebels, whom they always referred to as the 'nationalists'.

The campaign to control the Press in Kenya had borne all the marks of a communist-instructed semi-covert operation. When, that November, a correspondent of the London *Daily Telegraph* exposed some aspects of Russian influence, like the details of arms consignments to Kenya, he was immediately declared a prohibited immigrant. Within a bare year of *Uhuru* the techniques that were being used to undermine individual freedom in Kenya had not only been revealed, the situation they were producing had been defended by Kenya Ministers. 'When the time comes to exercise control over the Press,' Oneko was reported as saying, 'no one should come weeping and crying that the country is being tough.'

Having subordinated the media of communication to the national interest, the obvious next step is to attack foreign business interests. So far the wildcat demands for nationalisation have been turned down firmly and although the Minister of Finance, James Gichuru, has been forced to increase company taxes to 7/50 cts. in the £1, the official treatment of European business houses has been fairly exemplary. Dr. Julius Kiano is a Minister of Commerce who understands what economics are all about and while there are ever-increasing pressures for Africanisation the Government appears to realise that the business dynamism of Nairobi's expatriate community is a valuable asset.

Possibly Kenya is benefiting from mistakes in Tanganyika, whose Ministers have treated would-be investors remarkably cavalierly and who have in consequence lost valuable manufacturing projects—tyres and textiles among them. Furthermore whilst Nairobi is the commercial centre of all East Africa, a fact that arouses deep jealousy in the other countries, Kenya's economic position is actually not good. The adverse balance of trade with the outside world stands at over £25,000,000 a year.

After the Lancaster House Conference of 1960 capital left the country at the rate of £12,000,000 a year until barely any liquid capital was left. Gradually since Kenyatta came to power confidence has been re-established. Resisting the attractions of imposing exchange control has been rewarded by a new inflow of investment from Germany, Holland, Italy, Switzerland, Austria, Japan and the United States, as well as from Britain. Relatively few members of

K.A.N.U. want to jeopardise this build up, especially when the settlement schemes are bound to reduce agricultural exports and Government expenditure is rising steeply. The only purely doctrinaire point held to despite its cost so far is the boycott of South Africa. This was legally imposed before *Uhuru* and seriously affected the sale of the country's main mineral, soda from Lake Magadi. If the boycott is extended to refusing landing rights to any aircraft or ships bound for South Africa then the activity in the port of Mombasa would be cut to a quarter of its present volume, due to ships not bothering to call, and airline services would be drastically reduced. Kenya's business outlets would inevitably suffer, especially her tourist trade.

The tourist industry ought to boom. Kenya has coral beaches, good hotels, and above all, wildlife, in which the only real competitor is South Africa. In 1963 85,000 tourists visited East Africa, two-thirds of their collective stay being spent in Kenya. The hunting firms are based in Nairobi and while the development of tourism lies mainly in cutprice package tours, the full safaris still turn over a surprisingly large amount of revenue at charges of £30–£40 per day per client. Their business is also virtually unAfricanisable. While African gunbearers and trackers are renowned, no one quite envisages a rich American consenting to go out under the sole guidance of a black hunter. The hunters themselves, so beloved of fiction writers and film companies, deserve to be allowed to continue.

Hemingway took a good part of his tradition from them. Their knowledge and understanding of the African bush is a humbling thing for the city dweller to watch at work. Nor do they regret, indeed they are glad, that the object of more and more safaris is to photograph and not to kill. But there are no apprentices to their craft. When I last enquired there was literally not one youngster learning to be a hunter in Kenya, though many hunters are themselves still in their thirties. They don't advise anyone to follow in their footsteps. As one said to me: 'Ours is rather an anachronistic profession. Most hunters are people who have grown up here and don't much want to stay under an African Government.' If the farms they use as base camps are bought out for settlement there will be less incentive to stay, even though *Uhuru* was followed by a year of excellent business for them. Many of them served in the Kenya Regiment or the Kenya Police Reserve during the Emergency too. Though they have kept right out of politics what Odinga subsequently said of Henderson may be truer of them than of him. 'Unfortunately the Kenya Henderson belonged to and so fervently supported no longer exists. It disappeared in the ashes of our Independence bonfires.'

The crunch for the entire white community will come in December 1965 when residents have to decide whether to become Kenya citizens or not. They have been helped a little by the British Government's decision that anyone who takes a foreign nationality under these circumstances and subsequently wishes to revert to British citizenship will be able to do so under special arrangements. Those who do not care to take the risk will face the full force of trade-union and Youth Wing demands for Africanisation of their jobs. If Kenya follows Tanganyika's example then they will only be granted residence permits for one or two years at a time. Cancellation of the permit will be a neat little sword of Damocles hanging over every such expatriate's head, particularly if he has a substantial investment in the country. Work permits are bound to become more and more difficult for foreigners to obtain, especially for managerial as opposed to technical jobs.

Under the Bill of Rights all whites who take Kenya citizenship should be treated equally with Africans, as should Asians. I have already related the fury to which Nyerere's attempt to implement such an idea in Tanganyika was met by the unions in Kenya. Like the pigs in George Orwell's *Animal Farm*, they want some Kenyans to be more equal than others. If the present attitudes of the unions, the Youth Wingers and the wilder backbenchers are anything to go by, the white business community and the remnant of the settlers are in for a rough time, however much the Government wants to pursue its present attitude of encouraging expatriate investment. It often seems that only the common sense of Kenyatta, their erstwhile enemy, now stands between them and the wolves.

The trade unions have been in the habit of threatening European managers with deportation if wage demands are not met. Negotiations with the unions occupy at least as much of the managements' time as they do in Britain. The Government itself has had trouble in making them abide by agreements. The most important of these was part of a bold move to combat unemployment, introduced early in 1964. Under it the Government took on 15 per cent more employees and the private employers, except for householders, took on 10 per cent more. The *quid pro quo* was freedom from wage increases for a year and it was hoped that 50,000 unemployed would be absorbed. Inevitably the scheme was largely misunderstood. Africans swarmed off their shambas to join the queues outside employment offices in the towns. At one timber mill upcountry the while labour force quit to go and register for work in Nakuru. The problem in any subsistence economy is that enormous numbers of people making a bare living on the land are always ready to seek a job if one is to be had, and if it proves not to be obtainable then they declare themselves unemployed. Even if these are kept off Kenya's unemployment register, as strictly speaking they should be, there are still 80,000 youths leaving school each year who have to be fitted in somewhere.

The radicals in the unions profit from this situation and a fierce battle has raged within the Kenya Federation of Labour. An attempt to form a Ghanaian-aided rival Federation, headed by the Dock-workers' Union leader, Dennis Akumu, the Petroleum Workers' Union Leader, Mak'anyengo, and some others, failed when the Government refused to register their new organisation. They did manage to break the K.F.L.'s affiliation to the I.C.F.T.U., which dated from Mboya's days as General Secretary and indicated a pro-Western bias to which the radicals were totally opposed. They want to affiliate with A.A.T.U.F., based in Accra, which Lubembe calls 'a notorious Soviety stooge', and refuses to join.

Irresponsible union behaviour is also threatening another creation of Mboya's—the Industrial Charter, which is unique in East Africa. It lays down a code for handling industrial disputes, at the same time guaranteeing the unions' position. At the moment the K.F.L. enjoys a freedom of action and a freedom from K.A.N.U. party control which has long been lost in both Ghana and Tanganyika. In Ghana the trade unions are a wing of the Convention People's Party. In Tanganyika, where the likely parallel with Kenya is close, the wild irresponsibility of the unions and their constant challenges to Government policy have caused the right to strike to be withdrawn and the Tanganyika Federation of Labour to be put under the control of the Ministry of Labour. A number of Tanganyikan trade unionists are in preventive detention.

If the Kenya unions persist in acting against the Government, as they did in the threatened *Uhuru* bonus strike which Kenyatta himself dealt with, then they will court the extinction of their freedom,

Industrial Charter or no Industrial Charter. They have been exceedingly slow, perhaps deliberately, to realise that constant attacks on the capitalist basis of the economy are one thing when the Government is colonial, but another when the Government is African and perforce sensitive to the state of the economy, the cost of living, and revenue from exports and taxes. If the unions wage industrial warfare against certain sectors of the economy on an African Government's suggestion it's all right, but to agitate indiscriminately is to invite first legal curbs, and then suppression. Europe's democratic scruples, so helpful in the original formation of unions under colonial rule, are not necessarily observed by African rulers, nor is 'Striking in the spirit of *Harambee*' appreciated.

The chaos of passion, prejudice and militancy that boils beneath Kenya's surface was revealed when Kenyatta was away at the Commonwealth Prime Ministers' Conference in London in June 1964 and was assaulted by a fascist. An alarming wave of anti-British sentiment swept the country. Backbenchers demanded the British High Commissioner's expulsion and fulminated about a 'settler plot', the Agricultural Workers' Union ordered all European farmers out of the country within a month, the Youth Wing demonstrated. Only on Kenyatta's return did the storm subside. Then the backbenchers' action in breaking all the portraits of past Speakers of the Assembly was deplored by a vote of the House.

These outbreaks are much more than the work of a lunatic fringe, and are moderately co-ordinated. Rising prices, the unequal distribution of privileges despite *Uhuru*, the attractions of racialism and the sprouting seeds of communist propaganda all ferment in the minds of Africans, especially city dwellers, to unite them against many of the Government's policies, and particularly against those that seem Western-orientated. The Chinese-printed leaflets that arrive in crates by air from Hong Kong through London addressed to Odinga and which are then distributed to schools and the Youth Wing all emphasise the overthrow of capitalism and the need for revolution.

By this standard Kenyatta's Government is not a Government of the African Revolution. The Chinese and the Kenyan extremists want what they call the pattern of 'The Socialist Countries' established in Kenya, which is a technically correct way of referring to communism, since the fifth stage of Marxist theory, the communist stage, has officially not yet been reached by either China or Russia. This pattern is not quite Kenyatta's, with his neutralism and his encouragement of Western investment, though the founding of a Lumumba Institute with Russian aid will help 'align' the neutralism intellectually.

Just as Kenya's leaders had little more reason for joining the Commonwealth at *Uhuru* than that it was the accepted moment to join 'the Club' and would bring benefits in development aid, so I doubt if there is any long-term plan for establishing 'socialism' in Kenya, though there is certainly a long-term intention.

On the one hand many Kenyans feel it good that the Commonwealth is not aligned to any of the Power blocs, can help in the liberation of the rest of Africa, and does lend respectability to the retention of links with Britain. On the other hand the supporters of Odinga, Oneko, Paul Ngei, Bildad Kaggia, Fred Kubai, Senator Makasembo, and the other Eastern-orientated trade unionists and politicians, presumably feel as do their leaders, that the communist pattern can most benefit Kenya. The replacement of the white mixed farmers over the next three or four years by collectives and co-operatives may vindicate their belief. But it is not in the African nature to plan revolutionary change years ahead (which is why the young Arab element under Babu has such an interesting role in Zanzibar). If Kenya does become a 'socialist' state in five or so years' time, by when Kenyatta might well have died, the changes will be piecemeal and opportunist. One of the few certainties is that if there is a violent upheaval the Youth Wings will be at the forefront of it.

'The mistake Kenyatta made,' Harry Thuku told me once, 'was in letting the Youth Wing have its own Treasury.' Once the youth could organise their own finances they could break away from K.A.N.U.'s control, which to a large extent they have done. They have their own organisers and offices. As well as being stewards at political rallies they indulge in illegal and more or less secret periods of marching and drilling with dummy weapons. They can be frighteningly aggressive and display all the classic symptoms of childhood deprivation, which indeed many must have suffered. Thus although an organisation claiming 2,000,000 members contains plenty of quiet ordinary young men and women, the Youth Wing's overwhelming characteristic is militancy, as it was of K.A.D.U.'s rival Youth Wing too. When there were demonstrations in Nairobi against

United States policy in Vietnam, it was Youth Wingers who demonstrated despite Vietnam being somewhat remote from the consciousness of most Kenyans, although North Vietnamese guests did come unofficially to the Independence Celebrations, together with East Germans and North Koreans, and were looked after by Odinga's group. Needless to say Odinga is intensely popular among Youth Wingers, having long identified himself with them and helped formulate their aspirations. He invented the '*Uhuru* Chiefs', a title given to Youth Wing organisers in Nyanza who eventually had to be tactfully disabused of the idea that they were going to be real chiefs in Nyanza after *Uhuru*.

This concludes my brief sketch of the internal forces most likely to affect Kenyatta's Government in the future. The old man needs to be a master politician to keep them all in balance, though so far he has been remarkably successful at it. But to be so successful he has had to exert his own authority more and more in every sphere. It is not surprising that he is planning to make Kenya a one-party state, and in October 1964 started a campaign to convince Kenyans of its virtues. An opposition, even if not in itself in any way subversive, must seem to him like a constantly wandering flame that may at any moment find tinder and set the whole edifice afire. Or to use another metaphor, a degree of authoritarianism must appear the only way of converting the centrifugal forces that threaten to send Kenya's elements flying apart into a centripetal force that will bind them together.

Nor is it surprising that his external diplomacy is limited and unspectacular. He has frequently declared himself in favour of East African Federation, despite his revelation about the Declaration of Intention to Federate. He is himself the likely choice for first President of such a Federation, though the Kikuyu are known to dislike the idea, since his moving up a step would put Odinga into the local Headship of Kenya. But Ugandan fears have been a greater obstacle.

The ideal of Federation has been strongly taken up by the left-wing in K.A.N.U. since the Zanzibar Revolution and the Tanganyika-Zanzibar Union. The backbenchers actually decided that it must be achieved by August 21st, 1964, though, of course, it was not. This enthusiasm appears to spring from a hope that with left-wing influence newly predominant in Tanganyika, and Zanzibar still a Communist-run island, there would be every chance for a coalition of left-wing elements gaining power legally in a Federal Assembly. This may raise other doubts in Kenyatta's mind.

None the less he has agreed to Kenya making considerable trading concessions to Tanganyika[1] in order to meet Tanganyikan threats of leaving the East African Customs Union, if Nairobi's attractiveness to foreign firms were not counterbalanced by the direction of some industry to them. Thus the advantages of a common currency, civil aviation and railways, posts and telegraphs, have also been preserved, since they and the other East African Common Services Organisations functions might well have split up once the Customs Union was destroyed. Actual Federation remains unlikely to be realised soon.

1. The United Republic of Tanganyika and Zanzibar took the new name of Tanzania while this book was in production. The economic union of the two countries is gradually being achieved. Zanzibar did not formerly belong to the Customs Union.

14

An Abrupt Farewell

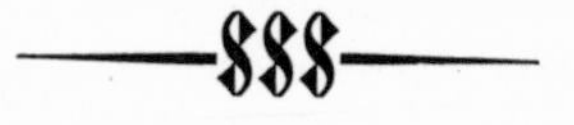

THE FOUR YEARS that I knew Kenya were the years of transition. The white man's country that Sir Charles Eliot's imagination foresaw when he was H.M. Commissioner in 1904 turned into the black man's country of Kenyatta. Africans not being noted for longevity, Kenyatta will presumably die before many more years have passed. During this time his bulky presence is impressing itself on all facets of the country's life. I have tried to give an impression of how he is setting about moulding Kenya, and what the other forces in the country underneath him are. Which of them will prevail after he is gone it is impossible to say, but there is certainly likely to be a struggle between Luo and Kikuyu in K.A.N.U., with the Youth Wing and trade unions actively involved.

It is absolutely clear that the multi-racial state—in which the races would share power on the lines Michael Blundell hoped for and which the Conservative Party affected to believe in when it launched the decolonisation—is as dead as the Dodo. The practical value given Kenya citizenship will reveal whether there may be a non-racial state, though the latent emphasis on citizenship in the ownership of land or the right to trade emphasises the gap between what the white man can expect in Africa and what the African Commonwealth citizen is allowed to do without question in Britain if he is resident there. Kenya is not alone in this. The much abused Commonwealth Immigration Act incidentally reflected the limitations placed on British subjects when they went abroad.

Few white Kenyans believe in their hearts that a settler community can finally reach the sort of *modus vivendi* with an African Government that English communities have with the Governments in Spain, Portugal, the Canaries and South America. The assumption of white superiority is not the best preface to integration. Equally economic pressures and political necessity, sharp with the unquenchable thirst of African aspiration for their country to be a black country, militate against a racial *rapprochement*. While no parallel of this kind is ever exact, Kenya might easily have passed through similar disgraces to Algeria's post-Independence removal of the French, had the British Government not been forced by its conscience to finance the massive settlement schemes and generally give Kenyatta's Government far more assistance than Uganda or Tanganyika ever enjoyed. Kenya always has been an Equatorial forcing house, whether breeding settlers or terrorists. Life as a far-from-rich tropical republic will be a comedown. Kenya the colony had standards that Kenyatta's country cannot afford. This however does not mean that Kenya's Africans are likely to look back on the colonial days as a golden age. They have no regrets about *Uhuru*. Happily the first year of freedom has seen the wild men kept under control and independent Kenya establish a reputation for stability.

My farewell to Kenya was abrupt, though some easement was given it by Kenyatta himself. Although it was the end of April, my own and the *Sunday Times* coverage of January events had not been forgotten, especially not the alleged libel against Odinga and Oneko. One morning a friend at the British High Commission woke me with a telephone call that began, 'Hearing your name on the radio reminded me . . .' and then continued maddeningly to discuss some arrangements he was making for me in West Africa. When I recalled to him his first sentence he said brightly, in the best Stiff Upper Lip tradition, 'Oh, didn't you know, old chap, you've been declared a prohibited immigrant in Tanganyika.' It had been on the early news bulletin. As far as anyone could discover Nyerere had flown into a rage at reading my account of Zanzibar's Union with Tanganyika, which, quite mistakenly I now realise, I had seen as being a blow to communist penetration of East Africa, instead of the reverse. Later that day I was given an assurance by Oneko's Permanent Secretary that since I had done nothing to offend Kenya I would not have action taken against me in Nairobi without first being given an answer to my written request not to be expelled.

Sure enough next day, May Day, I was rung by a local reporter and asked if I knew that the Ministry of Information was telephoning the newspapers to tell them I was a prohibited immigrant. I did not know. I was the one journalist they didn't bother to inform. Apparently I had twenty-four hours in which to leave. Things looked bad since it was a public holiday and my wife was in hospital in Mombasa 300 miles away recovering from a threatened miscarriage. However, the High Commissioner was extremely quick off the mark and tried repeatedly to trace Oneko, who had signed the order, if written order there ever was, in Odinga's absence. But Oneko was not available, although a journalist managed to get an interview with him for the Tanganyika Party paper, the *Nationalist*. The High Commissioner then approached Kenyatta, who agreed that the circumstances justified seventy-two hours' stay of execution.

That was a great relief. It also heightened the unreality of the whole affair. We had to telephone the Immigration Officer ourselves to be given the prohibition officially, if still only verbally. I was later told by an African Press officer that a Press release was an executive Government order. Be that as it may I never laid my hands on any document capable of being framed and hung on an office wall as a memento, which is the journalistic custom. May Day was a Friday and the weekend passed in an extraordinary mixture of activity, condolence and celebration. It's a very odd feeling still being in a place you love and knowing you will never see it again, like dying a little. Kenya has always had a capacity for getting under people's skin, carving out a shrine inside them where the memory of it aches. Happily I was allowed little time to dwell on this by my friends. Officers of my former regiment, stationed in Kenya, dined me out at Muthaiga Club. The Japanese Consul insisted on his wife cooking me a farewell lunch of traditional Japanese food, fried in front of us on the table and redolent with the strong flavour of edible chrysanthemums. Friends took me out for drinks and packed my belongings. I took an aircraft up and flew round and round over Nairobi for a good last look at my Spanish-style house near the Arboretum, at the race-course, as pretty as Goodwood, at the great flat Athi Plains and the animals in the Game Park, the lions, as usual, identifiable from the groups of motor-cars lurking round them. I had done the same the last time I had thought I was leaving Kenya for good in 1961.

On Monday the High Commissioner's official pleas on my behalf failed. As word had reached me the day before that the *Sunday Times* 'libel' was now being avenged, this was no surprise. What did take me aback was Oneko's attitude once he had turned down the official

British request. The Immigration Office, now headed by an African, had arranged for me to leave the following morning, there being a Comet flight then to Salisbury—the only place I had a ticket to. Kenya didn't care to burden herself with paying my fare to London. So that afternoon I went to the Information Service to sort out speeches by Kenyatta for this book. There at 3 p.m. a message reached me to return to the Immigration Office. Both the African and his European deputy were embarrassed. Oneko had ordered me out at once. A plane left at 5 p.m. for Salisbury via Northern Rhodesia. I pointed out that having acted on their suggestions I found myself not fully packed, my car not yet handed over, my dog still unkennelled. Friends were coming at 5 p.m. to cope with these things. So I was given a cup of tea while the African rang Oneko. Being in the room, I was told that Oneko had said, 'I don't care if he's not packed, or if you have to turn other passengers off the flight, he's to leave now.' Since he had earlier refused to see me personally this made it fairly clear that a policy statement he had recently made on always discussing matters with journalists who had offended the Government before instituting action against them was something of a fraud. With the help of an Asian friend I just caught the plane, semi-packed. (The dog was rescued and flown to London.) But as my aircraft turned over the city, and the air hostess announced that we could unfasten our seat-belts now, I felt acutely sorry for the Europeans whose homes and livelihoods are in Kenya and who might, any day, without reason or warning, be treated as I was. The aircraft was cool, ordered, civilised, a piece of the Western world bearing no relationship to the continent it now traversed. In the hands of the air crew one was safe, living in an age of logic and reason. But the white Kenyans, liable to be labelled 'ill-intentioned colonialist remnants' on any politician's sudden whim, were still down there on the ground, poor men.